Curriculum Provision
for the
Gifted and Talented
in the **Secondary School**

Curriculum Provision
for the
Gifted and Talented
in the **Secondary School**

Edited by
Deborah Eyre &
Hilary Lowe

David Fulton Publishers
London

David Fulton Publishers Ltd
The Chiswick Centre, 414 Chiswick High Road, London W4 5TF

First published in Great Britain in 2002 by David Fulton Publishers
Reprinted 2003
10 9 8 7 6 5 4 3 2

Note: The rights of the contributors to be identified as the authors of their work
has been asserted by them in accordance with the Copyright, Designs and Patents
Act 1988.

Copyright © 2002 David Fulton Publishers Ltd

British Library Cataloguing in Publication Data
A catalogue record for this book is available from the British Library.

ISBN 1 85346 772 3

All rights reserved. No part of this publication may be reproduced, stored in a
retrieval system or transmitted, in any form, or by any means, electronic,
mechanical, photocopying, recording or otherwise, without the prior permission
of the publisher.

Typeset by Textype Typesetters, Cambridge
Printed and bound in Scotland by Scotprint, Haddington

Contents

Preface   vi

Contributors   ix

1. **Introduction: Effective schooling for the gifted and talented**   1
   Deborah Eyre

2. **English and Literacy**   27
   Geoff Dean

3. **Mathematics**   42
   Roy Kennard

4. **Science**   59
   Pat O'Brien

5. **Art**   76
   Mary Fitzpatrick

6. **Design and Technology**   93
   Trevor Davies

7. **History**   113
   Sue Mordecai

8. **Geography**   128
   David Leat

9. **Modern Foreign Languages**   140
   Hilary Lowe

10. **Music**   164
    Frankie Williams

11. **Physical Education and Sport**   177
    Paul Beashel

12. **Religious Education**   188
    Mark Cope

Index   201

Preface

In the years since 1997, the issue of education for able/gifted pupils has moved from the margins of the educational arena towards the centre stage, with the dismantling of the Assisted Places Scheme and a government commitment to the establishment of a national strategy to help gifted and talented pupils in maintained schools to make the most of their educational opportunities. The national strategy is being developed using a two-stranded approach. The first strand is a national pilot project, located in inner cities as part of the Excellence in Cities initiative. In this strand, schools are required to have a policy on gifted and talented pupils, a designated member of staff taking responsibility for gifted and talented pupils and a distinct teaching and learning programme for the cohort in question. The second strand involves a greater recognition of the needs of gifted and talented pupils within wider educational initiatives such as the literacy and numeracy strategies.

The need for schools to look more closely at their provision for the able or, to use the adopted government terminology, 'gifted and talented' children has been evident for many years. In 1992, HMI stated: 'Very able pupils in maintained primary and secondary schools are insufficiently challenged by the work they are set' (HMI 1992). Five years later, after a period of immense change in education, OFSTED found that the problem of underachievement among the more able was still a feature of education in many schools: 'Provision for very able children, defined as the top 5% by attainment, is a significant weakness in one-third of maintained primary schools and about 30% of maintained secondary schools.' (OFSTED internal report 1997, quoted in House of Commons 1999).

Many reasons have been put forward for the lack of effective provision for able/gifted pupils, including comprehensive education, the National Curriculum, the British attitude to academic excellence, the private school system, etc. All these are possible factors, but in practical terms the most compelling reason seems to be that over a significant period of time educationalists did not see this issue as important. Few schools systematically addressed the needs of their able pupils, and for those who did, guidance on how to make improvements was in short supply.

An inquiry from the House of Commons Education Select Committee (House of Commons 1999) identified five main problems with provision: *THE PROBLEM - 1999*

- the needs of children of high ability are not seen as a priority by teachers and schools;
- schools do not set high enough levels of expectation for their pupils;
- the ethos of schools (and, more widely, society) does not value high academic or intellectual achievement;
- teachers are unsure about the most effective ways of recognising high potential or of teaching the most able children; and
- resources for providing the best education for such children are not available.

Since this report, the Department for Education and Employment (DfEE) and other government agencies have gone some way towards addressing these issues. The Excellence in Cities pilot provides in-service training for coordinators of gifted and talented pupils as well as resources for developing more effective school-based provision. National guidance on meeting the needs of the gifted and talented has also been produced by the Qualifications and Curriculum Authority (QCA) and additional material linked to the literacy and numeracy strategies has been produced. The needs of the gifted and talented are being given greater priority in schools, and standards are likely to rise accordingly.

Much has been written internationally regarding the educational and social needs of gifted children but relatively little research and publication has taken place in the United Kingdom. In 1998, OFSTED commissioned a review of the international literature (Freeman 1998) to provide an overview of what has been learnt. This document is particularly helpful in considering the psychological literature related to the nature of giftedness, but perhaps less helpful to the teacher in securing a whole-school approach to effective educational provision. This is not a criticism of the document itself but rather a recognition of the inherent weakness in reviews of this type; because educational systems vary greatly, educational provision, which must take account of the general educational context, will vary also.

The international research base has, however, been essential in providing a theoretical basis for school-focused research in England and for exploring effective provision in relation to the English educational context. Since the 1980s, small-scale work has been occurring in England. During the 1990s, a range of small-scale, school-focused research projects have been undertaken by researchers, resulting in the production of guidance to teachers (Clark and Callow 1998; Koshy and Casey 1998; Kennard 1996).

The purpose of this book is to assist secondary schools in making effective provision for gifted and talented children. The House of Commons (1999) found that teachers were unsure about the most effective ways of recognising high potential or teaching the most able. In recent years a number of good books have been published that help schools to understand the general principles behind making effective provision and also the management implications for schools. In this book we have chosen to focus specifically on a more detailed examination of curriculum provision because schools working to improve their provision for the gifted have highlighted the need for more detailed guidance in these areas.

New ideas on the education of the gifted

Educational provision for gifted pupils should reflect our understanding of what it means to be gifted. In this book we draw on the latest research into giftedness and consider its implications for school-based planning. We also link the research findings to the current educational context in secondary schools and highlight the opportunities offered by the National Curriculum, the KS3 National Strategy and post-16 developments.

The scope and organisation of the book

The book is divided into 12 chapters. The introduction (Chapter 1) looks at what schools should be trying to achieve and why. It draws on the substantial research base existing internationally and applies the findings to the context of the English secondary school. It deals in some detail with the complex issue of identification and its implications for curriculum planning. New ideas on giftedness have emerged in recent years which point to the developmental nature of giftedness and the differences in the educational needs of gifted children at different stages and to the importance of opportunity and motivation. The following 11 chapters focus on such issues as what it means to be gifted or talented in specific subject areas, the characteristics of effective provision within those areas, and ideas about how to develop aspects of good provision in and beyond the classroom.

References

Clark, C. and Callow, F. (1998) *Education of Able Children*. London: David Fulton Publishers.

Eyre, D. (1997) *Able Children in Ordinary Schools*. London: David Fulton Publishers.

Freeman, J. (1998) *Educating the Very Able: Current International Research*. London: HMSO.

HMI (1992) *Education Observed: The Education of Very Able Children in Maintained Schools*. London: HMSO.

House of Commons (1999) Education and Employment Committee Third Report, *Highly Able Children*. London: HMSO.

Kennard, R. (2001) *Teaching Mathematically Able Children*. London: David Fulton Publishers.

Koshy, V. and Casey, R. (1998) *Effective Provision for Able and Exceptionally Able Children*. London: Hodder & Stoughton.

Contributors

Paul Beashel has been Head teacher of the Deanes School in Essex since 1991. The Deanes School is a mixed 11–16 comprehensive Foundation School with 1,020 pupils and was designated as a DfEE Sports College in September 2001. Paul started his teaching career as a PE teacher in the London Borough of Barking and Dagenham. He then became Head of Middle School and, later, Deputy Head teacher in an 11–18 school in Brentwood, Essex. Paul has maintained his interest in physical education and sport, being co-author of a number of GCSE and A level textbooks, as well as a CD-ROM on the subject. He is an executive member of the Physical Education Association (UK).

Mark Cope is the Head of Religious Education, Citizenship, SMSC and PSHE coordinator at Alderbrook School, Solihull, West Midlands. In 1997, he was awarded the Farmington Fellowship, which he used to research into and write about religious education and more able students. He has published on the subject and contributed to reviews and journals. At the time of publication, Mark is involved in developing a new Citizenship and PSHE programme with the LEA in the light of Curriculum 2000, regularly coordinating summer schools for more able students and drafting the text of a book on the evolution of the relationship to authority in religion.

Trevor Davies is a Lecturer in the School of Education at the University of Reading. He has taught in secondary schools, up to deputy head teacher level, and has worked as a local authority adviser as well as an OFSTED Inspector. At the time of publication, he is completing a PhD thesis on the role of creativity in design and technology education and has additional major research interests in cognitive modelling in science and technology education. He has published in both national and international journals and in books on related themes. He also has considerable interests in international work and has been involved in EU-funded TEMPUS and COMENIUS projects, building new educational structures for democracy, linked to creative and autonomous teaching and learning in the eastern and western states of Europe.

Geoff Dean began his career teaching English and Drama in Northamptonshire, before becoming Head of English in Mildenhall, Suffolk. After a Deputy Headship at Sharnbrook, Bedfordshire, he went on to be English Adviser/Inspector for Oxfordshire, where he began researching more able language users. Having been Adviser for English in Cambridgeshire, where he implemented the Literacy Strategy, he was appointed English Adviser in Milton Keynes in 1999. He has published books on more able pupils in English, the teaching of reading in secondary schools, and he has contributed to a guide to the KS3 English Framework.

Deborah Eyre is Head of ReCAP (Research Centre for Able Pupils) and also Deputy Head of the Westminster Institute of Education, Oxford Brookes University. She is a former school coordinator and LEA adviser for able pupils and has worked extensively with schools on improving educational provision for able pupils. Her research interests lie in pedagogy and classroom practice and, in particular, the ways in which teachers can 'tinker' with their existing practice to create a classroom more conducive to the development of high ability. She has published three books on able pupils as well as a variety of papers and chapters. Deborah is a past President of NACE (National Association for Able Children in Education), a member of the government advisory group for gifted and talented, specialist adviser to the House of Commons Education Select Committee for its Highly Able Children inquiry and a consultant to QCA.

Mary Fitzpatrick is Assistant Principal at King Alfred's School, Wantage, Oxfordshire. She has previous experience in secondary schools as an art teacher, head of art and special needs and able pupils coordinator. She has held a research fellowship in the Research Centre for Able Pupils, Westminster Institute of Education, Oxford Brookes University, is a member of the NACE executive committee and was a leader of a National Mentoring Network research project in the mentorship of able pupils.

Roy Kennard is Maths Adviser for the City of Sunderland. He is a former co-editor of the NACE journal *Educating Able Children*, and has acted as maths consultant to QCA's Gifted and Talented guidance. He has published extensively in the field of maths and able pupils.

David Leat taught in the secondary sector for 12 years before becoming the PGCE geography tutor at Newcastle University. In conjunction with ex-PGCE students and mentors, he founded the Thinking Through Geography Group, which has produced two books and had a number of research grants. This led to a number of related subject and research-based partnerships with schools and teachers. His research interests are in teaching and professional development, which are mutually dependent. At the time of publication, he is on leave of absence working as Regional Director for TLF (Teaching and Learning in Foundation subjects), part of the KS3 strategy.

Hilary Lowe is Principal Lecturer in Education at the Westminster Institute of Education, Oxford Brookes University, and a member of the Research Centre for

Able Pupils. She specialises in the education of able pupils and in modern foreign languages and is Director of Studies for the national training programme for Gifted and Talented Co-ordinators in secondary schools within the government's Excellence in Cities programme. She was previously a head of modern languages and a deputy head teacher in secondary comprehensive schools.

Sue Mordecai is Principal Adviser with Bromley LEA, and currently the Vice-President of NACE. She was a member of the DfES Gifted and Talented Advisory Group and has worked with QCA on exemplification materials for gifted and talented pupils. Sue is an education adviser to the Charles Darwin Trust and she is an accredited secondary OFSTED Team Inspector.

Pat O'Brien is an independent educational adviser who has worked nationally and internationally in the field of science education and high ability. His main interests are in curriculum development, particularly differentiation and the use of ICT to support science. He has published widely, is a registered OFSTED Inspector and has acted as educational consultant to many national and international bodies. He also taught in a range of schools for many years.

Frankie Williams is a General Inspector for Cambridgeshire and has worked with primary, secondary and special schools. She has 20 years' experience in the advisory and inspection field, and is an OFSTED Inspector. She has particular interest and experience in pre-OFSTED reviews, LMS and efficiency, and the gifted and talented and music. She runs training for head teachers and is a consultant for the arts. She has represented the UK in Europe in the areas of music and information technology and youth music. At the time of writing, she is studying part-time for a doctorate in education. She is a member of European and national committees for music, is on the executive committee of NACE, and is a governor at Hills Road Sixth Form College.

THE NATIONAL ASSOCIATION FOR
ABLE CHILDREN IN EDUCATION
PO Box 242, Arnolds Way,
Oxford OX2 9FR

Registered Charity No. 327230

Tel: 01865 861879   Fax: 01865 861880
e-mail: info@nace.co.uk   www.nace.co.uk

MISSION STATEMENT

NACE . . . the association of professionals, promoting and supporting the
education of able and talented children.

AIMS
1. To promote the fact that able and talented children have particular educational
   needs that must be met to realise their full potential.
2. To be proactive in promoting discussion and debate by raising appropriate
   issues in all education forums and through liaison with eudcational policy
   makers.
3. To encourage commitment to the personal, social and intellectual development
   of the whole child.
4. To encourage a broad, balanced and appropriate curriculum for able and
   talented children.
5. To encourage the use of a differentiated educational provision in the classroom
   through curriculum enrichment and extension.
6. To make education an enjoyable, exciting and worthwhile experience for the
   able and talented child.

OBJECTIVES
1. To promote the development, implementation and evaluation in all schools of
   a coherent policy for able and talented children.
2. To provide appropriate support, resources and materials for the education of
   able and talented children.
3. To provide methods of identification and support to the education community.
4. To provide and facilitate appropriate initial teacher training.
5. To stimulate, initiate and coordinate research activities.
6. To develop a national base and establish regional centres.

STATEMENT
To make education an enjoyable, exciting and worthwhile experience for able and
talented children.

CHAPTER 1

Introduction: Effective schooling for the gifted and talented

Deborah Eyre

A school-wide approach to the gifted and talented

This chapter outlines the areas which need to be considered if a school is to improve its provision for the gifted and talented. The gifted and talented are not a homogeneous group and therefore provision needs to be responsive to individual needs and sufficiently flexible to take account of particular ages and contexts. This chapter aims to help schools to understand not only what they should do but also why it is appropriate and how to tailor the general guidance on provision to fit their own particular context. Finally, it provides guidance on how to monitor provision and judge whether the school really is an effective school for gifted and talented pupils.

What then constitutes good provision for the gifted and talented? A useful starting point is to recognise that for most schools, meeting the needs of their gifted and talented pupils is part of a commitment to ensuring suitable educational opportunities for all pupils rather than a separate activity. Schools are not looking to provide for their gifted and talented at the expense of other pupils but rather to ensure that all pupils, including those with gifts and talents, are receiving good quality educational provision. Therefore, in considering education for gifted and talented pupils it is not surprising to find that schools who are judged to be successful generally are also most likely to be among those successful in providing for their gifted and talented children. Schools who meet the criteria for effective schools set out by Sammons *et al.* (1996) (see Figure 1.1) are well placed to provide for the gifted and talented. Indeed any judgement regarding provision for gifted and talented pupils is likely to be influenced by two separate strands: firstly an assessment of the effectiveness of the general school offer, as this forms part of the educational experience of the gifted and talented pupils, and secondly the effectiveness of modifications made to meet the specific educational needs of the gifted and talented.

Gifted and talented pupils need access to broad, balanced and challenging curriculum opportunities. A good starting point for any school is to reflect on the extent to which these are provided as part of the general school offer. Does the general school offer really present a stimulating and challenging range of opportunities and are all those with the potential to benefit from them able to gain access? Specific questions to consider here might be as follows:

- To what extent does your general curriculum offer the potential to challenge the most able?
- Are there particular subject areas where significant challenge can only be provided through additional study opportunities?
- Are there subjects where demand is determined by the examination syllabus chosen or by the texts studied?
- Does the range of subjects on offer restrict opportunities to develop some types of ability?
- Does the general curriculum include opportunities to study for higher level exam and assessment papers?
- Do organisational arrangements mean that some individuals are denied access to appropriate opportunities because the system is designed to benefit the majority?
- How well does the general school offer meet the needs of the most able at different stages e.g. the Key Stage 3 curriculum, the Key Stage 4 exam syllabus, the 16 plus offer?

A summary of responses to the questions above provides a useful basis for determining what additional opportunities need to be made available for the gifted and talented to augment general school provision. The range of additional opportunities or curriculum modifications needed will vary from school to school and will reflect both the profile of the pupils and the curriculum profile of the school. For example, in a school where the majority of pupils are low to average achievers a significant amount of provision for the most able might be through enhancement of the general curriculum or fast tracking, whereas in a generally high achieving school most opportunities will be offered as part of general provision and the need for additional challenge will be less. Equally, in a specialist school it might be reasonable to expect that high quality opportunities will exist in the school's area of specialism as part of the general curriculum, but that additional opportunities may be needed in certain other areas.

When the quality of the provision for the gifted and talented is assessed consideration will be given not only to the incidence of activity specifically designed for the designated gifted and talented cohort but also to how this maps into general school provision to create a coherent whole.

Key point

Meeting the educational needs of the gifted and talented is about building on good general school provision, not about providing something entirely different. Therefore any assessment of effective provision for gifted and talented pupils will include a review of the school's general educational offer as well as of those elements specifically designed to meet the needs of the gifted and talented.

Eleven factors for effective schools	
1. **Professional leadership**	Firm and purposeful A participative approach The leading professional
2. **Shared vision and goals**	Unity of purpose Consistency of practices Collegiality and collaboration
3. **A learning environment**	An orderly atmosphere An attractive working environment
4. **Concentration on teaching and learning**	Maximisation of learning time Academic emphasis Focus on achievement
5. **Purposeful teaching**	Efficient organisation Clarity of purpose Structured lessons Adaptive practice
6. **High expectations**	High expectations all round Communicating expectations Providing intellectual challenge
7. **Positive reinforcement**	Clear and fair discipline Feedback
8. **Monitoring progress**	Monitoring pupil performance Evaluating school performance
9. **Pupils' rights and responsibilities**	Raising pupil self-esteem Positions of responsibility Control of work
10. **Home–school partnership**	Parental involvement in their children's learning
11. **A learning organisation**	School-based staff development

Figure 1.1 Eleven factors for effective schools

Elements of a school-wide approach

The DfES (Department for Education and Skills) suggests that schools consider a range of elements as part of their provision for gifted and talented pupils; a distinct teaching and learning programme, enrichment opportunities and study support. Organisationally it is useful for a school to consider the location for these activities.

The distinct teaching and learning programme

In the secondary school the majority of educational opportunities for gifted and talented children should be available as part of general classroom practice. The subject department should take responsibility for ensuring that opportunities are appropriate in terms of both range and level of challenge and should determine curriculum and organisation to support this aim. In any monitoring of school provision most attention will be paid to the role of the subject department in ensuring quality and range of opportunity as well as systems for assessing, tracking and guiding pupils in their progress.

Each subject area in the secondary school has its own conventions that determine the content and methodology for teaching. However the fundamentals of pedagogy remain the same. Kerry and Kerry (2000) describe pedagogy as being the key to the teaching and learning of able students and they assert that the key components to effective classroom provision are:

- defining learning objectives;
- setting effective classroom tasks;
- differentiating work;
- questioning effectively; and
- explaining effectively.

In providing well for gifted and talented pupils, a school needs to consider how each of these might operate in respect of those of high ability, since this forms the basis of the distinct teaching and learning programme. Therefore, in considering learning objectives, more challenging objectives for the most able will be a regular feature of classroom planning. This does not mean that different worksheets always need to be provided for the most able; learning objectives can be linked to understanding of additional or more complex concepts and may be achieved through careful questioning. It does, however, mean that a teacher should be able to demonstrate an understanding of the kinds of approaches that are most likely to provide challenge and justify the choice of a particular approach in a particular set of circumstances. The following goals for extension tasks (Eyre 1997) provide a useful aide memoire:

- critical thinking;
- creative thinking;
- increased independence;

- problem-solving ability;
- reflection; and
- self-knowledge.

School-wide opportunities

These are defined as opportunities not restricted to the identified gifted and talented cohort but offered outside normal departmental provision. While much of the provision in curriculum areas will be part of classroom practice, the development of the wider framework of opportunities is likely to be part of a school-wide offer. Good provision for the gifted and talented is broad-based and balanced. All pupils, including the gifted and talented, benefit from access to a wide range of experiences. If, as Gardner (2000) suggests, ability exists in a variety of possible domains, then pupils need to experience opportunities to operate within those domains if their ability is to be revealed. At secondary level these kinds of opportunities perform two functions. It may be that they offer a chance for pupils to develop their abilities in areas that they have not chosen to study. For example, pupils may play sport, act in plays, contribute to musical activity, etc. even though they are not chosen areas of study in Key Stage 4 and beyond. It is overly simplistic to suggest that pupils are only gifted *or* talented; many are both and while they may choose to study certain academic subjects they can also contribute significantly to a wider range of activity and derive considerable enjoyment from it.

School-wide opportunities may also provide the chance to try something new. Participating in a 'Model United Nations General Assembly' with other schools does not necessarily enhance examination chances but it does help to develop wider knowledge and broaden horizons. This same kind of outcome can be achieved by exposure to 'leading edge' experts in science or the arts as well as through potentially more mundane activities such as work experience. A good school for the gifted and talented does not see learning as restricted to exam classes but recognises the merit in stimulating thinking and challenging existing notions at every opportunity.

School-wide opportunities have always been to some extent dependent on the particular skills and interests of teachers in the school. A good school for the gifted and talented ensures a range of opportunities in different domains. If a school chooses to specialise by, for example, offering outstanding musical opportunities, then they need to ensure that the artistically talented or sporting child can also gain access to high-quality opportunities, whether this is provided within the school or beyond it.

School-wide opportunities might include:

- whole-school drama or musical productions;
- clubs and societies;
- competitions;
- access to experts, e.g. artist in residence or book week;

- residential visits;
- specialist workshops;
- visits and events;
- links with schools in other countries; and
- links with partner primary schools.

School-based enrichment opportunities

These are defined as opportunities that are offered to help selected pupils who have particular abilities and skills and are in the gifted and talented cohort. A good school for the gifted and talented aims to offer a wide range of experiences to many but also accelerated skills development for some. In deciding whether a particular opportunity should have open access or be for a selected group, this distinction is useful. The purpose and nature of the activity should determine to whom it is offered. If all additional opportunities are offered only to the gifted and talented cohort then the gifted and talented register serves to increase entitlement for some but at the expense of reduced entitlement for others. Conversely if open access is always the watchword then serious skills development will not occur.

Enrichment programmes invoke strong support and also extensive criticism in the research literature. On the plus side able/gifted pupils do benefit from the stimulation of their intellectual peers (Shore 2000) and increases in pace and complexity are easier to achieve in this kind of context. On the minus side no research evidence has proved significant long-term educational impact resulting from withdrawal programmes although increases in motivation and enjoyment are widely reported (Freeman 1998).

This research is important to note because schools tend to be drawn towards enrichment opportunities as a simple way to make provision, and to offer them without sufficient thought. Enrichment for skills development is only effective if it is carefully planned, usually part of an on-going scheme of activity and is led by someone with suitable expertise. The models used for skills development in sport provide a useful model for other areas. When monitoring enrichment activity the school should consider not only whether and how often enrichment occurs but whether it meets its skills development aims and how it enhances existing opportunities.

Community-based enrichment opportunities

A particular dilemma in the education of the gifted and talented is the extent to which the school is the primary context for the nurturing of abilities or talent. Of course, it will never be the sole educator, even for the most academic of subjects since home and school educate the pupil jointly. However, it is also the case that the school plays relatively little part in the development of some kinds of talent – a pupil learning karate or ballet may do so entirely in a location outside of school. Bloom (1985) in his retrospective study of high achievers found that some of the adults in his study began the development of their talent or ability in school but all later developed it outside the school context.

Advantages	**Disadvantages**
Some opportunities can only be offered in this form since they are unsuitable for the majority of children. Pace and complexity can be increased and so greater challenge offered in such sessions. Gifted children enjoy the stimulation of working with their intellectual peers. Feelings of intellectual isolation can be reduced through access to such opportunities.	Those who might benefit are not self-evident in the 4–11 age range and provision for some may reduce opportunities for others. Continuity of provision is difficult and expensive for a school to provide. Educational benefits only occur if the sessions are well planned, have clear goals and are linked directly to other learning.

Figure 1.2 Offering enrichment to selected groups of pupils

Key point

Overall, an effective school may choose to include enrichment for selected pupils as part of its provision. It will, however, have addressed the issues related to the rationale for this choice of approach, have clear learning outcomes for the sessions and have taken into account issues around continuity and progression prior to embarking on the project.

In the past schools have not seen their role in relation to the gifted and talented as extending beyond the school (and offering advice to parents on home support). Excellence in Cities (DfEE 1999), however, gives schools responsibility for alerting pupils and their parents to opportunities for talent development which exist on a local, regional or national basis. This is particularly important for the development of talents that are not well catered for in school. Local opportunities may include sports clubs and interest clubs (e.g. chess) as well as 'explorers' clubs', which are provided specifically for the gifted and talented. National opportunities include schemes run by museums and art galleries as well as the National Trust, etc. Finally, an increasing number of opportunities are appearing on the internet, and many families have found sites like 'nrich' to be invaluable in extending opportunities to develop skills in maths.

Key point

An effective school for the gifted and talented publicises local and national opportunities for the development of abilities and talent and alerts parents of pupils with particular abilities to the opportunities available.

Organisational arrangements

An effective school for the gifted and talented will consider the needs of high ability pupils when it makes decisions on organisational matters such as pupil grouping or assessment. Opportunities will exist to cater for the needs of able individuals, including the chance to work with others of like ability (even where this necessitates working with older pupils) and opportunities to access extension papers in SATs and higher level papers in GCSE. For the most part progress for gifted and talented pupils will be chartered through the school's general progress schemes but it is likely that a small number of gifted/talented pupils will need closer supervision. Such pupils include those with outstanding abilities who are subject to fast-track arrangements, those with special educational needs e.g. dyslexia, and those deemed to be significantly underachieving. Individual tracking is likely to be the responsibility of the Gifted and Talented Co-ordinator and may make use of an Individual Education Plan.

Pupil grouping arrangements also have an impact on provision for the gifted and talented. Effective schools for the gifted and talented may use any form of pupil grouping but are likely to set for at least maths, science and modern languages. Setting is not in itself a form of provision for the gifted and talented. Even within a top set, levels of achievement can vary considerably and differentiation will be needed. Setting is also problematic in that it requires a decision to be made about the pupil's potential for achievement at a time when talent development may be fluid and uneven. Setting does, however, provide a good context for presenting challenging opportunities and gifted pupils tend to prefer setted groups. However, for those pupils with latent potential or uneven skills, setting may lead to less challenge or a withdrawal of opportunities when they are relegated to a lower set. Research on setting in the secondary school (Ireson and Hallam 1999) suggests that there is a poor correlation between academic ability and sets in some schools and so setting arrangements need to be monitored carefully.

Social and emotional considerations

Stopper (2000) describes the relationship between intellectual and social/emotional development as complex. Work on definitions of high ability includes the role of emotional states, e.g. motivation, and work on high-achieving adults points to the role of emotional wellbeing in high achievement.

Pupils need to be confident and secure if they are to strive and take risks. This is the same for gifted and talented pupils as it is for others. Therefore, any provision made by schools for gifted and talented pupils should take into account its effect on the pupil or pupils. For one pupil, working with older pupils might be desirable and enjoyable; for another of similar ability it might be stressful and problematic.

Freeman (1998: 27) is unequivocal in saying: 'There is no reliable scientific evidence to show that exceptionally high ability *per se* is associated with emotional problems, or that inadequate education results in delinquent or disturbed behaviour.'

For adolescents social and emotional considerations are paramount. Csikszentmihalyi *et al.* (1997) in their study of talented teenagers identify a range of issues that should be of interest to any school: the desire of gifted and talented pupils to be part of the social group, the sacrifices they are forced to make in pursuit of high achievement and the resulting feelings of isolation. Gifted and talented adolescents are time poor, struggling to maintain social contact and yet give enough time to their chosen area. Without sympathetic support they may choose to disengage from academic study or talent development. Schools, in their desire to improve provision, must therefore be particularly careful to avoid adding to their overload.

In the effective school, the social and emotional needs of gifted and talented pupils are addressed in the same way as they are for other pupils. Their needs are not necessarily greater, but they do exist and intellectual progress should not be at the expense of social and emotional development.

Identification of the gifted and talented

Schools beginning to look at provision for gifted and talented pupils usually expect to adopt the approach which Freeman (1998) refers to as the 'diagnose and treat' approach. Under this system a decision is made as to who might constitute a gifted and/or talented cohort and then consideration is given to the educational treatment they may need. While this appears a logical approach, and one that may certainly constitute a part of effective school provision, it alone cannot lead to effective provision for the gifted and talented and indeed can lead to inequality of opportunity.

The main reason why this particular approach is flawed is that the identification of a cohort is not straightforward. Schools may make an attempt to identify their gifted and talented pupils and instead create an inaccurate cohort. This not only causes difficulties for the cohort in question, in terms of expectations, etc., but also, and perhaps more importantly, can cut off opportunities for those not identified.

Definitions of what it means to be considered gifted and talented vary. Freeman (1998: 1) defines the very able as: 'Those who demonstrate exceptionally high-level performance, whether across a range of endeavours or in a limited field, or those whose potential for excellence has not yet been recognised by either tests or experts.' She also draws a useful distinction between the recognised gifts of children and those of adults. In the case of adults, recognition is based on products which are the result of many years of dedication in the chosen domain, whereas for children it is usually precociousness in comparision to others of a similar age. It is possible to observe precocious ability or behaviour in some activities in the primary or secondary school. However, not all abilities or talents show themselves in this way at an early stage and even where they do only a limited range can be accurately measured. For example, pupils with precocious linguistic ability may be achieving at a level well in advance of their peers by the time they reach secondary school, however those with scientific ability may be less obvious. Even where precocious behaviour is observed, it is important to remember that it is only one indicator of giftedness.

For giftedness, as it is displayed by adults, research shows there are various developmental stages. Bloom and his colleages (1985) looked at 120 young adults performing very highly in sport (swimming and tennis), fine arts (music and sculpture) and science (maths and neurology). They identified three general phases in their childhood development:

- the playful phase;
- the precision phase; and
- the personal style phase.

The playful stage is characterised by a playful immersion in a field of interest. A child may find this activity rewarding and become interested in pursuing the field further, but this is largely a phase which involves enjoyment rather than striving for achievement. The second stage concerns the mastery of technical skills and a reaching for perfection. Here the child learns the 'rules of the game' and begins to master the techniques required for excellence in a given domain. The third or personal phase comes when a child is able to express their talent to create something new and uniquely different. In some activities or domains the personal stage does not come about for most gifted pupils until adolescence. Winner (1996) suggests that art may be an example of this, where the move from the conventional phase to the post-conventional phase may not take place well into adolescence. It is therefore difficult to identify on entry into secondary school those who might excel in the third and crucial stage in some, or indeed many subjects.

Gardner (2000) also suggests that the first and second phases can produce results which are confusing. The pupil in the playful phase encountering what Walters and Gardner (1986) call 'crystallising experiences' can, almost by chance, produce work which appears precocious. However when they enter the second phase, precision or mastery, the ability to convert this into a more recognised and accepted form may not be demonstrated. Equally the mastery stage may itself produce outcomes that are so satisfying and rewarding for the pupil that they choose to remain at stage two and become technically proficient but not in any way original. These pupils often achieve well up to GCSE but may have difficulty making the transition to more advanced study.

Yet another problem for the school seeking to identify the gifted and talented is that giftedness is a complex phenomenon. As Zorman (1998: 65) indicates:

It is not enough to measure specific abilities and talents. It is not even enough to measure the ability to learn when given mediation. Rather one must also search for the non-intellective components that may aid or deter development of talent and abilities.

What are these 'non-intellective components'? Jackson (2000) states that most current conceptualisations of giftedness in children stress the fortunate coincidence or interaction of multiple factors. These have been identified by various researchers as including motivation, personality, task commitment, opportunity, support from home, school and peers (Renzulli 1978; Monks 1992; Sternberg and Lubart 1992; Tannenbaum 1983; Feldman and Goldsmith 1996 and Gardner 1983).

Finally, there is the growing awareness that giftedness is multidimensional. It has long been recognised that children or adults may be gifted in a single area or in a range of domains. Gardner (1999) cites eight possible domains of intelligence in which an individual may display outstanding ability (see Figure 1.3).

In his 'triarchic theory', Sternberg (1986) cites three areas:

- analytic intelligence;
- creative intelligence; and
- practical intelligence.

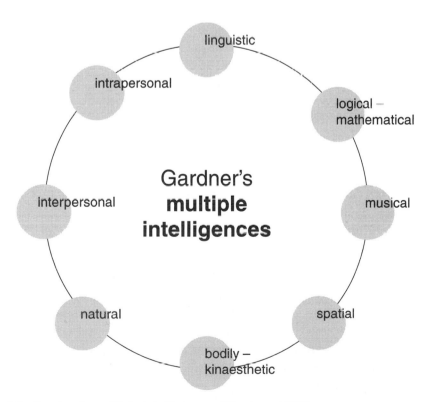

Figure 1.3 Gardner's multiple intelligences (Gardner 1999)

What may be less familiar are findings from such researchers as Achter *et al.* (1997) and others, who have shown that significant disparity exists between abilities in one domain and another. Differences in ability in language and maths was found to be the norm rather than the exception. Ninety-five per cent of the 1,000 gifted children they looked at had a considerable difference between their abilities in language and maths. As Winner (1996) puts it: 'Unevenness is the rule among academically gifted children while global gifted . . . is the exception.'

Implications of perspectives of giftedness

The most obvious conclusion from this review of the literature is that identification of the gifted and talented might at best be described as problematic. Yet, even when all these factors are taken into consideration it is obvious to any teacher that some of the pupils in his/her class are significantly brighter than others and that curriculum opportunities need to be adjusted to take account of this.

So how might the effective secondary school undertake identification and what might be the purpose? The chief purpose must be to create a better match between the curriculum opportunities on offer and the pupil's cognitive needs. The most obvious first step in identification is to make use of the wide range of achievement data available from primary schools in the form of SATs, World Class Tests, etc. To this can be added outcomes from cognitive ability tests (CATs) and recommendations on subject-specific abilities from staff. However, if the school is to avoid over-simplifying the identification process then a consideration of the possible 'talent pool' is another way to approach inclusion in the cohort.

Categories of pupils who have the potential to be gifted:

- pupils who appear to be exhibiting precocious talent or ability, i.e. they are achieving at a level significantly above that of their peers in one or a range of areas;
- pupils who are interested in an area and actively seek to pursue it, enjoying it for its own sake;
- pupils who appear to master the rules of a domain easily and can transfer their insights to new problems;
- pupils who observe their own behaviour and hence utilise a greater variety of learning strategies than others;
- pupils who exhibit any of the characteristics above plus a tendency towards non-conformity in the given domain.

Some of these categories can be measured, others cannot. It may be possible to create a register of gifted and talented pupils based on the first category, but in doing so it is likely that some gifted pupils will be overlooked. The creation of a register is not in itself straightforward or even a universal good. Any school creating a register must recognise its limitations and avoid directing challenging opportunities only to the pupils on the register.

> **Key point**
>
> The universal dilemma for schools seeking to make effective provision for gifted and talented pupils is the need to provide well for the group of pupils already recognised as gifted or talented and at the same time create opportunities for those who are not yet recognised to display their ability. This leads me to conclude that effective identification will be a combination of the assessment of precocious achievement or behaviour plus an emphasis on creating the conditions which will allow giftedness to develop and reveal itself.

Methods for identifying precocious ability

The DfEE in its Excellence in Cities initiative requires secondary schools to identify a cohort of pupils of between 5 per cent and 10 per cent of the overall school population who form the gifted and talented cohort and for whom a distinct teaching and learning programme should be available. This approach has been very successful in raising awareness of the needs of the gifted and talented and in encouraging curriculum experimentation. Even so, the creation of the cohort has been the most problematic aspect of the policy and tensions have arisen in 'thinking' schools regarding the extent to which the cohort should consist primarily of those who already demonstrate high achievement or of those who may have potential to do so but currently do not achieve highly. In the secondary sector many pupils will have reached the third stage of development (personal originality) and providing that the curriculum is structured to value such original thought and ideas (and generally the National Curriculum and exam syllabuses are) then achievement should be the norm for most gifted pupils. Exceptions to this general rule come largely in relation to pupils who are underachieving for a variety of reasons. Underachieving pupils are difficult to spot and may easily be overlooked. Common causes of underachievement are disaffection, lack of familiarity with the English language, dyslexia and poor organisational skills.

In seeking to create such a register, three broad forms of information are available to schools. All these forms have strengths and weaknesses and therefore the use of a combination is thought by most researchers to be essential. Montgomery (1996) states: 'What is quite clear is that uni-dimensional methods and tests are not successful in identifying the able.'

Available information

1. Tests
   - SATs, World Class Tests
   - cognitive ability or non-verbal reasoning tests
   - reading, spelling, maths
   - school progress and module tests
2. Diagnostic assessment
   - based on the work pupils produce (portfolios)

- performance in class, especially in question/answer sessions
- based on checklists of characteristics (general or subject specific)
3. Opinion
    - teacher nomination
    - parental nomination
    - self nomination
    - peer nomination

The fashion for testing in school has increased in recent years as part of an overall approach to the use of data as a measure of school improvement. SATs and other forms of assessment undertaken by pupils at various stages in their school career can provide useful data to demonstrate that a pupil is achieving at a level in advance of their peers. Therefore, pupils achieving highly in SATs might reasonably be included in the gifted cohort although, as has already been mentioned, high achievement in SATs tends to focus on mastery of what Gardner (2000) calls the 'rules of the game' and therefore is a better indicator of a competent expert than of a potentially gifted adult.

Other forms of testing can also provide useful data, although they too have their limitations. The strengths and limitations of tests, and in particular IQ tests, are well covered in OFSTED's review of current international research (Freeman 1998). In fact Howe (1995) suggests that we will never find a test that can be administered in childhood that will reliably predict eventual adult achievement. Yet IQ tests are still used to identify the gifted. In 'Highly Able Children' (House of Commons 1999), evidence given as part of the inquiry into provision for the highly able suggested a discrepancy of view amongst experts as to the value of using tests as an indicator of ability. Evidence submitted to the inquiry suggested that parents find IQ tests useful in providing 'observable hard evidence' in discussing the issue with schools. (Perhaps this is an indicator that schools are not always as open-minded as they could be when considering high ability). Overall the inquiry found as follows: 'the consensus of the evidence is that tests have some value in the recognition of both ability and achievement but are merely one form of evidence and cannot, in themselves, provide a definition of high ability' (p. xii).

Diagnostic assessment overcomes some of the problems related to tests and can help teachers to become better at recognising some aspects of high achievement. The English National Curriculum is helpful in assisting teachers to look up the 'levels' to decide how a piece of work might be judged and in providing a notional performance norm for pupils of a given age. Since the introduction of this type of national assessment framework, increasingly tighter judgements are being made on pupils' progress and this is obviously helpful in the identification of the gifted. 'Procedures for assessing pupils' attainment have continued to improve' (OFSTED 1999).

Portfolios are a useful way of recording the achievements of pupils and are particularly useful for charting the development of outstanding individuals or those whose talents are uneven. Portfolio-based evidence of achievement at a level significantly in advance of one's peers should be sufficient evidence for inclusion on a gifted register.

Checklists have proved a popular form of identification in schools but also have their problems. Few checklists are based on research evidence and many make use of anecdotal evidence so reducing their validity. In addition a checklist can only ever be a guide and give an overall sense of what it means to be gifted. Even experts disagree to some extent on the characteristics for inclusion. Hence checklists must be viewed with caution. (Subject-specific checklists can be more helpful in identifying domain-specific ability as is demonstrated in later chapters of this book.)

The most reliable forms of checklist are those based on actual research. The checklist below is based on the outcomes of work by Shore in which he was exploring the ways in which gifted pupils think (Freeman 1998, adapted from Shore 1991):

- Memory and knowledge – excellent memory and use of information
- Self-regulation – they know how they learn best and can monitor their learning
- Speed of thought – they may spend longer on planning but then reach decisions more speedily
- Dealing with problems – they add to information, spot what is irrelevant and get to the esssentials more quickly
- Flexibility – although their thinking is usually more organised than other children's, they can see and adopt alternative solutions to learning and problem solving
- Preference for complexity – they tend to make games and tasks more complex to increase interest
- Concentration – they have an exceptional ability to concentrate at will and for long periods of time from an early age
- Early symbolic ability – they may speak, read and write very early

Finally, the category of opinion. Parents are likely to be effective in identification since they observe their children most frequently. Robinson (2000) in her study of 100 kindgergartners found that the responses of parents clearly correlated with their children's assessed behaviour. Of course, such identification is reliant on an understanding of the indicators of ability and therefore parents in American studies are often given checklists of characteristics to help them in their assessment. Much work has been done to consider the effectiveness of teachers in identifying gifted and talented pupils. Once again the research base for this is well covered in Freeman (1998). The overall finding is that teachers can be effective in identifying the gifted and talented provided they have been trained in what to look for. Without training, they tend to confuse ability with neat, tidy, conforming pupils. My view would be that teacher identification is an essential part of the on-going identification process but that untrained teacher assessment can be inaccurate and dangerous.

> **Key point**
>
> Teachers in school should see themselves as 'talent spotters', constantly on the lookout for signs of ability or talent.

Methods for revealing ability

If revelation of ability is to be a partner to the more formal identification of precocious ability it must in its own way be rigorous and systematic. There are three key areas for schools to consider if they are to ensure effectiveness in identification through provision.

a) Providing the context

Here a school has two responsibilities: it must ensure range of provision and quality of provision. Range is important because it allows pupils to discover their talents. A pupil never introduced to improvised drama is unlikely to know that they have a talent for this. Many adults discover new abilities and talents in later life and this will always be the case. It is not possible for schools to offer opportunities in every area, but it is a strong argument for a broad and balanced curriculum. This also applies to pupils who demonstrate precocious ability in a particular domain. While they may wish to pursue their initial domain of interest, it is important to continue the process of offering opportunities in new areas because they may find they have additional domains of talent. Just because a pupil is good at maths it does not mean they should be excused art; they may discover they are equally talented in this area.

The quality of what is offered is equally as important as the range. If schools have low expectations of their pupils and set tasks accordingly, then it is difficult for those with the ability to achieve highly. Equally, if challenging opportunities are always offered to a restricted group then those outside the group are unable to demonstrate high levels of achievement. Where challenging opportunities are a regular feature of classroom provision, pupils will demonstrate their abilities through high level responses.

b) Observation of emerging ability

For identification through provision to occur it is necessary for outstanding outcomes to be observed. These outcomes might be in the form of written work, practical work or class discussion and debate. Two forms of observation should operate in the effective school. Firstly, the teacher should be involved in an on-going process of talent spotting. She or he may keep a log of significant responses or comments and these together form a body of identification evidence. Secondly, systematic observation may take place from time to time with another adult observing the pupil's responses while the teacher teaches. This second option allows for close observation which is difficult for the teacher to achieve while also teaching the lesson.

c) Recording of outcomes

As part of the regular process of updating the gifted and talented register, outcomes from the 'identification through provision' process should be collected and submitted. In this way new talents will be uncovered and pupils can be added to the list. An effective school is likely to revisit its identification framework at least annually, although of course individual teachers will adjust their cognitive demands on individual pupils as soon as significant ability is demonstrated.

Key point

For a school to provide high-quality identification procedures, its framework must include both methods for recognising precocious ability and for revealing emergent ability.

Modifying the curriculum to create challenge

The fundamental question facing schools when looking to improve provision for gifted and talented pupils is: What do we need to change in our existing curriculum in order to make it sufficiently challenging and motivating for gifted and talented pupils? This question has a uniquely English context and must be addressed accordingly. The National Curriculum outlines in considerable detail the knowledge, skills and concepts to be taught and even links them to specific recommended ages. This is quite different from other countries, for example the USA and Australia.

The National Curriculum

Much of the influential international literature on curriculum planning, e.g. Van Tassel-Baska (1992) and Maker and Nielson (1995), focuses on *creating* a curriculum which meets the needs of the gifted and talented. Here in England we are not actually creating a curriculum but rather assessing the effectiveness of our existing, nationally determined, curriculum and making necessary adjustments or modifications to it. This has both advantages and disadvantages. The most significant disadvantage is highlighted by Montgomery (2000: 131): 'We now have the situation where the National Curriculum and the methods by which it is taught have especially not led to a stimulating and educative experience for the gifted and talented.'

A preoccupation with content coverage and skills acquisition has led some teachers to focus on delivery rather than learning. They concentrate on what is being taught, rather than how it is being taught and what is being learnt. At worst this has actually reduced access to the kinds of learning opportunities most appropriate for gifted pupils.

The advantages of having a National Curriculum surround the possibilities of exploiting its requirements in an imaginative way. The National Curriculum is not in itself prescriptive as regards teaching methodologies and does include opportunities for higher order thinking – indeed it is actively required. While some teachers have become focused on didactic content delivery, others have used the same curriculum requirements to create challenging, stimulating and imaginative lessons. Even where teaching methodologies have been centrally prescribed in England, i.e. the literacy and numeracy strategies, some teachers have used the approaches to challenge their gifted pupils.

Key point

The National Curriculum can provide an effective context for exploring possibilities for using particular theoretical models or approaches.

How might a curriculum be changed?

Researchers looking to improve provision for gifted pupils are generally looking to provide a curriculum that Maker and Nielson (1995) call 'qualitatively different from the programme for all students'. Gallagher (1985) suggested that changes could be made to the content, method and learning environment. Figure 1.4 is adapted from Maker and Nielson (1995) and outlines the various possibilities available.

Changes to content (including process and product):
- enrichment – variety;
- extension – complexity/abstractness;
- higher order thinking – analysis, synthesis, evaluation;
- enquiry/problem solving;
- scaffolded learning (Vygotsky 1978);
- social interactional approaches.

Changes to method:
- task modification;
- questioning;
- increased pace;
- increased independence;
- increased direction;
- intellectual risk taking.

Changes to the learning context:
- programmes for the gifted;
- withdrawal groups;
- selective classes;
- mixed ability classrooms (differentiation);
- classes with older children (acceleration);
- non-school contexts.

Figure 1.4 Curriculum changes (Adapted from Maker and Nielson 1995)

In practice the range of possibilities can be bewildering and most teachers seeking to improve their practice begin by selecting a small range of approaches and deploying them where possible.

Changing the curriculum for selected gifted pupils or changing it for all?

When Maker and Nielson refer to creating a programme for the gifted that is 'qualitatively different' from the programme for all students they make an assumption that such a curriculum would only be suitable for the gifted. This perspective has dominated the work on the gifted and talented in the USA and Australia and led to the creation of special programmes for the gifted. The question of whether these 'qualitatively different' aspects of curriculum provision are useful for all children is only beginning to be explored in the USA and Canada (Shore 2000). In England it has been more thoroughly explored, although comprehensive empirical research studies of any scale are still lacking.

Teacher-researchers looking to develop their classroom practice in England have largely focused on in-class programmes. Therefore a body of small-scale work now exists spanning approximately 20 years. Two interesting findings have emerged from this work. First, it is possible for teachers to adjust their regular planning to provide work which meets the 'qualitatively different' requirement of Maker and Nielson and to provide this as part of the ordinary classroom offer (Eyre and Marjoram 1990). Second, where teachers have focused on planning to create challenge for the most able/gifted pupils, they often then choose to make the task available to a wider group of pupils, sometimes offering additional support to allow other pupils to access the same task. The reasons given for this by teachers are both pragmatic and pedagogical. In terms of classroom management a reduction in the number of tasks on offer allows for smoother operation and time for the teacher to work with individuals. In pedagogical terms the challenging tasks require more 'expert behaviour' or 'higher order thinking' and lead to higher levels of attainment, but are also intellectually stimulating and likely to be highly motivating regardless of a pupil's ability level.

The significance of these findings should not be underestimated. They provide compelling evidence of the benefits of an inclusive approach to the education of the gifted as advocated in Eyre (1997), Freeman (1998) and Montgomery (1996 and 2000). This kind of approach also goes some way towards solving the problems created by difficulties in the identification of young gifted pupils. If the 'qualitatively different' curriculum is a regular feature of general classroom provision then those who can demonstrate 'gifted behaviour' should reveal themselves. In 1992 HMI found that where specific attention was paid to the needs of gifted pupils there was often a general increase in the level of expectation of all pupils. This is likely to be as a result of teachers adopting an inclusive view of provision.

Of course, not all challenging opportunities can be made available in this way. Sometimes a task is only suitable for the small group who can demonstrate particular skills (e.g. working with very complex text) and therefore flexible ability grouping does have a significant place in effective curriculum provision. Equally, as Shore points out, the stimulation provided by intellectual peers aids cognitive development and, therefore, gifted or talented pupils need a chance to work with others of like ability. This may mean some access to extra activities for those gifted in a particular area (enrichment opportunities).

What do we mean by a challenge?

Much is said about the need to create more challenging opportunities for gifted and talented pupils. These can be achieved by any of the methods above, but what do we actually mean when we describe something as challenging? Hertzog *et al.* (1999), in a paper on challenging young gifted children, describe it as follows: 'A challenging activity would be one that would cause the students to perform at a level that extends beyond their comfort zone.'

Vygotsky (1978) introduced to education the idea of the zone of proximal development:

> The difference between the actual developmental level as determined by independent problem solving, and the level of potential development as determined through problem solving under adult guidance or in collaboration with more capable peers.

Both Vygotsky and Hertzog *et al.* indicate that in order for an activity to be challenging it must require the individual to strive for success rather than achieve it effortlessly. For gifted children many requirements of the school curriculum, deemed appropriate for children of their age, can be achieved effortlessly and are not challenging. Modification of the curriculum for gifted pupils should seek to increase challenge through the introduction of higher level thinking, skills development and problem solving. It is worth noting at this point that much 'so called' extension work provided in schools does not meet this criterion. Rather it focuses on increasing the volume of work undertaken by gifted pupils, often meaning more work at the same level.

The Vygotsky zone of proximal development does not just focus on increased levels of difficulty but also recognises that work which is over-demanding may prove impossible and demotivating. This is the same for gifted pupils as for those who find learning difficult. Hence effective assessment of pupils' current levels of understanding is absolutely crucial to creating effective challenge.

Csikszentmihalyi (1990) uses the term 'flow' to describe a state of mind in which suitable challenge is linked to appropriate skills. To achieve a state of 'flow', expectations must be high enough to require an individual to strive while skills levels must be good enough to allow for the goal to be achieved. Where expectation is too high and skills too low frustration is the result; where expectation is too low and skills too high, boredom.

Of course each individual has a different set of circumstances in which they encounter flow. Some individuals can cope with more challenge than others; some find risk taking exhilarating, others find it frightening. Modifications to the school

high challenge low skill	low challenge low skill
high challenge high skill	low challenge high skill

Figure 1.5 Flow (Mihaly Csikszentmihalyi 1990)

curriculum for gifted pupils should aim for flow, not for pressure. Too much low level activity does not lead to flow and too much acceleration of learning can lead to pressure. Learning should be fun and, if the development of ability or talent loses that element of fun, then we are unlikely to produce rounded, fulfilled individuals.

How gifted pupils think and learn

If a school is to adjust or modify its curriculum provision to make it more appropriate for gifted and talented pupils, then an understanding of how gifted children think and learn is essential. Gilhooley (1996) describes thinking thus:

Thinking is an activity that has long intrigued and puzzled psychologists and philosophers – and continues to do so. Since all valuable innovations in the arts and sciences originate from fruitful thinking, it is a process of evident importance. At a more prosaic level, thought is frequently required to deal with various frustrations that arise in everyday activities. Even when not dealing with any pressing problems, thinking is always occurring, during periods of wakefulness, albeit often in a free flowing daydreaming fashion.

In recent years, in England, growing attention has been given to the importance of developing pupils' thinking. Fisher (1992) has led the way in primary schools with his work on teaching thinking, and Shayer and Adey's (1981) pioneering work on using cognitive conflict in science (CASE) has been highly influential in secondary schools. McGuinness (1999) provided a review of current research into thinking skills and related areas for the DfEE. She concluded, perhaps not surprisingly, that successful approaches tend to have a strong theoretical underpinning, well-designed and contextualised materials, explicit pedagogy and good teacher support. What must concern the school looking at creating effective provision for gifted and talented pupils, is whether a general increase in a focus on thinking will in itself improve provision for gifted pupils.

Bruce Shore and his team at McGill University in Montreal have been exploring the thinking and learning of gifted pupils for many years and conclude that gifted learners do seem to use strategies that others never use (Shore 2000). These strategies include a three-way interaction between speed, flexibility and metacognitive knowledge. Shore found that gifted pupils could usually work with both speed and accuracy but that *accuracy* was the salient characteristic in high ability. Most gifted pupils who are prone to make careless errors learn to concentrate on accuracy because *self monitoring* is one of the strategies they invoke frequently. The ability to reflect on our thinking processes (*metacognition*) is seen by Shore as linked to both flexible thinking and to high ability. Some gifted pupils were found to be flexible thinkers whilst others were less so, but all gifted pupils were aware of the need to explore alternative solutions when obvious ones failed to work. What is interesting here is that gifted pupils are using the approaches which are recognised as those used by adults expert in their field. They may not be producing outstanding results but they are using the same strategies. Shore suggests that gifted pupils draw on a repertoire of skills that are available to others but use them more imaginatively and self monitor or regulate their use in order to produce outcomes of increasing sophistication.

This would suggest that for a school to provide effectively for its gifted and talented pupils a focus on the development of critical and creative thinking linked to metacognition would provide a good basis for the approach. This is in itself not a new or original idea. Most of the recent literature in this field in England (Montgomery 1996; Eyre 1997; Koshy and Casey 1998, Freeman 1998) reaches this conclusion. What is more interesting is to examine the extent to which the thinking skills approach, which is being widely advocated for all pupils, can provide the basis for gifted and talented provision. In essence a focus on the development of thinking will lead, in part, to the use of problem solving, problem creating and higher order thinking. It will also promote self regulation of ideas and metacognition. Therefore this approach, if well handled by the teacher, can prompt gifted pupils to invoke creative or innovative solutions and begin to produce unique or original ideas. However, even when thinking skills approaches are used to provide challenge for the gifted, suitable learning goals need to be identified.

Key point

Well-grounded approaches which focus on developing thinking are good for all pupils. However, appropriately used, they can also provide a vehicle for the deployment of the complex repertoire of intellectual skills that gifted pupils utilise.

A second issue related to the learning of gifted and talented pupils concerns differences in learning styles between the precociously talented child and the potentially gifted adult. If all giftedness were related to precocious ability then an appropriate educational response might be to allow pupils to progress rapidly through the curriculum in order to succeed early and move on further than others. However, the research evidence suggests that achievement is not merely a race with the gifted being the faster runners. Giftedness or expertise is the result of efficient learning and a good deal of hard work and practice. Howe (1995) says:

> Exceptional people climb higher than the rest of us do, though they may climb faster and more efficiently. But they do climb all the same, just like everyone else. No-one miraculously arrives at the peak of their accomplishments.

So all pupils, including the gifted, need to learn to concentrate and persevere, even when outcomes are unrewarding. Even gifted pupils need to learn the 'rules of the game'.They need to learn the techniques required to play the piano or the skills needed to make a good football player. They need to learn how to create a beginning and an end to a piece of writing and how to calculate quickly in mental maths. They will, however, tend to learn these skills efficiently and progress rapidly in skills acquisition, and so they will need either to move on to learning new skills before their peers or to begin to use and apply the skills learnt with increasing rigour. If a pupil has learnt a skill more quickly than others then two options are available. The pupil can move on to a new skill or they can 'apply' that skill. In the literature this is defined as *extension* (Eyre and Marjoram 1990) and can provide a viable alternative to moving on to the next concept (*acceleration*).

An effective classroom for the gifted and talented

This book is concerned to offer practical ideas on how to make effective classroom provision for the gifted and talented. This section, therefore, has restricted itself to looking at cross-curricular or generic approaches and to considering measures of effectiveness. Determining what might constitute effectiveness in classroom provision is a key consideration for any school. This chapter has looked at the range of issues that might be taken into account and how these might influence school and provision. The checklist in Figure 1.6 is based on a synthesis of the research findings mentioned at earlier points in this chapter and presents an overall framework for reviewing classroom provision.

For teachers reviewing their own practice or that of others, there is a need for a more detailed set of indicators that are linked to existing practice in the school. Figure 1.7 takes the points made in Figure 1.6 and expands them to provide a framework for staff discussion and also for possible monitoring. Each of the points in Figure 1.7 provides a stimulus for staffroom discussion and could usefully form an agenda for school improvement in the education of gifted and talented pupils. Why, for example, is it necessary to have a combination of subject expertise and teacher enthusiasm? One answer may be that while subject expertise is vital in recognising the progression routes within the subject and the potential for

---

Effective classroom provision for gifted and talented pupils:

1. builds on what we know about how gifted and talented children think and learn;
2. offers opportunities to reveal ability as well as operate at high levels;
3. offers structured access to higher levels of achievement;
4. uses assessment for determining learning as well as assessing learning outcomes;
4. requires children to strive, persist and self regulate;
5. makes learning enjoyable as well as challenging and rewards intellectual risk taking and innovation.

Figure 1.6 Effective classroom provision

challenge within tasks, it does not in itself motivate pupils. Gifted and talented children are motivated by both knowledge and fun (Joswig 1998) and therefore an effective teacher of gifted and talented pupils will provide both.

Classroom considerations

- Agreement regarding higher level skills children might acquire within the subject
- High teacher expectation
- Subject expertise and teacher enthusiasm
- Variety in teaching styles and nature of tasks
- Teacher–pupil relationship which encourages questions, personal reflection and the formulation of personal opinions
- Clear outcomes both generally and for most able
- Balance between structure and independence
- Recognition of prior learning
- Honest feedback and target setting
- Assessment which relates to objectives and does not overmeasure
- Interest in teaching and learning the subject, not just the syllabus
- Fun and laughter and maybe a little quirkiness
- No artificial ceilings
- No MOTS (more of the same) or overload

Figure 1.7 A framework for discussion

References

Achter, J. A., Benbow, C. P. and Lubinski, D. (1997) 'Rethinking multipotentiality among the intellectually gifted: A critical review and recommendations'. *Gifted Pupil Quarterly*, **41**, 5–15.

Bloom, B. (ed.) (1985) *Developing Talent in Young People*. New York: Basic Books.

Clark, C. and Callow, F. (1998) *Educating Able Children*. London: David Fulton Publishers.

Csikszentmihalyi, M. (1990) *Flow: The Psychology of Optimal Experience*. New York: Harper and Row.

Csikszentmihalyi, M., Rathunde, K. and Whalen, S. (1997) *Talented Teenagers: The Roots of Success and Failure*. Cambridge: Cambridge University Press.

DfEE (1999) *Excellence in Cities*. London: HMSO.

Eyre, D. (1997) *Able Children in Ordinary Schools*. London: David Fulton Publishers.

Eyre, D. (1999) 'Ten years of provision for the gifted in Oxfordshire ordinary schools: insights into policy and practice'. *Gifted and Talented International*, **14**, 12–20.

Eyre, D. and Marjoram, T. (1990) *Enriching and Extending the National Curriculum*. London: Kogan Page.

Feldman, D. H. (with Goldsmith, L.) (1996) *Nature's Gambit: Child Prodigies and the Development of Human Potential*. New York: Basic Books.

Fisher, R. (1992) *Teaching Children to Think*. Cheltenham: Stanley Thornes (Publishers) Ltd.

Freeman, J. (1998) *Educating the Very Able: Current International Research*. London: HMSO.

Friedman, R. C. and Shore, B. M. (eds) *Talents Unfolding: Cognition and Development*. Washington DC: American Psychological Association.

Gallagher, J. J. (1985) *Teaching the Gifted Child*. Newton: Allyn and Bacon Inc.

Gardner, H. (1983) *Frames of Mind: The Theory of Multiple Intelligences*. New York: Basic Books.

Gardner, H. (1999) *Intelligence Reframed: Multiple Intelligences for the 21st Century*. New York: Basic Books.

Gardner, H. (2000) 'The giftedness matrix: A developmental perspective', in Friedman, R. C. and Shore, B. M. (eds) *Talents Unfolding: Cognition and Development*. Washington DC: American Psychological Association.

Gilhooley, K. J. (1996) *Thinking: Directed, Undirected and Creative*. London: Academic Press.

Hertzog, N. B., Klein, M. M. and Katz, L. G. (1999) 'Hypothesising and theorising: challenge in an early childhood curriculum'. *Gifted and Talented International*, 14, 38–49.

HMI (1992) *Education Observed: The Education of Very Able Children in Maintained Schools*. London: HMSO.

House of Commons (1999) Education and Employment Committee, Third Report, 'Highly Able Children'. London: HMSO.

Howe, M. (1995) 'What can we learn from the lives of geniuses?', in Freeman, J. (ed.) *Actualizing Talent*. London: Cassell.

Ireson, J. and Hallam, S. (1999) 'Raising standards: Is ability grouping the answer'. *Oxford Review of Education*, 25(3), 343–58.

Jackson, N. E. (2000) 'Strategies for modeling the development of giftedness in children', in Friedman, R. C. and Shore, B. M. (eds) *Talents Unfolding: Cognition and Development*. Washington DC: American Psychological Association.

Joswig, H. (1998) 'Motivational learning conditions in gifted pupils', *Gifted and Talented International*, 13, 28–33.

Kennard, R. (1996) *Teaching Mathematically Able Children*. Oxford: NACE (National Association for Able Children in Education).

Kerry, T. and Kerry, C. (2000) 'The centrality of teaching skills in improving able pupil education', *Educating Able Children*, 4(2), 13–19.

Koshy, V. and Casey, R. (1998) *Effective Provision for Able and Exceptionally Able Children*. London: Hodder and Stoughton.

Maker, C. J. and Nielson, A. B. (1995) *Teaching Models in Education of the Gifted*. Texas: pro-ed.

McGuinness, C. (1999) 'From thinking skills to thinking classrooms'. DfEE research brief no. 115. London: DfEE.

Monks, F. J. (1992) 'Development of gifted children: The issues of identification and programming', in Monks, F. J. and Peters, W. (eds) *Talent for the Future*. Assen/Maastricht: Van Gorcum.

Montgomery, D. (1996) *Educating the Able*. London: Cassell.

Montgomery, D. (2000) 'Inclusive education for able underachievers: Changing teaching and learning', in Montgomery, D. (ed.) *Able Underachievers*. London: Whurr.

OFSTED (1999) *Annual Report of Chief Inspector for Schools 1998/99*. London: The Stationery Office.

Renzulli, J. S. (1978) 'What makes giftedness? Reexamining a definition', *Phi Delta Kappa*, **60**, 180–84.

Robinson, N. M. (2000) 'Giftedness in very young children: How seriously should it be taken?', in Friedman, R. C. and Shore, B. M. (eds) *Talents Unfolding: Cognition and Development*. Washington DC: American Psychological Association.

Sammons, P., Hillman, J. and Mortimore, P. (1996) *Key Characteristics of Effective Schools*. Ringwood: MBC Distribution Services.

Shayer, M. and Adey, P. (1981) *Towards a Science of Science Teaching*. Oxford: Heinemann.

Shore, B. M. (1991) 'How do gifted children think differently?' AGATE (*Journal of the Gifted and Talented Education Council of Alberta Teachers Association*) 5(2), 19–23.

Shore, B. M. (2000) 'Metacognition and flexibility: Qualitative differences in how gifted children think', in Friedman, R. C. and Shore, B. M. (eds) *Talents Unfolding: Cognition and Development*. Washington DC: American Psychological Association.

Sternberg, R. J. (1986) 'A triarchic theory of intelligence', in *Conceptions of Giftedness*, ed. Sternberg, R. J. and Davidson, J. E. Cambridge: Cambridge University Press.

Sternberg, R. J. and Lubart, T. I. (1992) 'Creative giftedness', in Colangelo, N., Assouline, S. G. and Ambroson, D. L. (eds) *Talent Development: Proceedings from the 1991 Henry B. and Jocelyn Wallace National Research Symposium on Talent Development*. Unionville, New York: Trillium, pp. 66–88.

Stopper, M. J. (2000) *Meeting the Social and Emotional Needs of Gifted and Talented Children*. London: David Fulton Publishers.

Tannenbaum, A. J. (1983) *Gifted Children: Psychological and Educational Perspectives*. New York: Macmillan.

Van Tassel-Baska, J. (1992) *Planning Effective Curriculum for Gifted Learners*. Denver, Colorado: Love Publishing Company.

Vygotsky, L. S. (1978) *Mind in Society*. Cambridge, Mass.: Harvard University Press.

Walters, J. and Gardner, H. (1986) 'Crystallizing experience', in Sternberg, R. J. and Davidson, J. E. (eds), *Conceptions of Giftedness*. New York: Cambridge University Press.

Winner, E. (1996) *Gifted Pupils: Myths and Realities*. New York: Basic Books.

Zorman, R. (1998) 'A model for adolescent giftedness identification via challenges (MAGIC)' *Gifted and Talented International*, **13**, 65–72.

CHAPTER 2

English and Literacy

Geoff Dean

Introduction

There is little research or published material currently available about gifted and/or talented pupils in English. No one clear reason can account for this shortfall. Explanations might include former attitudes to the subject by its teachers, the lack of attention paid to notions of learning in English, or the ways in which the gifted and talented in English have been historically treated, relative to, for instance, those who display similar early ability in subjects such as mathematics.

> In the English teaching profession there are no doubt many differing views about what ability in English might mean but it is highly significant that the issue of ability itself does not seem to generate much debate. (Goodwyn (ed.) 1995: 2)

Bothering about the reasons for this lack of knowledge concerning the more able pupils in English, however, is less important than actually beginning properly to meet their needs.

Establishing exactly what 'gifted and talented' might mean in English has not been without its problems. Most people would probably agree that Lenny Henry, or any other stand up comic of equal stature, should undoubtedly be regarded as 'gifted and talented'. The ability to think quickly, make witty and unrehearsed responses or, sometimes, fully developed discourses are obvious examples of advanced linguistic abilities. Readers familiar with the writing of James Joyce would also certainly describe him as 'gifted and talented'. He was capable of subverting and redefining notions of written text, bringing about significant change to accepted contemporary views of the novel. Reviewers writing in the literature sections of most broadsheet newspapers have carefully read considerable numbers of texts, and successfully mediate the meanings of those books to interested potential readers in their carefully crafted critiques. All these 'gifted and talented' users of English display obvious skills within the broadest understanding of the subject, yet those skills have been deployed in quite different ways. Recommending a programme of studies to support, challenge and develop all their possible areas of language growth appropriately can be seen as an extremely difficult project. Yet, every day teachers face groups of pupils in classrooms evidencing equally broad language-based capabilities and are expected to provide differentiated lessons to encourage suitable progress for them all.

Before the arrival of comprehensive schools there had been little perceived need in Britain to offer separate and directed provision for more able/gifted and talented pupils. They were, so everybody believed, already being separated from their peers in grammar schools and educated appropriately there! Much of the early attention given to the more able was the result of a growing interest across all subjects in 'differentiation', possibly influenced by the work of Freeman (1980, 1991), Gallagher (1985), Gardner (1983), and Renzulli (1986). An HMI publication (1992), drawn from inspection evidence, made an uncompromising case for giving proper attention to the more able: 'Very able pupils in maintained primary and secondary schools are often insufficiently challenged by the work they are set' (HMSO 1992: vii).

Deborah Eyre drew together much of the material of this 'quiet revolution', as she called it, in her book *Able Children in Ordinary Schools* (1997), deflecting attention from the 'all-rounder' to pupils with marked abilities in separate subjects:

> At the heart of this work is the recognition that the number of pupils who have significant ability is much greater than had previously been considered. This is because previous assessment methods had always relied on the identification of all-round or overall ability. This is fairly rare, but significant ability in certain subjects is more plentiful: outstanding musicians may not be good at history, good mathematicians may not be good at art, etc. A focus on specific ability as well as all-round ability helps to maximise pupil potential and has the added advantage of helping to raise school standards and examination results. (p. vi)

Only since the mid 1990s has any significant attention been paid to gifted and talented pupils in English. The most important books about the subject of that time, *The Challenge of English in the National Curriculum* (Protherough and King (eds) 1995) and *Teaching English* (Brindley (ed.) 1994) make no mention of this topic. An article by Peter Daw in the *English & Media Magazine*: 'Differentiation and its meanings', had a genuinely influential effect on the way this topic was discussed among English teachers:

> The term 'differentiation' does not have a long history as educational jargon but it currently occupies a central place in most discussions of teaching and learning . . . Two of the influences that have led to its increased use are the development of the National Curriculum, with its assessment, and the emergence of the Ofsted inspection. (1995: 11)

Andrew Goodwyn, researching English at the University of Reading, offered a tentative exploration of what ability in English might mean:

> The most able can be male or female and can be identified by their noticeable maturity beyond their years. They tend to enjoy challenging texts but they are

more interested in wide reading than in a few canonical texts. They have immediate responses to their reading but are marked by a wish to return to those responses and re-evaluate them. They write in very imaginative ways and are technically proficient. (Goodwyn (ed.) 1995: 26–7)

His studies with teachers showed their reluctance to develop such criteria further, hampered as they were by their adherence to developing the 'personal growth' of their pupils. My own research in Oxfordshire, culminating in the publication of *Challenging the More Able Language User* (Dean 1998), directly influenced by Deborah Eyre's book quoted above, confirmed the difficulties of provision discovered by Goodwyn.

The emergence of a new interest in the more able coincided with changing attitudes about how pupils 'learn' language and the development of ideas about what might constitute 'progression' in the subject (Carter (ed.) 1990; Bain *et al.* (eds) 1992). Nationally, educational researchers and new curriculum initiatives began shifting attention from the issues of teaching to those of learning in classrooms of all subjects. Researchers in language learning were hugely interested in the work of Vygotsky (1986), eager to explore the possibilities of the notion of 'scaffolding', with its potential to support and direct learning in more structured ways.

It was commonly accepted, until this time, to think of the subject 'English' as the natural vehicle for teaching language and literacy skills in primary and secondary classrooms. Yet, since the introduction into primary schools of the National Literacy Strategy in 1998, it has become clear that the subject was insufficiently defined in the primary sector. Too little systematic learning of language and literacy was being planned for pupils in Key Stages 1 and 2, despite the considerable number of language-based activities taking place in lessons. Those concerned with language development in the earlier stages have been surprised about the accelerated pace and the broader range of their pupils' learning in a context where planning and teaching have been more successfully focused. As a consequence of this realisation, many secondary teachers of English are vigorously reconsidering some of the long-standing assumptions behind their own practices and attitudes. These sorts of re-evaluations have, in their turn, led to changing views about the relationship between the subject and its more able pupils.

Until very recently, teachers of English rarely discussed the most suitable ways in which pupils, already displaying advanced linguistic skills when they arrived in secondary school, could be assisted to attain even greater ability.

Although there seems to be a valuable match between pupil and teacher perceptions, teachers themselves are somewhat at a loss when it comes to providing for the more able. For example, many teachers interviewed in the study felt very ill at ease with any strict definition of ability in English and they also expressed considerable uncertainty about what to do with very able pupils; they felt they could recognise them as individuals but were unclear how to help them. As one experienced teacher put it when asked what should be done about the more able in English, 'I wish I knew.' (Goodwyn 1995: 15)

Usually, those pupils labelled as 'more able' were given 'tougher' (mostly meaning longer) writing assignments or 'harder' books to read as a consequence of being so identified. Because differentiation in English was most regularly described as 'through outcome', the more able pupils were expected to perform better in whatever tasks they had been allocated. By definition they usually sat on the top of the pile, and were expected, as a matter of course, to produce superior written outcomes or offer the more perceptive insights in their textual encounters, not necessarily of a kind designed to lead to further learning. Not much special preparation was offered and few extension activities were planned to enable these particular pupils to not only demonstrate, but also further develop their advanced capabilities in specified ways. It was not surprising that some young people deemed 'able', or 'gifted', or 'talented' in English felt that they were being 'punished' for being better in the subject than their peers. There were instances (Dean 1998) of pupils not prepared to inform their teachers about the demanding books they were reading for pleasure beyond the classroom, as they 'might have to write about them!'

> Talented and gifted pupils in English became a further focus of interest when the Labour government introduced the National Literacy Strategy into primary schools in 1998 (HMSO 1998). The Strategy, designed and implemented to raise generally low standards of literacy across the whole population, was mistakenly interpreted by some trainers, and the teachers they trained, as a 'straitjacket' of restrictive, mechanistic methodologies, their order and organisation determined by the clock. A survey by the Association of Teachers and Lecturers, reported in the *TES* (29.1.99), suggested that many teachers believed that the Literacy Hour was not capable of meeting the needs of the more able. Where the circumstances described above prevailed, the most able pupils in English did indeed quickly become bored with their 'Literacy Hours', causing important rethinking about how the needs of these particular pupils could be best met. (Dean 1998: 57)

With the extension of the principles of the Literacy Strategy into secondary schools in September 2001, the same concerns will need to be addressed for the more able pupils in Key Stages 3 and 4. They have to be enabled to gain the greatest benefits from planned programmes that build on their current attainment.

In 1999 a House of Commons Education and Employment Committee, investigating provision for the highly able, had no doubts about the importance of giving proper attention to this group of pupils:

> In recent years, education policy has concentrated on ensuring that all children reach at least a minimum level of competence. However, the Government and those involved in education are now taking a greater interest in the education of highly able children. Why should we be concerned about the provision for highly able children? Because the commonly held view that they can 'get by on their own' is not borne out by the facts: they are entitled to have their needs

addressed as much as any other children. There is also evidence of an association between good provision for the most able in a school and for all the children in a school. (The Stationery Office 1999: v)

English departments catering appropriately for their most able pupils have, similarly, discovered that they are making the best provision for all their pupils. It follows that if the most worthwhile learning programme leading to genuine progression has been established for those pupils who can go furthest, then all other language learners will have been attended to.

This committee's report was part of a wider government interest in, and exploration of, gifted and talented pupils. Projects such as Excellence in Cities have drawn attention to able pupils attending schools in some of the, apparently, least supportive circumstances experiencing appropriate curriculum programmes designed to enable them to reach their full potential. The government's Qualifications and Curriculum Authority (QCA) has been involved in research and evidence-gathering about best practice in educating and developing gifted and talented pupils in all National Curriculum subjects during 2000 and 2001.

So, gradually but inevitably, primary teachers and teachers of English in secondary schools have had to become aware of the challenge presented by more able pupils, and are beginning to recognise that there will be an increasing imperative to provide properly for them. The rest of this chapter will set out ways in which that provision could be approached and put into practice.

Identification

There are no exact measurements to help identify gifted and talented pupils in English, but there are a number of common characteristics of this small proportion of pupils with more advanced literacy skills. Being more able in regard to language and literacy usually refers to that group of pupils who enter secondary school each year:

- capable of demonstrating close reading skills and attention to detail;
- more sensitive to the nuances of language use as they attempt to make meaning through their own writing, drawing on the models of texts they have read (it is not a coincidence that the most able pupils in English usually have a very well developed, sophisticated sense of humour);
- likely to be more fluent and confident readers, possibly having read a broader range of texts (although not necessarily just fiction texts);
- with readier, incisive critical responses, displaying more marked pleasure and involvement in language tasks than that of other pupils;
- already able to read with more meaning, drawing on inference and deduction; 'reading between and through the lines';
- probably able to articulate their insights by speaking more confidently and precisely about their own writing intentions, or those of other writers they have read (although their speaking skills may need further support);

- able to approach writing tasks more thoughtfully and make more careful preparation for them, readily considering issues such as the way in which the text type fits the purpose, and making more precise choices of language;
- likely to be able to explain how their written work can be improved;
- able to make relationships between different sorts of texts already read, and choosing future reading with greater purpose;
- most importantly – able to *reflect* carefully on the sorts of language and linguistic engagements they are encountering, and having some insight into their own abilities.

Gifted and talented pupils in English do not, however, necessarily arrive in their secondary schools fully formed. Some might not even be regarded as displaying any sort of outstanding or notable characteristics when compared with their main-stream peers in the early stages of their secondary education. Unlike more able mathematicians, for instance, skills in this particular area of learning are not always precociously apparent. Because much textual interaction and meaning making, and a closer attention to the effects of language, require certain levels of maturity and some experience of life, a large proportion of the more able might not be identifiable until their adolescence. Even then, a sympathetic or stimulating teacher, or a strik-ingly powerful text, could be the reasons for a pupil adopting a new and noteworthy approach to literary/literacy studies. Another obstacle to easy identification might come about because potentially able pupils have not been provided with the necessary contexts to enable them to demonstrate their skills. If the tasks they are expected to take part in have been commonplace and the prevailing atmosphere of lessons not conducive to lively and exploratory language engagement, there is little likelihood that young people will be sufficiently stimulated to produce remarkable outcomes. All of these issues require teachers of English to be continually alert and sensitive to the linguistic development of their pupils, and regularly planning the sorts of textual engagements, in a variety of discourses, likely to bring the best results from them.

There will, of course, be a proportion of students whose advanced attainment has been noticeable from the time they started school, and about whom the primary schools will already have clear evidence to share with their receiving secondary colleagues. Occasionally in the past, such pupils might well have been identified, but in the transfer arrangements their needs have not been fully met. Increasing attention to and greater understanding of 'progression' in language and literacy learning will go a long way towards ensuring that these young people are given appropriate attention from the moment they arrive in Year 7, and that subsequent planned teaching and learning are based on their already established abilities.

The National Literacy Strategy, properly implemented, offers the opportunity for encouraging a different dialogue between primary teachers and their secondary colleagues about the nature of 'progression' and continuity, from one phase of education to the next. Only two or three years ago secondary English departments were often dismissive of the standards achieved by their incoming pupils in their feeder primary schools, and took little account of the levels of attainment described by the Key Stage 2 tests. That attitude has altered since the implementation of the Strategy, as teachers in secondary English departments have increasingly discovered that many primary pupils are being asked to undertake and manage a programme of language learning in advance of the sorts of expectations asked of their own, older, students.

An English department in a school already confident about identifying and providing fully for its more able pupils, and supported in its procedures through agreed policy, is likely to be at an enormous advantage. Such a department will be already looking out for these pupils, because it realises the strong probability that a proportion of each year group will qualify for this attention. It is also more likely to begin providing appropriately for its more able pupils, with resources and programmes to hand, as soon as they have been identified. But this well-prepared department will still need to have ready essential, clearly articulated and properly understood theories of how pupils make progress and grow as language and literacy users.

Progression in English

Until very recently, gifted and talented pupils were often recognised in the English departments in which they worked, but they were rarely expected to make progress in carefully focused ways. In grammar and independent schools, English departments would assume that most of their pupils were, indeed, more able and many would be 'gifted and talented'. Usually these pupils had already displayed their superior linguistic skills by succeeding in their difficult entrance examinations, and had probably used those same skills to demonstrate the extent of their learning in other subjects. Even where there was a preponderance of such pupils, however, it was rare to find that the department had devised teaching and learning schemes of work designed to enable them to become more accomplished readers, or writers, or speakers and listeners, across a broad range of skills associated with each of those modes of language. There is so often an assumption that these pupils have already been fully taught how to read and write by the time they arrive at secondary school, and they require no further teaching. What they really need, so the thinking goes, is plenty of practice of these skills.

Teachers in these circumstances would, of course, want their pupils to read and study more 'challenging' texts, and they would set essays or comparable written tasks requiring pupils to respond in a 'sophisticated' manner. There would usually be debates and class discussions on taxing and demanding subjects. Very regularly, in departments with large numbers of capable pupils, the teachers would 'accelerate' individuals, whole classes or even year groups, entering them for examinations in the subject at least a year before the normal chronological age. The relevant pupils would certainly have gained benefit from these organisational arrangements, and most would have responded positively to these high expectations. But, there are important fundamental issues of learning and personal development also needed by such pupils, which are not addressed through the provisions described above, and they are not always suitable in schools where fewer pupils qualify for gifted and talented support.

A helpful starting point for an English department reconsidering the provision for its more able pupils is to anticipate how teachers might respond to the stark, but fair, question posed by a parent of a very able pupil as the child approaches the end of Year 9: 'How can you demonstrate and produce evidence to show that my child has made real progress as a reader (or writer etc.) during the time that s/he has been taught by this department?' To be ready with a confident answer the department would need to have already agreed what it might mean by the term 'reader', to have a working sense of the qualities defining a 'good reader', and a planned programme for ensuring that 'good readers' could become even more accomplished. Recognising that most work in the subject is designed within what the linguist George Keith calls 'the four gerunds of English: reading, writing, speaking and listening', the department would need to be similarly prepared with answers embracing writing, and speaking and listening. Few departments would currently be able to offer a spontaneous, collective response to such a challenge.

Knowledge about language learning, and the ways that pupils make headway as language users, has grown enormously during the last 30 years of the twentieth century. The history of the teaching of English in different countries, from the early days of mass education, was regularly bedevilled and influenced by predominant political pressures over all other considerations. Modern research and the outcomes of classroom practice on three continents, America, Australia and Europe, has contributed to the development of new learning programmes with a more assured pedagogical rationale.

The theories of 'social semiotics' developed by Professor Michael Halliday and his department at the University of Sydney, itself drawing on the research of Vygotsky, have been extremely influential in the new understanding. This work, in turn, touched directly on 'genre theory', bringing about quite different ways of making relationships between and across texts, and has caused a wholly new interest in the language of texts. From these backgrounds blossomed seminal classroom-based studies, such as the *First Steps* programme in Western Australia, the 'reading recovery' scheme devised by Dame Marie Clay in New Zealand, and the projects of the Centre for Language in Primary Education (CLPE) in London. Simultaneously, Marilyn Jager Adams and her team at the University of Illinois were looking closely at the necessary prerequisites for the successful teaching of reading. Many related procedures grew from these lines of action and have been gaining increasing recognition and credibility in the work of teachers in schools, during the 1990s. The Literacy Strategy itself, originally implemented in the majority of primary schools since 1998, and disseminated into all secondary schools in September 2001, is a culmination of considerable numbers of these projects (Beard 1998).

Planning for language learning and learning through language has been revolutionised by the findings from these studies. Far greater importance has been discovered in the relationship of *text, sentence* and *word* knowledge in approaches to language learning, and the necessity to ensure a balanced provision of all three. English teachers have gained a better insight into the intimate, symbiotic relationship of reading and writing and recognise that their pupils should have oversight of such knowledge if they are to progress effectively. From their understanding of the research findings of Vygotsky, those concerned with the language development of young people have recognised the power of 'modelling' reading, writing and speaking interactions, as ways of providing 'scaffolding' to support and give direction to pupils' linguistic growth.

From this new learning about language it is possible to see how improving pupils' *reading* capabilities would mean giving greater planned and systematic attention to, and further practice in:

- alerting pupils to the many ways they make intellectual engagements with texts, beyond mere decoding;
- empowering pupils in their skills of raising a broad repertoire of questions to 'interrogate' texts, before, during and after reading engagements;
- assisting pupils' experience of developing skills of prediction, at all stages of reading;
- continually seeking opportunities to make comparisons of and seek similarities with a wide range of texts, recognising universal intertextual relationships;
- identifying the patterns in and the structuring of texts;
- seeking levels of meaning in and attempting 'different' readings of texts;
- identifying features of text-type and genre, in terms of content and language, and recognising consistency and density of language;
- drawing inferences from and detecting the nature of voice and tone across a variety of texts;
- making judgements about the levels of personal enjoyment, interest or fitness for purpose of a range of texts;
- recognising that other readers might have experienced very different 'readings' of the same text;
- increasing powers of pupil reflection on the extent and depth of engagement in encounters with a range of texts.

It is possible to improve every one of the 'reading qualities' described above, and each might be considered a 'strand' along which progress could be planned and made. These 'qualities' are not exclusive to readers in English; they could be applied to readers undertaking engagements with texts in any school context. By adopting an overview of reading, such as the one outlined, and directing their teaching to each one of its 'strands' depending on the needs of the pupils relative to them, English teachers would be able to articulate a far more directed programme of language improvement. It can also be seen that by attending to the needs of the more able pupils, all pupils will have benefited, as the House of Commons Committee (quoted in the introduction to this chapter) suggested.

From the evidence of the research into language development explored earlier, it is also possible to suggest learning 'strands' to support planning for intensive progression in *writing*. English teachers would need to help their pupils to:

- become absolutely clear about the purpose(s) of any writing;
- understand and meet the needs of the intended audience of any writing;
- rehearse and prepare writing in its earliest stages, through discussion, drawing on and paying attention to previous textual material already read and studied;
- understand the process of writing, and the necessity for reworking material to bring about new, different or alternative meanings at various stages, to suit overall purposes;
- practise making clear decisions about choices of language to underpin and specify deliberate meanings and effects;
- attempt occasional short, focused, intensively controlled pieces of text, able to explain all its features;
- use writing for a range of different purposes, including communicating information, narrating, exploration and explanation of ideas, and speculation;
- reflect regularly on writing outcomes, exploring and attempting ways in which it could be improved.

These 'strands' or headings for learning, just as those describing areas of reading development, are capable of incorporating the requirements of schemes such as those contained in the Key Stage 3 Framework for teaching, or any of the English GCSE syllabuses.

In a similar fashion, for directed and detailed progression in *speaking* and *listening*, teachers should be assisting pupils to give greater attention to:

- a developing awareness of speaking as a deliberate textual construct, to meet the demands of a range of purposeful contexts;
- the ability to meet the needs of particular audiences and contexts;
- the ability to identify, discern and listen out for, with increasing concentration, specific issues in spoken discourses;
- knowing how to respond appropriately to matters and issues raised in a variety of spoken discourses;
- the skills of organising ideas before and during speaking encounters;
- the ability to raise more reflective questions about own developing speaking and listening skills.

The adoption of 'strands' of learning in reading, writing, speaking and listening, as illustrated above, has the potential to enable the teachers who use them to make more sophisticated assessments of their pupils' growing attainment. At Key Stages 3 and 4 schools have only minimal descriptions of pupils' 'knowledge, skills and understanding', as articulated by the 'levels' described in the National Curriculum attainment targets; themselves, 'end of key stage . . . best fit' judgements, not expected to contribute further formative learning. The pupils should also be privy to these 'strands' or 'qualities'. They cannot be asked to improve the reflective questioning of their own learning progression without having a very clear idea of the language learning in which they are expected to be involved.

Suggested ways of raising the abilities of gifted and talented pupils in English

Gifted and talented pupils in English do not like having to do more work just because they are better at the subject than others of the same age. Some of these pupils will naturally enjoy writing, and may well already be putting together an impressive portfolio of prose or poetry texts. A considerable proportion will be voracious readers, without extra urging from their teachers. A few will be readily displaying their oral language talents in contexts such as drama or debate. Further practice is not what they require in these areas of accomplishment; they need to be seeking real improvement. Like athletes aiming for the Olympics, the more able should be helped to achieve 'higher', 'faster', 'deeper' – not 'longer' – but 'broader' attainment, in their textual interactions.

Good readers should be shown how to work appropriately in independent ways, and then given opportunities to:

- interrogate texts more confidently with a growing repertoire of enquiry – at text/sentence/word level;
- make relationships between texts and across texts and trace intertextual associations, leading to a growing confidence about recognising range of genre and text types;
- compare texts – in terms of theme/content/language/voice/intent/density/ structure/genre etc.;
- relate texts to their contexts and times; and
- consider different/alternative 'readings'.

More able writers should be challenged to:

- construct texts with very particular purposes, for clearly identifiable audiences, within specified text types and genres;
- articulate confidently the linguistic choices and grammatical constructions they have chosen to make their texts operate as they are intended;
- relate their writing to the reading 'models' on which it is based;
- rework written material in different text types and genres;
- practise a range of processes contributing to improved outcomes; and
- discuss their work with others.

Pupils with impressive speaking skills should be helped to progress further by:

- speaking in a range of contexts, reworking material for different audiences;
- facing and properly responding to different degrees of challenge to their spoken texts;

- having opportunities to support other speakers, with whom they are interacting, more effectively; and
- being supported in attending more carefully to oral texts, and putting their responses to those texts to more demanding uses.

Classroom activities to bring about progression for gifted and talented pupils in English

It is not necessary to separate gifted and talented pupils in English from others in their year group in setted arrangements to be able to make proper provision for their progress. More able pupils can, and regularly do, flourish in mixed ability situations where they study exactly the same texts as their more mainstream peers. To grow in their linguistic insights, their critical confidence and their greater textual overview, however, they should be given more challenging tasks, explorations and inquiries to carry out with those same and related textual materials. These pupils do, however, enjoy and readily contribute to sessions where they have the chance to work, read or discuss language activities or texts, with others of similar ability, not necessarily in the same year group. They also appreciate and are happy to call on the occasional assistance of a named 'mentor', in order to explain ideas, sort out problems related to their greater attainment, or seek reassurance.

Below are a few broad ideas which have been successful in classrooms, and from which teachers can construct many supportive study activities.

Reading

- When a class is about to study a text representative of a particular text type/genre, the more able pupils should be encouraged to read, simultaneously:
    either a parallel text of similar kind, to seek for related characteristics;
    or, a quite different example of text type/genre with which to compare important differences;
    or, a text by the same author, to explore related/dissimilar themes, approaches etc.;
- where the class might be studying, for instance, a prose text exploring a particular theme, or characteristic of genre, etc., the more able are provided with lists of related texts in poetic/dramatic form, and challenged to explore ways in which the same meanings are made;
- before the study of any text, invite the more able pupils to compile, add to and rehearse the repertoire of questions they are becoming accustomed to using to interrogate texts;
- encourage the more able pupils to make predictions – with clear explanations – about likely plot development/textual structuring/relationship of characters/the use of linguistic devices – at different stages of reading, readjusting original predictions where necessary;
- while a whole class is studying a text to improve their knowledge of two or three characteristics, more able pupils should be given other challenges to explore – possibly invited to raise their own 'problems' about the text;

- a class might be studying a whole fiction text, but not reading every word/ chapter; the more able are expected to read, in their own time, the parts not considered in class – and are expected to summarise the 'missing' sections for the rest of the class;
- more able pupils are regularly given opportunities to consider the broadest ideas of 'meanings' in texts over a 'cross-section' of texts; i.e. they might be exploring similar ways of plot structuring/revelation of character/density of description in picture books/texts for newly independent readers/more challenging reads;
- the gifted and talented readers should be challenged to explore some extracts/ selected passages from texts:

    to make *very* detailed grammatical/linguistic analysis in the manner of George Keith's model in Chapter 3, 'Noticing grammar', from *Not Whether but How: Teaching Grammar in English at Key Stage 3 & 4* (QCA 1999) – to confirm and speculate on consistency/inconsistency of style through a whole text;

    having made this sort of analysis, to rewrite the passage, or parts of it, to deliberately change the meaning;

    rewrite parts of the text, using a different narrative voice or viewpoint;

    to identify and explain a focused relationship between the language and the purpose of the text;

- the more able should be given many opportunities to make comparisons between the written published versions of texts and their interpretation into film, television, theatre or other media, considering such issues as:

    what has been left out or added to the alternative media version?

    which aspects of the original text have been highlighted/neglected in the media version?

    what new insights, not discovered in the original, might the new media interpretation of the text bring to light?

    are there significant differences between the television/film/theatre versions which can be explained in terms of the medium in which the text is now represented?

    what relationships can be made between the language grammar of the original and the visual 'grammar' of the media version?

- Where the text is an example of non-fiction, more able pupils should be asked to consider and collect a number of examples of that text type, to establish clearer criteria characterising the type.

Writing

- More able writers should, as a matter of course, be expected to take part in extensive and detailed discussion of their planning of written tasks, to explain clearly their decisions about embarking as they intend on the task;
- the gifted and talented should be regularly challenged to write focused, short pastiche passages in the manner of the original model, explaining the effect they are attempting to create;

- it should be possible for more able writers to rework passages or texts into an alternative text type or genre, to point out the devices of language and style that change the effects and impact on an audience;
- gifted and talented writers should be asked to rework the same written material to meet the needs of different audiences;
- more able language users should be given opportunities to devise their own written tasks, with the guidance of their teachers, to allow them to make reference to those areas of their work requiring more attention;
- more able writers benefit considerably from learning advanced keyboarding skills, to allow them to write at the pace of their thinking;
- more able writers should always be asked to consider 'what next' about their written outcomes, even if time prevents them from actually addressing the changes and adaptations they might suggest.

The study and exploration of language is continuous and unending. The gifted and talented in English can always find out more about the textual material in which they are expected to take an interest – or seek out alternative material in which to be interested. They can, however, only continue with those expectations in a culture where their abilities have been recognised, those talents begun to be developed and where their capacity for improvement is regarded as their fundamental right.

References

Adams, M. J. (1990) *Beginning to Read; Thinking and Learning about Print.* Cambridge, Mass: MIT Press.

Bain, R. *et al.* (eds) (1992) *Looking into Language: Classroom Approaches to Knowledge about Language.* London: Hodder and Stoughton.

Beard, R. (1998) *National Literacy Strategy: Review and Research and Other Related Evidence.* London: DfEE.

Brindley, S. (ed.) (1994) *Teaching English.* London: Routledge.

Carter, R. (ed.) (1990) *Knowledge about Language and the Curriculum: the LINC Reader.* London: Hodder and Stoughton.

Clay, M. (1977) *The Patterning of Complex Behaviour.* London: Heinemann Educational.

Daw, P. (1995) 'Differentiation and its meanings', *The English & Media Magazine,* **32**, Summer, 11–15.

Dean, G. (1998) *Challenging the More Able Language User.* London: David Fulton Publishers.

DfEE (1998) *The National Literacy Strategy: Framework for Teaching.* London: HMSO.

Eyre, D. (1997) *Able Children in Ordinary Schools.* London: David Fulton Publishers.

Freeman, J. (1980) *Gifted Children.* London: Cassell.

Freeman, J. (1991) *Gifted Children Growing Up.* London: Cassell.

Gallagher, J. (1985) *Teaching the Gifted Child.* Newton: Allyn and Bacon.

Gardner, H. (1983) *Frames of Mind: The Theory of Multiple Intelligences*. London: Fontana.

Goodwyn, A. (ed.) (1995) *English and Ability*. London: David Fulton Publishers.

Halliday, M. (1975) *Learning How to Mean: Explorations in the Development of Language*. London: Arnold.

Halliday, M. (1978) *Language as a Social Semiotic*. London: Arnold.

HMI (1992) *Education Observed: The Education of Very Able Children in Maintained Schools*. London: HMSO.

House of Commons (1999) Education and Employment Committee: *Highly Able Children*. London: HMSO.

Pemberton, L. and Davidson, N. (1999) *First Steps Literacy Development Continuum*. Oxford: GHPD.

Protherough and King (eds) (1995) *The Challenge of English in the National Curriculum*. London: Routledge.

QCA English team (1999) *Not Whether But How: Teaching Grammar in English at Key Stages 3 & 4*. London: QCA.

Renzulli, J. (1986) 'The three-ring conception of giftedness: a developmental model for creative productivity', in Sternberg, R. and Davidson, J. (eds) *Conceptions of Giftedness*. Cambridge: Cambridge University Press.

Vygotsky, L. (1978) *Mind in Society*. Cambridge, Mass.: Harvard University Press.

Vygotsky, L. (1986) *Thought and Language*. Cambridge, Mass.: The MIT Press.

CHAPTER 3

Mathematics

Roy Kennard

Introduction

Discussions about provision for very able children are often beset by difficulties encountered in trying to define what we mean by 'very able' or any of the plethora of other terms in this field. A common approach is to quantify in percentage terms a proportion of a year group. Thus, the 'very able' might be regarded as the top 10 per cent nationally. However, the government's Excellence in Cities initiative requires each participating school to identify the top 5–10 per cent of pupils in each year group as a 'gifted and talented' cohort. It is important to realise that this is a relative definition since the performance of pupils in one school may exceed that of another. It also reserves the use of the term 'gifted' for academic subjects like mathematics. The Excellence in Cities initiative goes on to say that gifted pupils will perform '*at a level significantly in advance of the average for their year group in their school*' (DfEE 2001, EiC Phase 2–Paper 11: 39). Whether we are trying to identify the top 10 per cent nationally or at local school level it is helpful to rely on mutually supportive sources of evidence. Testing is one key form of evidence. Another is to evaluate the strength of the aptitudes which able pupils exhibit in response to suitably challenging tasks. This is often referred to as *identification through challenge* to distinguish it from an approach that relies on testing. As such, 'This is a day to day process going well beyond the notion of a classification in percentage terms' (Kennard 1996: 2).

In part this chapter looks more closely at how teachers can be more discerning in their own classrooms. The analytical framework for doing this is provided by the model in Figure 3.1.

The recognition of mathematical ability goes hand in hand with its development. The teacher's view of the nature of mathematical ability is at the heart of this model; consequently the first step for a mathematics team seeking to develop a distinctive curriculum for its 'gifted' mathematicians is to consider the question, 'What does it mean to be mathematically able?' This question and other aspects of the model above are amplified in the following sections.

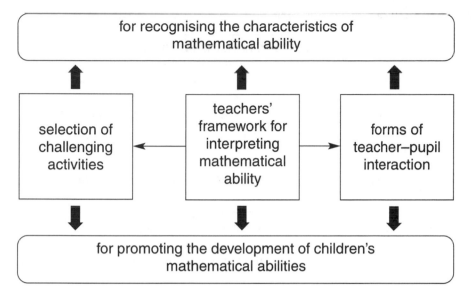

Figure 3.1 The discerning teacher model of provision in ordinary classrooms (Adapted from Kennard 1996: 20)

The nature of mathematical ability

Most characterisations of mathematical ability draw on a twelve-year research study by V. A. Krutetskii (1976). His profile of mathematical abilities has proved helpful in interpreting the work of able pupils in primary and secondary contexts as shown in Table 3.1. (Kennard 1996). His structure of abilities is summarised below; the comments in italics indicate links with key process abilities in mathematical thinking.

According to Krutetskii able children display these characteristics to a stronger degree than their less able peers. In one case study he posed the following question. 'There are two supplementary adjacent angles. One angle is equal to 45°. The bisectors of these angles are constructed. What is the angle between the bisectors equal to?'

For this specific question a diagram soon reveals a particular answer (see Figure 3.2).

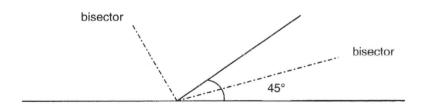

Figure 3.2

Table 3.1 The structure of mathematical abilities (Kennard 1996: 53)

Able children have the ability to:
Grasp the formal structure of a problem in a way that leads to ideas for action.
Generalise from the study of examples. *Search for and recognise pattern, specialise and conjecture.*   Generalise approaches to problem solving.
Reason in a logical way and as a consequence develop chains of reasoning. *Verifying, justifying, proving.*
Use mathematical symbols as part of the thinking process.
Think flexibly; adapt their ways of approaching problems and to switch from one mode of thought to another.
Reverse their direction of thought. Work forwards and backwards in an attempt to solve a problem.
Leave out intermediate steps in a logical argument and to think in abbreviated mathematical forms.
Remember generalised mathematical relationships, problem types, generalised ways of approaching problems and patterns of reasoning.

However, Sonya (an exceptionally able 8-year-old) replied: 'For all supplementary adjacent angles the bisectors should form a 90° angle, since the sum of supplementary adjacent angles is 180°, half the sum will always be 90°.'

Sonya's solution is represented symbolically in Figure 3.3.

Figure 3.3

$$a° + b° = 180°$$

$$\frac{1}{2}(a° + b°) = 90° = \frac{1}{2}a° + \frac{1}{2}b°$$

What does Sonya's solution reveal about her mathematical abilities? A striking feature of her solution is that it is perfectly general. Her argument relates to 'all' supplementary adjacent angles and not simply the pair comprising 45° and 135°. She reasons logically from a known fact (the sum of supplementary adjacent angles is 180°) to her conclusion. The latter is possible because she has grasped the essence of the problem; she recognises that bisecting two adjacent supplementary angles is equivalent to halving their sum. Thus, three key abilities from the above profile are exhibited in her response.

In his Theory of Multiple Intelligences, Howard Gardner (1993) puts forward a case for viewing human potential as comprising several 'intelligences' of which logical–mathematical intelligence is one. In a similar way to Krutetskii he has sought to characterise mathematical ability by examining the essence of mathematics and the work of eminent mathematicians. In so doing he concurs with many aspects of the profile put forward by Krutetskii, most notably the characteristics of:

- Sensing the direction of a problem.
- Sustaining long chains of reasoning.
- Using mathematical notation.
- Specialising or breaking down a problem into simpler but related parts.
- Abstracting general features from mathematical material.
- Memory for general arguments based on mathematical reasoning.

A national survey of secondary mathematics teachers found strong support for this structure of mathematical abilities (Chyriwsky and Kennard 1997). Recent guidance from the National Numeracy Stategy aimed at primary teachers also refers to the characteristics outlined above (DfEE 2000a; DfEE 2000b). The key to effective provision in the future is to *utilise* this model to simultaneously recognise and promote mathematical ability. In subsequent sections the work of pupils from schools in Sunderland will be interpreted using this model.

Selecting activities to promote mathematical ability

A challenging mathematical activity will give pupils the opportunity to display some or most of the characteristics identified in Table 1. The history of mathematics provides many useful starting points that allow pupils to probe more deeply into topics within the normal curriculum. The mathematical strand of 'shape and space' is rich with possibilities for this type of work. The examples below begin with the relevant teaching objective in the National Numeracy Strategy's Framework for teaching mathematics: Years 7 to 9 (DfEE 2001b), or a reference to the Key Stage 4 Programme of Study in the National Curriculum for Mathematics (DfEE/QCA 1999).

i. Deduce and use the formulae for the area of a triangle, parallelogram and trapezium (Year 8, Shape, space and measures, NNS Framework, section 3:9)

The key word here is 'deduce'. Will this be done *for* the pupils? Typically, teachers 'demonstrate' arguments to pupils. However, there is also scope for pupils to think mathematically; that is, to do the mathematics for themselves. Following consideration of the diagrams given in the Y7, 8, 9 examples, p. 235, pupils could be referred to a sixteenth century Indian mathematician who wrote: 'The area of a triangle is given by the product of the base and half the height.' No further explanation was given, just a diagram similar to the one below (Figure 3.4).

Is it obvious? Is the diagram really that powerful? After seeking explanations from pupils, which are likely to feature reasoning based on congruent shapes, *adapt* the problem to focus on different shapes. For example:

The area of a kite is given by half the product of its diagonals; invent a diagram to explain this. Try to invent rules and diagrams for the area of parallelograms and trapezia.

This task was set to some Year 9 pupils on a Saturday morning 'masterclass'. Lindsay's result appears in Figure 3.5.

Lindsay's work is indicative of high ability. It reveals that she can:

- relate the area of a kite to the area of a rectangle; she has grasped the essence of the problem;
- establish the relationship between the area of a kite and the rectangle which surrounds it through reasoning based on congruent triangles;
- use mathematical symbols to express equivalent forms for the area of the kite; and
- think flexibly and offer more than one diagrammatic solution.

   ii. Know and use the formulae for the circumference and area of a circle (Year 9, Shape, space and measures, NNS Framework, section 3: 11)

A possible starting point here is a diagram which appeared in the Ahmes Mathematical Papyrus which was written approximately 4000 years ago. The diagram shows an octagon inscribed inside a circle. Challenge pupils to find the Egyptian formula for the area of a circle. One pupil's reponse is shown in Figure 3.6.

Equate this formula to the conventional formula: what approximation are the Egyptians using for π

   iii. Understand, recall and use Pythagoras' Theorem (Ma 3, Key Stage 4, higher programme of study: 66)

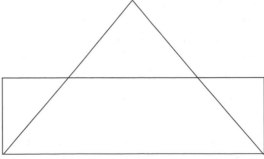

Figure 3.4 (Adapted from Popp 1978: 47)

The area of a kite is given by half the product of its diagonals.

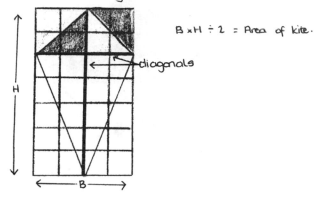

B × H ÷ 2 = Area of kite.

diagonals

H

B

The area of the rectangle surrounding the kite is twice the size of the kites area.

The relationship between the rectangles and kites area can also be shown like this.

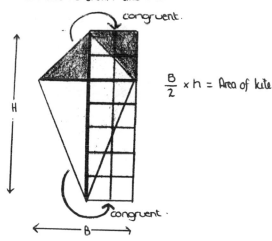

congruent.

$\frac{B}{2} \times h$ = Area of kite

H

congruent.

B

The kite fits into half of the rectangle

Figure 3.5 Lindsay's work

Able pupils can be challenged to consider alternative proofs of Pythagoras' Theorem. Some excellent versions can be found at *http://www.argonet.co.uk/oundlesch* (go to Mathematical Links, Mathematical Resources, Japan, Mathematical Java Applets, Middle School Geometry); at this site pupils get the opportunity to work dynamically by 'transforming' shapes on screen. Alternatively, ask pupils to develop a relationship between the lengths a, b and c by considering the areas in the diagram in Figure 3.7, which appears in an ancient Chinese text known as the Chou Pei (700–200 BC).

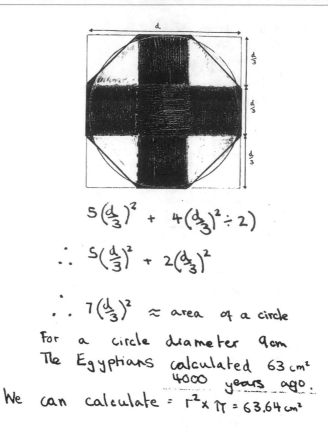

$$5\left(\frac{d}{3}\right)^2 + 4\left(\frac{d}{3}\right)^2 \div 2)$$

$$\therefore \; 5\left(\frac{d}{3}\right)^2 + 2\left(\frac{d}{3}\right)^2$$

$$\therefore \; 7\left(\frac{d}{3}\right)^2 \approx \text{area of a circle}$$

For a circle diameter 9cm
The Egyptians calculated 63 cm²
4000 years ago.

We can calculate = $r^2 \times \pi = 63.64$ cm²

QUITE BRAINY PEOPLE,
.WOULDN'T YOU SAY!

Figure 3.6 Egyptian

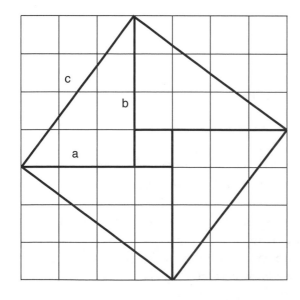

c
b
a

Figure 3.7 (Adapted from Joseph 1991: 180)

Pupils should be encouraged to encode the relationship between the area of the 'tilting square', c, and the sum of the areas of the triangles, 2ab, and square (b-a) within itself.

iv. Understand similarity of triangles (Ma 3, Key Stage 4, higher programme of study: 66)

A Greek mathematician called Thales, who lived around 624–547 BC, used shadows to help him find the heights of the great pyramids of Egypt (see Figure 3.8).

Ask pupils to interpret this diagram and to use their knowledge of similar triangles to find the height of the pyramid. (Note: L, h, m and b can all be found by measurement.)

All of the above activities provide able pupils with opportunities to engage in mathematical reasoning. They also complement the 'geometrical reasoning' strand in Ma 3 of the National Curriculum which places more emphasis on notions of

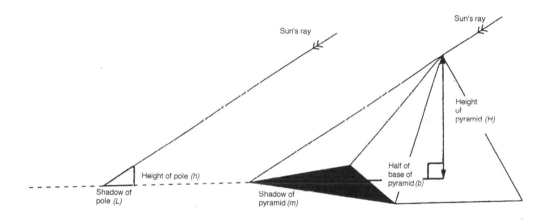

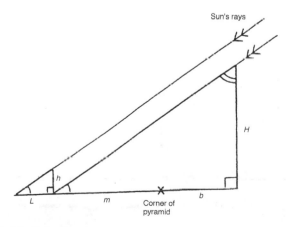

Figure 3.8 Thales diagram

proof than its predecessor. For example, pupils are expected to: 'distinguish between a practical demonstration and a proof' (Key Stage 3, Ma 3: 36), 'explain a proof that the exterior angle of a triangle equals the sum of the two interior opposite angles' (Year 8, NNS Framework, section 3: 9), 'provide a convincing argument to 'explain that a rhombus is a parallelogram but a parallelogram is not a rhombus' (Year 8, NNS Framework, Y7, 8, 9 examples: 187), 'prove and use the fact that the angle subtended by an arc at the centre of a circle is twice the angle subtended at any point on the circumference' (Ma 3, Key Stage 4, higher programme of study: 66).

Problem solving and the investigation of novel starting points are important ways to stimulate and challenge the more able mathematician. For example, the following sequence (Figure 3.9) appears in the Reception to Year 6 Framework for Mathematics, Y4, 5, 6 examples: 79 (DfEE 1999).

Able Year 6 pupils will be able to continue the sequence pattern and conjecture the form of the function rule as: 'The number of counters is three times the position number plus one' and to write this symbolically as $c = (3 \times p) + 1$. Later, in Key Stage 3, a distinction can be made between a result based on experimental evidence (it works for all the cases considered), and a result obtained by direct reasoning from a general case (see Figure 3.10).

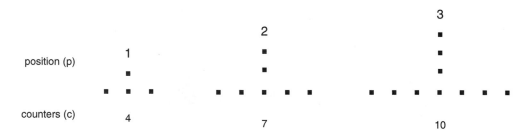

Figure 3.9

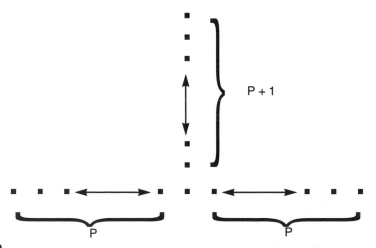

Figure 3.10

This visualisation leads to $c = p + (p + 1) + p = 3p + 1$.

Providing opportunities of this nature would be consistent with the added emphasis on proof in the 'Solving Problems' strand of the new Key Stage 3 Framework. At Key Stage 4 the National Curriculum for Mathematics states that pupils should be offered 'activities in which they progress from using definitions and short chains of reasoning to understanding and formulating proofs in algebra and geometry' (p. 72). Whilst these references to proof in the National Curriculum are intended to apply to a wide group of pupils they should be seen as opening the door to a curriculum for very able pupils based on achieving greater depth of understanding. Very able pupils will demonstrate a greater aptitude for the logical reasoning demanded by 'proving' mathematical results. The activity of establishing convincing mathematical arguments is one which provides a strong basis for challenging very able pupils and is consistent with the demands of the National Curriculum for Mathematics.

At A level, proof skills can be refined and developed. At the end of their course we should expect that the students understand different notions of proof. That is, proof in terms of deductive reasoning, proof by contradiction, proof by exhaustion, inductive reasoning and the use of counter examples in mathematical argument. Other opportunities arise to use newly learnt mathematics and to revisit earlier mathematical formulae for which substantive proofs were not previously discussed for example, using the calculus to prove the formulas for the area of a rectangle or the volume of a cone. A strong case can be made for using 'logical argument' to present A level mathematics as 'an inter-connected logical system' (Waring 2000). In this way A level students can also be challenged through the activity of proving.

Forms of teacher–pupil interaction

Mathematically challenging activities are ones which promote the mathematical abilities identified in Table 3.1. With these abilities in mind teachers are in a position to be more 'discerning' about pupils' responses to such challenges especially if teacher–pupil interaction provokes reflective discussion. This can be achieved through questioning which probes pupils' understanding. For example, following a brief introduction to the notion of mathematical proof and discussion of a similar problem in the context of two-digit numbers, Year 9 pupils were set the task of proving that 'any three-digit whole number is divisible by 9 if the sum of the digits is divisible by 9' (NNS Framework, Year 9, Solving Problems, Y7, 8, 9 examples: 35).

Richard's solution is shown in Figure 3.11. Richard's approach reveals that he can:

• Generalise the form of a multiple of nine, use his understanding of place value to generalise the structure of a three-digit number and to work towards an alternative form for the latter; he understands the essence of the problem.

General = abc
$a + b + c$

If $a + b + c = 9 \times n = 9n$

$a = 9n-b-c$
$b = 9n-a-c$
$c = 9n-a-b$

$$
\begin{aligned}
a(100) + b(10) + c &= (9n - b - c) \times 100 + (9n - c - a) \times 10 + c \\
&= 900n - 100b - 100c + 90n - 10c - 10a \\
&= 990n - 110b - 111c \\
&= 990n - 100b - 111\,c
\end{aligned}
$$

Rewrite substituting for c as well

$$
\begin{aligned}
&= (9n - b - c) \times 100 + (9n - c - a) \times 10 + (9n - a - c) \\
&= 900n - 100b - 100c + 90n - 90n - 10c - 10a + 9n - a - b \\
&= 999n -
\end{aligned}
$$

I have had difficulty subsituting b, when it wasn't necessary

$900n - 100b - 100c + 10b + c$
$900n - 90b - 99b$

This number is obviously a multiple of 9. We have proved that if the digits of a 3 digit number add to a multiple of 9. The number can be divided by 9.

Figure 3.11 Richard's approach

- Reason logically.
- Think flexibly; initial substitutions did not work!
- Use mathematical symbols.
- Generalise previously learnt methods.

The key lines of questioning employed by the teacher comprised:

- Tell me in your own words what you are trying to prove. Is it true for particular cases?
- What would a general three-digit number look like?
- What would a general multiple of nine look like?
- What are we told about the sum of the digits? How can that be written?
- What do each of the letters of the three-digit number represent? How can you make that expression look like a multiple of nine?
- What do you hope to get after substituting?
- What does your reasoning tell you? What makes your reasoning a mathematical proof?

The questions are used to provoke and support pupils' reasoning and anticipate that they will be able to articulate the purpose behind each step.

Organisational issues

(a) Grouping, enrichment and acceleration

Secondary mathematics departments typically group pupils into 'sets' for teaching purposes. This is often seen as an appropriate way to cater for differing abilities. However, setting *per se* does not ensure this; the effectiveness of the teaching within the context of setted groups is still the over-riding factor in determining pupils' progress. In other words, it is still possible for pupils in a top set to be insufficiently challenged by the work that they are set. For example, there may be too much emphasis on repetition and rehearsal and insufficient emphasis on problem solving and enquiry. Whatever the form of grouping that able pupils find themselves in, the development of their abilities still depends on how discerning the teacher is.

Setting is also typically regarded as a helpful way of accelerating able pupils through the normal curriculum. In many schools this practice is associated with early entry to GCSE Mathematics. This may then be followed by a course in Statistics or Additional Mathematics. Some schools run the extra course in parallel with the normal GCSE Mathematics programme. When schools adopt early entry policies it is clearly important to evaluate pupils' grades. For example, 'Do all the pupils achieve high A*/A grades?' If not, then it is reasonable to ask, 'What is the point of accelerating pupils to low grades?' This latter question has added significance if there are doubts about how well pupils understand the mathematics they have been taught. Behind this last point lies a concern that for many able pupils fast-tracking means that opportunities to gain deeper mathematical understandings have been overlooked.

In some schools there will be exceptionally able pupils for whom acceleration is an appropriate strategy. Where individuals are moved up whole year groups for mathematics, or because of all-round abilities, full consideration should be given on a regular basis to their social and emotional development. The key point here is that the move to meet a pupil's academic needs should not have serious adverse consequences for other aspects of their development. Whether individuals or groups of pupils are accelerated, schools will always need to face what a recent report called 'the inevitable question' of 'What next?' (UK Mathematics Foundation 2000: 11). In other words, what are the organisational implications of pupils finishing the normal curriculum early? Is there something suitable for them to go on to? Are the resources available? This report is strongly critical of acceleration as a strategy and makes a strong alternative case for enrichment as the most suitable way to provide for very able pupils. This is consistent with the results of a national survey of secondary mathematics teachers which found that 94.3 per cent of teachers favoured enrichment as a strategy but only 17.9 per cent agreed with early entry to an older year group (Chyriwsky and Kennard 1997). The UK Mathematics Foundation Report goes on to say that an enrichment strategy should expect the following from its able pupils:

- a higher level of technique in,
- a greater depth of understanding of, and
- a willingness to reflect on
  standard curriculum material, together with supplementary material which . . . does not pre-empt standard curriculum work from subsequent years. (p. 12)

Many of the examples in the section on 'Selecting activities to promote mathematical abilities' reflect this standpoint. One of these is discussed below in the context of how a mathematics department might approach the design of such a curriculum.

(b) Planning

The Key Stage 3 Framework for Mathematics provides strong guidance on long-, medium- and short-term planning. Mathematics departments can construct a challenging curriculum for their most able pupils by identifying links between key objectives in Yearly Teaching Programmes, intended for the majority of pupils, and challenging enrichment materials. For example, with respect to one of the illustrations above, a medium-term planning format might look like the example in Table 3.2.

Of course, space in the planning grid might be reduced by reference to a corresponding worksheet activity. It will sometimes be appropriate to provide additional challenge by selecting objectives from a higher year group. A small adjustment to the planning grid can cater for this (see Table 3.3).

Table 3.2 Year 8 autumn term: shape, space and measures

Topic	Hours	Teaching Objectives	Enrichment
Measures and Mensuration	2	Deduce and use the formula for the area of a triangle, parallelogram and trapezium.	Refer to 16th century Indian mathematician who wrote: 'The area of a triangle is given by the product of the base and half the height.' No further explanation was given, just a diagram similar to the one below. Demonstrate using OHT. The area of a kite is given by half the product of its diagonals. Invent a diagram to explain this. Try to invent rules and diagrams for the area of parallelograms and trapezia.

Table 3.3 Year 8: Numbers and the number system

Topic	Hours	Teaching Objective	Enrichment	Extension taken from Year 9
Integers, powers and roots	2	Use squares, positive and negative square roots, cubes and cube roots and index notation for small positive integer powers.		Use ICT to estimate square roots and cube roots.

This 'objectives led' approach showing the distinct nature of provision for very able pupils is easily adapted to form a planning basis for pupils in Key Stage 4.

(c) Effective departments

A departmental team will have successfully met the needs of its most able pupils when:

- Pupils attain the highest grades in examinations.
- Pupils achieve a depth of understanding demonstrated by the use of mathematical reasoning to prove results and to make connections between areas of mathematics.
- Pupils are highly motivated by mathematics.
- Enrolment on A level courses increases.
- Enrolment on mathematical-science degrees increases.

The first three points above can certainly be influenced by teachers within a department; pupils' decisions relating to further study may, however, be influenced by a range of factors including the possibility that they have stronger interests in other subjects. For all sorts of reasons, not least a chronic shortage of mathematics teachers, it would be desirable to see enrolment rates increase in the future.

A departmental approach to securing effective provision would need:

- To plan a distinct scheme of work that aims to develop pupils' mathematical abilities and consequently a deeper understanding of the normal mathematics curriculum.
- Joint observation of teaching with subsequent discussion to explicate forms of teacher–pupil interaction which provides pupils with appropriate challenge. For example, questioning which specifically promotes mathematical reasoning.
- Joint scrutiny of pupils' work to evaluate abilities demonstrated and standards achieved. This information would be used to modify future planning.

The second set of points above, relating to effective provision, could usefully be incorporated into a Mathematics Action Plan whilst the first set of points might be adapted to constitute success criteria for those actions. The DfEE 'audit booklet' could be used for this purpose (DfEE 2001a: 14).

Resources, texts and organisations

1. Enrichment:

These associations sell excellent enrichment resources:
Mathematics Association, 259 London Road, Leicester, LE2 3BE. (0116 2210013)

For example:

- Are you sure? Learning about proof.
- Can you prove it? Developing concepts of proof in primary and secondary schools.
- Problem pages. A photocopiable book of thought provoking mathematics problems for sixth form and upper secondary school students.

Association of Teachers of Mathematics (ATM) Publications, 7 Shaftesbury Street, Derby, DE 23 8YB (01332 346599)

For example:

- Eight Days a Week. Puzzles, problems and questions to activate the mind.
- Points of Departure Booklets 1–4.

2. Other very useful texts for secondary mathematics departments include:

- *Maths Challenge Books 1 to 3*, edited by Tony Gardiner (2000), Oxford University Press.
- *The Crest of the Peacock. Non European Roots of Mathematics*, Joseph, G. (1991), I B Tauris.
- *Fermat's Last Theorem*, Singh, S. (1998), Fourth Estate.

3. An excellent website for enrichment activities is:
http://nrich.maths.org.uk

4. National competitions are organised by:

United Kingdom Mathematics Trust, University of Leeds, 0113 2332339.

5. Masterclasses are supported by:

- The Royal Institution of Great Britain at *www.ri.ac.uk*
- Gabbitas Truman and Thring Educational Trust at *www.masterclass.co.uk*

6. Assessment and testing:

Information focused on mathematically able pupils can be found at: *www.qca.org.uk*

Look for *World Class Tests for 13 year olds* and *Advanced Extension Awards for 18 year olds*.

References

Chyriwsky, M. and Kennard, R. (1997) 'Attitudes to able children: a survey of mathematics teachers in English secondary schools.' *High Ability Studies*, **8**, 47–59.

DfEE (1999) *The National Numeracy Strategy: Framework for Teaching Mathematics from Reception to Year 6*. London: HMSO.

DfEE (2000a) *National Literacy and Numeracy Strategies: Guidance on Teaching Able Children*. London: HMSO.

DfEE (2000b) *Mathematical Challenges for Able Pupils in Key Stages 1 and 2*. London: HMSO.

DfEE (2001a) *Auditing a Subject in Key Stage 3*. London: HMSO.

DfEE (2001b) *The National Numeracy Strategy: Framework for Teaching Mathematics: Years 7 to 9*. London: HMSO.

DfEE/QCA (1999) *National Curriculum for Mathematics*. London: HMSO.

Gardner, H. (1993) *Frames of Mind: The Theory of Multiple Intelligences* (2nd edn). London: Fontana.

Joseph, G. (1991) *The Crest of the Peacock: Non European Roots of Mathematics*. London: British Academic Press.

Kennard, R. (1996) *Teaching Mathematically Able Children*. Oxford: NACE.

Krutetskii, V. A. (1976) *The Psychology of Mathematical Abilities in Schoolchildren.* Chicago: University of Chicago Press.

Popp, W. (1978) *History of Mathematics.* Buckingham: Open University Press.

UK Mathematics Foundation (2000) *Acceleration or Enrichment?* University of Birmingham.

Waring, S. (2000) *Can You Prove It? Developing Concepts of Proof in Primary and Secondary Schools.* Leicester: The Mathematical Association.

CHAPTER 4

Science

Pat O'Brien

Introduction

A workshop session. Year 9 pupils have been put into groups for the activity. They are introduced to the science problem and the visiting speaker moves through the group talking to the pupils. One is very difficult to communicate with. She has the name Hayley on her badge. The speaker comments on the difficulty of communicating with Hayley and is told there is no such pupil in the group. Confusion: 'Who is Hayley and why is she acting in this way?'

Hayley turns out to be Charlotte, a reluctant gifted and talented pupil. She hates the idea of being identified as one of the group. Throughout the morning technology/science activity she works on the edge of the group doing the minimum to enable the group to progress with its task. The group compensates for her, and when challenged they reply that she will come into her own soon.

The afternoon workshop starts with an art/science based task; one that requires a high degree of creativity. Hayley has become Charlotte with a new badge and very much the leader with the consent of the group. The concluding product is one of very high quality and links the morning's work clearly, with a presentational flair.

Hayley reveals some of the problems of dealing with gifted and talented pupils in science. They are very able and know about themselves. This makes it difficult to deal with them. The scientifically gifted and talented child is not simply one who can show good knowledge about science; there are other characteristics a teacher can identify. A range of the following is evident in the gifted and talented child:

- concentrates effort and attention upon reaching a specific goal, outcome or purpose;
- concentrates upon a specific task for a long time;
- recognises patterns and relationships in science data and links it to a conclusion;
- good use of specific subject words and vocabulary beyond that of other pupils of their age. Words are part of the way they create abstract ideas;
- processes complex data and information quickly. They mathematically model

ideas and can spot inconsistencies and inaccuracies in the science knowledge supporting any conclusion;

- uses relevant science data when presented with a mass of information;
- continually tests ideas and makes critical evaluation of the outcome to support a prediction and form a scientific conclusion;
- forms scientific hypotheses and makes predictions supported by science knowledge, illustrating an understanding of the principles using relevant evidence;
- uses new science ideas very quickly and frequently makes links between differing areas of science. This makes them good at solving problems;
- good memory for general science ideas and principles enabling them to form models to scientifically explain situations and events;
- very aware of how the context influences interpretation of the science content, and how this then affects the degree of difficulty of solving a problem. They frequently identify a personal role to help them focus on the task in solving a problem. They will make use of the context and role to create an interest for themselves. This often means they enjoy a cross-curricular approach to learning;
- prepared to try different science ideas and alternative modelling approaches to solve a problem;
- a dreaminess or withdrawn approach to life;
- deep interest in reasoning logically and finding out about things by reading or solving science problems or puzzles;
- can demonstrate extremes of unacceptable behaviour because of frustration such as a lack of interest in school work and an aggressive attitude towards staff, but they do excel and persevere at self chosen activities to produce a high standard of work;
- a perfection in completing the thinking aspect of the work;
- very creative ideas often linking science concepts from areas not studied in school science. Often use science ideas to embellish other work;
- often very mature in their emotional behaviour.

Metacognition

Gunstone (1994) advances the view that the nature of the specific content offered to pupils in a teaching situation can foster particular styles of behaviour that relate to the way pupils are aware of, and consciously use, their thought processes to enhance their learning of the subject. Gunstone pursued much of his research in the field of science.

Gunstone indicates a model of conceptual change as a process of:

- recognising the ideas and making links;
- evaluating those links with regard to solving the problem;
- deciding to reconstruct the conceptual frameworks in the light of things learnt;

- constructing knowledge into models of understanding which are applied to solve problems.

All pupils are capable of thinking about their cognitive processes and making appropriate choices about using a learning style that matches the context and content and which best suits them at that time. This is called metacognition.

The gifted and talented are well advanced in their metacognition ability and are able to evaluate their learning very efficiently. A gifted and talented 11-year-old working on a science problem thinks in similar ways to the average 14-year-old. They can accept a more quantitative approach and search for less obvious connections.

Wittrock's generative model for teaching

Wittrock (1994) proposed a practical plan for teaching, which uses the pupil's awareness of metacognition to help the pupil become more proficient in their learning. This approach is very successful with gifted and talented pupils and the steps are:

- Teaching should indicate the science knowledge, previous experience, language and conceptions to be taught as clear objectives for learning and relate them to the pupil's everyday world by placing it in a strong real context. For the more able this can be made quite complex.
- Teachers should have a good understanding of the preconceptions and science misconceptions a pupil has about the way the world works in order to construct experiences which allow these preconceptions to be challenged.
- Teachers should challenge the pupil's ideas and models using examples and applications, and facilitate comprehension by identifying links between science ideas, models and experience.
- The teaching should rely upon developing the idea that learning is a generative process, which emphasises the use of one's own thoughts and models to predict and solve problems.

Generative teaching relies upon the student's ability to become more responsible for their own learning but with direct help in learning how to learn. The goal is not to cover content but to lead pupils to generate ideas and models to explain.

Pupils should be aware that they can succeed in understanding complex ideas by using their own knowledge. This requires them to concentrate upon the development of models to enable them to explain events, rather than affix facts to explain phenomena. They need to be taught learning strategies, in order to learn to develop and monitor their own learning approaches by identifying the range of strategies they use in solving problems and to evaluate their learning by examining how efficient they were at comprehending the problem and developing a solution.

If these ideas about science education are common elsewhere, and other researchers such as Freeman (1998) indicates that they are, then one conclusion must be that the National Curriculum structure for science is too restricting for the gifted and talented pupil. The results might indicate the reason to be that the gifted and talented are well developed in terms of Wittrock's generative model and already very efficient in using Gunstone's conceptual change model.

What are the good design features for the gifted and talented?

The gifted and talented pupil in science is frequently quick to pick up knowledge and solve problems but many display, either overtly or covertly, a frustration with the highly structured nature of school subjects.

They appear well aware of how to use their thinking and the best approach to use to learn more effectively. They use this awareness of their thinking to maximise their learning strategies by using a number of techniques like: mnemonics, and other work-based approaches relating to a sequence of text; words or numbers; mind mapping to organise their knowledge; concept-mapping to indicate links or brainstorming to search for plausible ideas, and modelling to explain difficult ideas.

The ability of the gifted and talented pupil to use generative learning more efficiently and be responsible for their own learning could be a strategy that schools might adopt to design a curriculum for them. This would mean teachers acting in the main as facilitators for developing independent learning and designing science problems which involve creative thinking, selected focused teaching and quality exposure to high levels of teaching from outside agencies.

Within the curriculum there is a need for both enrichment and extension that can pick up on the nature of language, methodology, type of mental model or the nature of context in which a problem is set; extension that is not an add-on, but content specially designed for the gifted and talented science pupil; enrichment that is not just additional work after school but carefully designed problems, which use cross-curricular topics.

The challenge is the ability to find appropriate starting points for the gifted and talented and to free their curriculum of material with which they are already very familiar and which they can use, and to concentrate upon areas of advanced thinking. One line of thinking is that the design of work should encompass the full chain of progression as outlined in Figure 4.1.

In this approach it is expected that all pupils will require activities that follow this progression with the least able finding the knowledge, comprehension and application activities relatively straightforward. However, they find the analysis and synthesis difficult unless these are founded in familiar contexts that possess a direct relevance to themselves and their experiences. The gifted and talented, however, are excited by the challenge of the activity set in an unfamiliar context and will develop a new knowledge base to ensure success.

Progression in levels of complexity

• Knowledge –	*What do you know about......? Know the following words......*
• *Knowing*	*Collect more ideas and facts about...... Complete the following......*
• Comprehension –	*How does.....happen? What is the difference between .....?*
• *Show knowledge*	*Describe...... What would you do to......? How accurate......?*
• Application –	*What can you do if......? Explain using diagrams how......*
• *Make use of*	*If you change......what will happen?*
• Analysis –	*Make a crossword on...... Explain how......affects......*
• *Break down, relate*	*Decide which is best and why*
• Synthesis –	*Write a biography of...... Describe the ideal......*
• *Creative – What if*	*What would happen if there were a complete reversal of.....?*
• Evaluation –	*What have you learnt well? What was difficult to learn?*
• *Personal reflection*	*It......happens what would be the comments of......?*
	Imagine you are......what would be your response to......?

Figure 4.1 *(After Bloom's Taxonomy)*

Assessment and finding starting points

To be successful it is important that we identify notionally a starting point for the learning. This will require carefully designed summative assessment tools like concept maps, brainstorming, or Observation-Prediction-Explanation (OPE), problem solving, etc. These are powerful tools, allowing the teacher to identify initial points for the learning by indicating something of the level of understanding.

Assessment of understanding is a process of using specific techniques or probes to determine the level of knowledge, range of associations and an ability to apply models. Our appreciation of a pupil's understanding is dependent upon what the probing techniques reveal and what we understand from that process of revealing. Dealing with the gifted and talented is a difficult area and one in which the tools we use for assessing should be carefully chosen with knowledge of their limitations. This requires more adventurous use of assessment techniques (see Figure 4.2).

What is the place of thinking skills in designing the science curriculum?

Young children have the potential to learn but do not always receive the right conditions to learn the skills of effective thinking. Gifted and talented pupils are not necessarily good thinkers! Some may develop a thinking style orientated towards considering certainties as answers rather than considering probabilities and using deductive thinking. This may make them impulsive thinkers who react quickly with definite answers or who are reluctant to answer when uncertain.

Types of assessment techniques available

- Word association and word burrs
- Concept map
- Relational drawings/Venn diagrams
- Prediction–Observation–Explanation
- Fortune lines
- Word association
- Question setting
- Drawings with explanations
- Word/concept walls
- Modelling
- Observation and mastery tasks
- Investigations with brainstorming
- Interviewing and conversation
- Problem solving

Figure 4.2

Lewin (1987) makes a clear distinction between putting more emphasis on cleverness than upon wisdom; a situation in which the child learns to use verbal fluency to construct answers and yet does not display rational use of knowledge. Lewin identifies this as the intelligence trap. A child knows, but not how to use, an answer. Renzulli (1977) defines giftedness by suggesting it includes not only ability and task commitment but also creativity. In science this creativity is crucial in developing answers to problems. It often marks a lateral dimension in thinking rather than just pure vertical development of knowledge.

It is important to consider all intellectual abilities when constructing a curriculum and to include thinking skills. The qualities we desire in capable pupils are:

- to be confident thinkers, clear about the means;
- the capacity to enjoy thinking and consider the beauty of the process rather than the chore of the operation;
- to consider concepts with care and not to dismiss them in haste;
- to trawl widely for ideas, to encourage originality and creativity but to be on target with that breadth;
- to use the fine tools of thinking like a surgeon's knife for incisive conclusions.

This could be done using CASE (Cognitive Acceleration through Science Education) or any other tool that assists the development of higher order thinking skills, supplemented with other more lateral thinking exercises such as those designed by de Bono (1989). For example:

- *Breadth of perception* – In a genetic experiment there is an opportunity to redesign the human body; what things would be candidates for redesigning and why?

- *Alternatives, possibilities, choices* – A mysterious disease strikes in the South East. It strikes quickly and is very contagious; so much so that everyone in contact catches it. They are left severely deaf. Brainstorm how you would communicate with each other.
- *Consequence and sequel* – A new medicine involving some genetic engineering is discovered that will allow people to live to the age of 120. This medicine is expensive and has not been trialled over a longer period than the statutory seven years. What are the consequences and sequel of the immediate use of such a drug without control? What could be the long-term implications if its use is controlled?
- *Hypothesis, speculation and provocation* – Why do you think mice have long tails? Put forward two different hypotheses – or – because of genetic variations and environmental effects, cows have recently been born very small. This is resulting in the large species of cow being quickly swamped and overtaken in numbers. What would be the consequences of this event?

Creativity is the ability to play imagination games – thought experiments. Tony Buzan observes that breakthroughs in science have often come about as a result of a dream, a daydream, an accident, or a chance happening that moved the dreamer to diverge from the dominant paradigm. To help the development of lateral thinking in science such problems as those in Figure 4.3 (see pages 66–7) could be used.

Thinking can also be better organised by adjusting the curriculum for the gifted and talented, and using Kennard's (1996) model, we can represent the strategy for redesigning the curriculum to include thinking development as shown in Figure 4.4 (see page 68).

This model is appealing because it emphasises the need to develop the individual child alongside the teacher's skills. A mixture of enrichment and extension is required to develop an effective curriculum for gifted and talented children in science. Enrichment and extension should develop out of the taught curriculum and not be an appendix to the classroom work and, more importantly, it must be linked with a range of extra-curricular activities such as reading about science, viewing science programmes, science clubs and science challenges. These ideas (see Figure 4.5, on page 68) are represented in the following model developed from Kennard's (page 65) model by Berkshire Science team for developing a science curriculum to suit the gifted and talented pupil.

Once the department has developed a shared view of the key abilities of able children, the first task is to design a curriculum to include extension and enrichment activities. The second hurdle is the design and inclusion of continuous assessment to determine the daily and overall progression of pupils. Once a level of expectation is determined, the content can be extended using appropriate science models and generalised theories. Great consideration should be given to language, the nature of its usage, text and the context used for developing ideas. Developing an awareness of the origin of words used in a subject can be a valuable way of offering extension.

1. Describe what will happen when the tap in the middle of this device is opened.

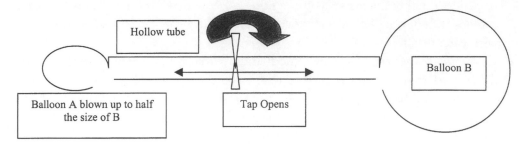

2. Describe what will happen when the candle burns at both ends. Explain why the candle does what it does and what is causing the effect.

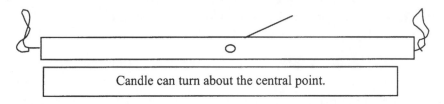

3. Describe what will happen to the temperature in the following experiment when the hotplate is turned on. Explain why the temperature does what it does and what is causing the effect.

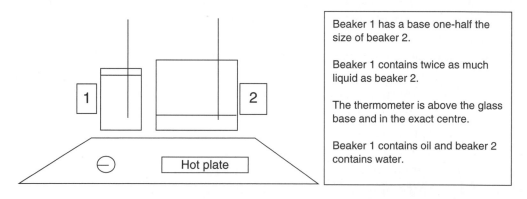

4. A candle is placed on the pan of A. A torch is placed on the pan of B. The mass of each is taken. The candle is lit and allowed to burn for some time until it is half its size. The torch is turned on and left to run for the same time as the candle burns. The mass is then taken of each. What do you think the result will be? Why do you think it will be that?

5. People like to dunk biscuits and recent research has shown that dunking biscuits into a milky drink enhances the flavour since the fat forms around the food flavours and locks it in. This dunking weakens the biscuit because it melts the fat, which holds the biscuit together. What would be useful to know would be a relationship linking the 'dunkability' of different biscuits to temperature of drink and amount of milk. Design an experiment to determine the 'dunkability coefficient' of different biscuits.

6. Take 100 cubic centimetres of water and put a $3 \times 3 \times 3$ centimetre cube of ice into the water in a beaker. Mark the water level and now predict the new level of the water when all the ice has melted. Explain the results.

7. Scientists ask questions about events and try to answer them using observations relating to the event. Here are some science questions. Try to explain the event and identify the important evidence that would allow you to explain the event.

   • Kestrels hover above busy motorway verges.
   • Turtles swim many miles to a beach they know and at night they lay their eggs in the warm sand.
   • On a cold day when you breathe out you can see your breath as a thin mist.

8. Scientists look for patterns in data that can help to indicate relationships or solve problems. Look at a pine cone and note the scales form regular left and right spirals. If you count the numbers of scales at each level you can see they follow the Fibonacci sequence. Try to explain why the segments in a pine cone or the arrangement of leaves on a flower follow a Fibonacci sequence such as 1, 1, 2, 3, 5, 8, 13, 21, 34, etc.

9. Scientists also model ideas by drawing pictures or using logic solutions. Try this problem. Two glasses are equally filled with water. Into one a spoonful of red dye is added. To the other is added a spoonful of green dye. Is the number of red particles and green particles in the two likely to be the same? Explain your answer. Now a spoonful of red dye solution is taken from the red glass and added to the green glass. It is stirred. Now a spoonful of the dye mixture in the green glass is taken and added to the red dye glass. Is the amount of green water in the red glassful greater than the amount of red in the green glassful? Explain your answer.

10. Sometimes scientists have to devise new methods for measuring objects or changes. Devise a way to measure the volume of your hand. Why does that method work? How does this problem link with Archimedes?

Figure 4.3 Sample problems

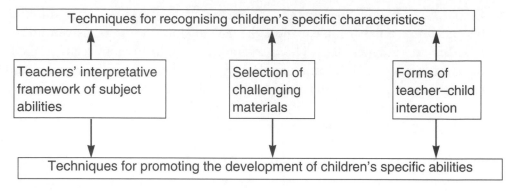

Figure 4.4

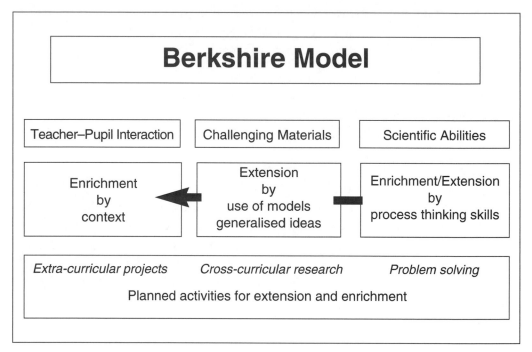

Figure 4.5

Clive Sutton (1992) has looked at the interplay of language and meaning in science and he writes: 'When circumstances are right they [words] can excite people's minds and move their imaginations, in science as in any other active area of human activity.'

It can help to develop a consideration of the relationship of word structure to a description of meaning. This etymological exercise can be a valuable extension in the form of homework and in this way the pupils can build their own etymological dictionary or glossary of terms. This approach has been found to give the subject language, life and meaning for pupils who like to experiment with words. A modern science expression like *messenger RNA* can be seen to be explicit in its meaning because the language is familiar, but sometimes the meaning is not so well defined, e.g. *computer virus* or *dissolve*.

Some schools have found the material from the next key stage textbooks helpful in extending the content but the difficulty is that in most cases the knowledge will be further developed but concepts left untouched. Some schools couple focused classroom teaching with more independent learning styles involving extensive library searches linked with focused writing tasks and more complex problem solving as part of science investigation activities and many of these use SATIS (1996) (Science and Technology in Society) materials.

Enrichment can be achieved by placing content in a different and more demanding context than for the rest of the class. This will give children an opportunity to reflect on ideas and be creative in the way they use and connect ideas because the context can be unfamiliar and require the application of ideas or contain cross-curricular aspects. This develops science understanding and an appreciation of the culture of science. The context can be set in an historical or technological situation. One can couple active work within the curriculum to extra-curricular experiences, e.g. visits to science lectures, entry into science competitions or BAYS awards. Use can be made of outside agencies such as sixth formers, postgraduate students or industry link people to come into school and work with children. The internet can be used to extend the classroom by linking with another school in a cooperative investigation.

Enrichment and extension is used to develop children's process and thinking skills. It extends content by using scientific models and generalised theories within an enriched context to develop the culture of science. It also makes use of the higher order skills in dealing with information.

Teachers' skills for questioning need to be well developed to ensure that gifted and talented pupils are really challenged. This does not mean asking more difficult knowledge questions but ones that use the higher order cognitive skills.

- Observation – 'What do you see?' 'Look carefully and describe how it happens.'
- Prediction – 'What will happen if?' 'What's the next thing to happen when . . .?'
- Causal reasoning – 'This happens because . . . happened.' 'If you do this then . . . will happen.'
- Correlational reasoning – 'It could be . . . are connected and so . . . will happen and . . . will change by . . . .' 'These two factors could be connected.'
- Application – 'If we consider this problem . . .' 'What do you think will be the important thing to do to make . . . happen?'
- Synthesis – 'What would you want to investigate to explore this problem?'
- Evaluation – 'What would be the consequence of that event?' 'Would it happen every time or are there other conditions which would help it to happen?'

To further extend a practical task, the pupil should be asked to question the purpose and relationship of what they are doing – i.e. the method – to the attainment of a solution to the problem. This makes them think about the nature of experimental method and the reliability of the approach.

To extend a science task it is possible to use one of the following context enrichments:

- use a philosophical idea (e.g. concept of proof versus statistical reliance);
- use a mathematical context to promote mathematical modelling;
- economic (e.g. perceived economics of using different sources of energy);
- historical issue (e.g. debate about gravity and falling);
- societal issue (e.g. morality of using genetic engineering);
- environmental context (e.g. transportation of oil to keep an oil based industry going).

For example the following use everyday life, mathematical and historical contexts. They also extend the work in the Key Stage 3 Programme of Study and enable the pupil to attain level 8 in the context of Key Stage 3 content.

1. You will have a good idea of particles and the way a particle model can be used to explain the way a material acts. In this challenge you need to devise a simulation involving people in your class or other materials to model and help explain how particles:

   - make a material form a crystal
   - make a substance brittle
   - make a substance very runny
   - make a liquid thick and viscous
   - make a substance elastic
   - how a substance dissolves
   - why rubber is stretchy
   - how metals can be pulled into thin wires
   - how a wax sets into a shape in a mould.

2. Ben Franklin wrote a letter to the Royal Society in 1774. In it he wrote:

   At length being at Clapham where there is, on the common a large pond, which I observed to be one day very rough with the wind, I fetched out a cruet of oil and dropped a little of it on the water. I saw it spread itself with surprising swiftness upon the surface . . . the oil, although not more than a teaspoonful, produced an instant calm over a space several yards square, which spread amazingly . . . making all that quarter of the pond, perhaps half an acre, as smooth as a looking glass.

Franklin repeated the experiment and found the same result each time. A teaspoon contained 2 cubic centimetres of oil. So what had Benjamin Franklin found out and could you make the same calculation? You will need to carry out some conversions from imperial to metric.

Using grouping to help enrich the work of gifted and talented science students

The design of activities should be carefully thought through. Bennett (1994) indicates that teachers find the design process of activities difficult because there are two facets to the design problem: the cognitive demand linked to a social objective. It has been argued that teachers often abdicate responsibility for one of the most powerful tools for directed learning; that of group composition and role effectiveness. The student's response to a group is to identify with a specific role to achieve both a personal and group objective.

The cognitive demand is related to a body of knowledge, concept, model or general theory and this sets the relevant context for the pupils to work in. It is often set at a mid-ability level to ensure the group can succeed at the task.

The structure of the group matches the social demand and will require the group to work in specific roles. This will require a high degree of cooperation within the group, with subsequent valuing of each other's work. In cooperating, pupils will be engaged in a process of decision making that will require some structure to ensure equal sharing. The overall structure decided upon for the activity can be represented as shown in Figure 4.6.

The careful composition and organisation of groups help planning for specific purposes. When working with groups it is worth constructing groups with reference to three possibilities:

Home groups – normal pupil working groups for the start of an activity. These can be paired or larger and self-chosen. They provide security and support because the pupil can work in a comfortable, undemanding environment.
Sharing groups – reconstituted groups in which pupils are directed to share their work. These are also called expert groups. They are reconstituted by teacher choice according to criteria to suit a particular outcome.
Whole class – useful for questioning or discussion work but does require focused and careful management using a balance of open/closed questions involving everyone.

This way of thinking about group work allows greater flexibility, particularly when dealing with mixed ability groups, because it can mean all pupils work in groups with clearly defined targets.

In the planning process it is important to identify individual pupils with an objective and task that will contribute to the success of the whole group. To be effective in the use of some group work can require the teacher to constitute the group by ability and renegotiate using different objectives for different groups so each pupil is being challenged appropriately.

Careful mixing of individuals can control the possibility of domination by pupils of ability. To control the domination by personality, regulate the group dynamics using specific roles for pupils and make clear the task outcome.

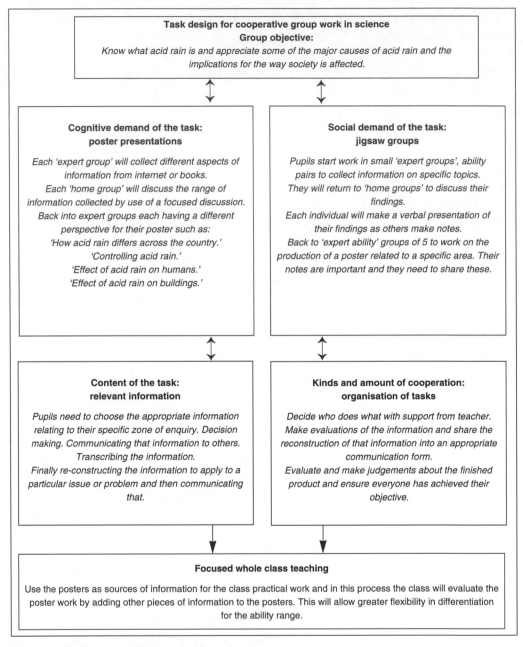

Figure 4.6 Groupwork planning in science

This strategy will allow extension of the work based upon a common starting point for all. Because the gifted and talented are generally more accomplished at hypothesising, manipulating variables and theorising, their task can be matched to this level. It is a successful strategy in managing differentiation in mixed ability groups.

Physical domination is more difficult because groups have a notional state of membership. When groups are constituted they must relate to some structure that ensures they have a common factor denoting belonging, such as ability, skill or friendship. Groups also have an underlying pattern of roles. These two factors can be heavily influenced by the systems of norms the pupil brings to the group as a result of belonging to a particular peer group. In this context the pupil will both have an identity and be secure, or be dominated and feel threatened.

In some evaluations of classroom learning it has often been noted that gifted and talented pupils bury their talent under a cloak of mediocrity to make sure they are part of the group. Their metacognition skills are such that they can do this convincingly. Others become frustrated and troublesome in the group and become the centre for distracting or disruptive behaviour. Others become loners, preferring seclusion to the strength of the group. Not all the gifted and talented have the strength of character to over-ride others who appear more physically dominating. To overcome these problems requires a range of strategies to ensure that individuals are forced to be included or work upon their particular strength, and cooperative group work effectively allows these strategies to be used.

Groups are powerful tools for differentiation when designed well with clear objectives for individuals and when the success criteria for the whole group are identified (Figure see 4.7).

Example of writing an activity for groups including gifted and talented pupils

Cognitive demand: **Apply knowledge about atoms**	**Chemistry example KS3** Work as a team of three. Each of you is a science journalist researching the development of the atomic theory for a magazine like *Focus*. Through history many scientists have pictured what matter is made up of and some of those have advanced an atom model. Find out about the following scientists' atom model and list the similarities and differences in the proposed model: Dalton J.J. Thompson Lore Rutherford Neils Bohr Modern ideas
Use of role definition to determine style of work **Analysis of the knowledge in an historical context**	Work as designers to make models for photographing for a magazine article. Make visual models of each atom and compare them by producing a timeline tracking the development of the atom. Explain the changes by linking them to evidence of the times.
Synthesis of ideas within a creative context **Evaluate the ideas in a journalistic context**	Work as individuals in the role of a science writer. Each selects a different scientist from the list. Bring them through time to have an imaginary conversation with a modern day atomic scientist. What would be the focus of the conversation? How could they be helped to understand the changes?
Context is a story but based upon hard science ideas	Work as a group of three journalists to edit an article of three sides of A4 on 'The Development of Atomic Theory'. In the article you must compare and link the three conversations into a single article. You must indicate the major developments that have led to the modern ideas of atom structure. Show the important contribution the scientists made and also indicate some of the 'wrong' ideas they held.

Role determined comprehension of climate and natural cycles	**English, Geography and Science Vertical grouping approach KS3/4** The pupils work in a vertical set group Year 7 to Year 11. Use the short story 'All Summer in a Day' by Ray Bradbury and the poem 'Sunflakes' by Frank Asch as a stimulus.
Application of ideas to indicate correlational reasoning **Analysis and synthesis**	*The story concerns Margot, who was born on earth and remembers the sun. The children who were born on Venus do not know of the sun, they know only constant rain. Today the sun is expected to shine for one hour and everyone waits expectantly.* Work as theoretical meteorologists in teams of 5, one from each year group. Brainstorm what the earth would be like with constant rain for seven years.
Knowledge, comprehension, application and synthesis	● What natural cycles would be affected by the climate? ● What might be the effect on living things? ● What would be the effect on the surface of the earth and the rocks? ● How would the earth's surface feel, smell and sound? ● What would be the effect on temperature, chemistry and other physical factors?
Knowledge and comprehension	
Application and analysis	**Divide into three different groups. Year 7, Year 8/9 and Year 10/11.** Year 7 pupils work together as ecobiologists to research and brainstorm. If there was a period of heavy rain and dim light how would life on the earth be different from that around us at present? What types of life might be expected to survive and thrive and what might the food chains look like?
Analysis and synthesis **Evaluation**	Year 8/9 pupils work together as earth scientists to research and brainstorm the conditions on the young earth and the young planet Mars. What are the similarities and what are the differences? How and why have things changed over the years to the present day? What might have been the cause of those changes?

Year 10/11 pupils work together as behaviour scientists to research and brainstorm the concept of a human going a year without seeing the sun and discuss what the effects of this might be on the individual both physiologically and psychologically. What would the conditions be like? How do you think the human might adapt to this environment?

Reform into the bigger group as designers and planners for a future venture to Mars. Consider the following problem. You will need aspects of the above research to solve the problem.

Consider the idea of landing on Mars and attempting to colonise it. Research and draw out what the surface of Mars is like. Select a likely area for the landing, i.e. at the poles, or equatorial or mid between equator and pole.

● What resources are present on the planet surface?
● What resources could be present locked up in the rock structure?
● What conditions and materials would we need to make it habitable? How could these conditions be developed with the planet's present conditions?
● How could we use the interaction of plants and natural geological events to help the process of colonisation?
● Determine the conditions needed for the successful carrying out of the project. You are not asked to consider the economics of the project.

Pupils could be asked to make a final response by a presentation in one of the following: prose, music, poster or drawings.

Figure 4.7 An activity for groups

References

Association for Science Education (1996) *Science Resources.* Birmingham Association for Science Education.

Bennett, N. (1995) *Co-operative Learning in Groups in Schools.* (ed. Kutnick and Rogers). London: Cassell.

de Bono, E. (1989) *Teach Your Child to Think.* London: Penguin.

Freeman, J. (1998) *Educating the Very Able: Current International Research.* OFSTED Reviews of Research. London: HMSO.

Gunstone, R. F. (1994) 'The Importance of Specific Science Content in the Enhancement of Metacognition', in Fensham, P., Gunstone, R. and White, R. (eds) *The Content of Science: A constructive Approach to its Teaching and Learning.* London: Taylor & Francis.

Kennard, R. (1996) 'Providing for mathematically able children in ordinary classrooms', *Perspectives on Educating the Gifted and Talented Child,* Worcester Papers in Education, 1. Worcester College of Higher Education.

Lewin, R. (1987) *A Practical Problem Solver's Handbook for Teachers and Students.* Royal County of Berkshire County Council.

Renzulli, J. (1977) *The Triad Enrichment Model: A Guide for Developing Defensible Programs for the Gifted and Talented.* Mansfield Center, CN: Creative Learning Press.

Sutton, C. (1992) *Words, Science and Learning.* Buckingham: Open University Press.

Wittrock, M. C. (1994) 'Generative Science Teaching', in Fensham, P., Gunstone, R. and White, R. (eds) *The Content of Science: A Constructive Approach to its Teaching and Learning.* London: Taylor & Francis.

CHAPTER 5

Art

Mary Fitzpatrick

Introduction

Secondary school art education has evolved quite dramatically over the last 15 years. It has changed from a curriculum designed by individual teachers who had the freedom to decide what should be taught and how it should be taught, towards a model which now provides a clear framework, with a prescribed content, but also stresses the importance of critical thinking.

Clark, Day and Greer (1987) believe that this new approach sees art as an academic subject for study with a focus on aesthetics, art history, art criticism and art production rather than a vehicle for developing creativity and self-expression. They feel its written sequential curriculum takes account of other curriculum areas as opposed to a non-sequential curriculum developed in isolation by individual teachers. It provides opportunities for students to study adult artwork and use adult images to serve as a focus for integrating learning from the other art disciplines, in contrast to the previous approach which was based on the assumption that adult images might have a negative influence on the students' self-expression and creative development.

Able artists respond well to the kind of curriculum that provides them with the opportunities to think critically about art. They are able to use their superior technical skills to show how they think about the visual world. Art can be seen as a means of developing a student's overall intellectual growth. Eisner (1982) argues that far from being a trivial pursuit, visual representation makes a unique contribution to the process of education and the student's cognitive development. Research conducted by Wang and Lindvall cited in Montgomery (1996) showed that critical thinking activities not only lead to improved acquisition of subject content, but also to improved generalisation and transfer of knowledge and skills.

What does it mean to be able in art?

It is important to be clear about just how we define high ability in art. Many secondary school students can produce artwork that demonstrates an ability to use a variety of materials and tools, which is technically accurate and is visually interesting. However, the most able artists are more than competent technicians. They are likely to:

- think deeply about their work, show ability to analyse and interpret their observations and then present them in a creative way;
- be able to draw on existing knowledge, make connections and draw comparisons with the work of others;
- display enthusiasm and interest in all the visual aspects of the world around them;
- enjoy experimenting with a wide range of materials and may exceed the bounds of convention;
- be able to sustain concentration and persevere with work, sometimes with a degree of obsession, constantly refining ideas and, in some cases, finding it difficult to accept their work as finished or complete;
- have confidence in their ability to use a range of skills and techniques and readily acquire new skills and transfer skills developed in one activity to another.

With inspirational and appropriate teaching the most able will develop an interest and an appetite for discussing and evaluating the work of other artists. They will begin to use a more extensive artistic vocabulary and will be able to make connections between art and design over time showing an understanding and interest in the social, religious and historical context of artwork.

Artistic ability and academic achievement

Some students who are talented in art do not show a tendency to be scholastically capable and may even have difficulties with some aspects of their learning. For example students gifted in drawing have a higher incidence of reading problems such as dyslexia in comparison with the normal population (Winner 1996). The most systematic study to date of academic achievement in the artistically gifted was conducted in the USA by Csikszentmihalyi *et al.* (1993). They observed a group of teenagers who were gifted in art, music, mathematics, science and athletics over a period of four years and found that the artistic talented adolescents did not do as well in school as the musically gifted teenagers. They also discovered that the artistically talented group, while being highly committed to their art, actually had a lower commitment to academic achievement than all of the other groups, including the athletes. This singleness of purpose was also demonstrated when Csikszentmihalyi found that art students rated aesthetic values above all others, rating them, in fact, more highly even than theology students rated religion.

Savant artists

Very occasionally you may come across an individual student who possesses extraordinary artistic ability but who is limited in all other fields. These 'savants', as they are called, show us that a form of giftedness can operate in the absence of 'normal' intelligence. Winner (1996) believes that savant syndrome occurs six times more often in males than in females and that a third of all savants are also autistic although most have some autistic characteristics. Unlike the normally gifted artist the savant's gift is more constricted. They rarely show people relating to one another and rarely paint or draw expressively. They are able to faithfully reproduce scenes from the external world but are not able to analyse and interpret their observations.

Identifying the gifted artist

The identification of the most able artist is a complex affair and relies heavily on the understanding and expertise of art teachers. It is a process made easier in schools where the education of gifted and talented students is given a high priority and where whole school systems exist to coordinate and monitor this work. In such schools departments will have worked together to establish a shared definition of what it means to be able in their field and will have devised systems to track student progress. This is particularly important to avoid underachievement. For example, an able student may be inspired to produce some outstanding ceramics work in response to a particular stimulus in Year 7 but may then revert back to a mediocre standard in following years.

The identification of the most able artists must not be seen as an end in itself. There is only value in identifying the able if it has a direct influence on provision and enables teachers to differentiate more effectively. The strategies and approaches used to identify able artists need to be ongoing and varied and may include the following:

- information from primary schools, end of Key Stage 2 assessment details with accompanying sketchbook and examples of work;
- end of Key Stage 3 assessment – exceptional performance descriptors;
- teacher assessment based on observation of students' achievements both in terms of two and three dimensional outcomes but also in the form of oral dialogue with students regarding their ideas and the thinking behind their art work; and
- parental nomination.

Characteristics of effective provision for the gifted and talented in art

Art departments which are effective in meeting the needs of the most able foster a climate of real enthusiasm and intense interest in all aspects of the visual arts. Provision for the able is not seen as separate but builds on the general provision available to all students. Identification of the able is seen as important and systems exist to monitor and record progress.

Successful art departments are well organised, offer a stimulating environment and plan efficiently within the context of their own school community. The size of the school, the layout and arrangement of the art studios, the proximity to ICT facilities and the way the students are grouped will all have an impact on how the department caters for the needs of the able. What works well in one situation may not be the best way forward in another.

Able students need teachers of art who have high expectations and who display a real passion and enthusiasm for the subject. It is particularly important that relationships are formed that are based on the mutual respect that derives from sharing personal ideas. Able students will need time with their teachers to engage in rigorous intellectual debate exploring the context, media, social and historical connections of the student's or artist's work.

Within the framework of a structured national curriculum, able students must have the opportunity for in-depth learning experiences, at specialist events or with artists in residence. Where necessary they should be taught how to develop the critical thinking skills and advanced art vocabulary required to analyse and evaluate artwork. Emphasis should be placed on establishing a range of research skills using the internet and CD ROM material to enrich and inspire ideas. Wherever possible a flexible approach should be adopted so that the able students can experiment with different media and ideas.

At KS4 and beyond able students should have the opportunity to spend more time on their artwork constantly revisiting and reworking their original ideas. With encouragement they should develop an extensive knowledge and understanding of the various movements and theories that have influenced the art world. Ideas outlined in the A level syllabus can provide additional guidance. Older students should be encouraged to remain open to the distinctive qualities of each movement or trend rather than engage in speculative value judgements. Art, like poetry, almost always seeks a deeper, less obvious reality; the challenge for the student is to learn from the truths it conveys.

Ideas for classroom provision

As stated earlier, what works well in one situation may not be possible in another. The individual interests and specialisms of the teaching team, together with the physical layout and configuration of the art studios, will have an impact on provision. Inspirational and creative art teachers take account of their individual situations to develop provision for their most talented students. The following case studies illustrate some of the approaches and ideas that have been used to provide challenges for the most able artists in three different settings.

Case studies of three art departments

Art department A

This department is located in an 11 to 18 co-educational comprehensive school on the edge of a provincial town in Berkshire. There are 1,000 students on roll, many of whom travel to school from the surrounding villages. There is a long-standing interest in provision for the most able students, a whole school policy and a register of students who are considered to be gifted and talented. A senior teacher oversees all aspects of this work.

The art department is housed in a separate single storey building, purpose built as a resource for students with special needs although it has not been used for this purpose for over 15 years. Access to the four studios is via the large central studio with very little natural light. The toilets have been converted into a well-equipped dark room. The kiln and the ceramics material are stored in a cage within the largest studio. The small staff area contains the filing system, student records and a very comprehensive library of books, slides and CD ROMs. The teaching team consists of four full-time members of staff, all of whom have a solid grounding in fine art but can also offer specialisms in ceramics, photography, textiles and history of art. One member of the team has special responsibility for the most able. There is no obvious house style. It is a young team; no one has been teaching for more than eight years.

The main features of this department are teamwork, flexibility and accessibility to a range of resources and materials. The head of department has deliberately worked towards appointing staff who can offer a wide range of specialisms but who are very flexible in their approach to their students. Lesson planning is a team exercise and lessons are evaluated and refined at the end of each unit. It is not uncommon to find a small group of Year 7 or 8 students working alongside Year 11 or sixth form students. Because the studios are so close there is a great deal of cross fertilisation and movement between groups not only by teachers but also by students. There is a culture of high expectation and genuine excitement about all aspects of the visual arts. Exam results at both GCSE and A level are outstanding. All available wall space together with a number of easels are covered in glorious examples of students' work. Students are encouraged to talk about their work and evaluate the work of both established artists and fellow students. The main difficulty for this department is a lack of space. There is nowhere within the department to create space for an artist in residence nor is there much space for storage of both materials and students' work. So far there have been no restrictions on the size of the work attempted by students in the upper school but this may have to change.

All members of the department are expected to identify the students who are seen as most able using the departmental checklist (see Figure 5.1) and then monitor progress. For all students each unit of work is assessed using the National Curriculum descriptors at Key Stage 3 or GCSE grades at Key Stage 4. Great use is made of the digital camera to provide evidence of achievements for departmental records.

At Key Stage 3 the department is working towards adopting the QCA schemes of work but there are some resourcing issues that have not yet been resolved. They are very pleased to have been able to move to mixed ability teaching groups and are already seeing significant improvements in the overall standard of work. The previous grouping arrangements were based on the students' linguistic and mathematical ability, not their artistic ability, so had little relevance for art.

All students are expected to use a sketchbook to record ideas, experiment with a range of media, produce evidence of planning showing a structured sequence of activities and undertake research about art.

Thinking and talking about a diverse range of visual stimuli is seen as a vital prerequisite for extending the most able artists. They are exposed to technical vocabulary directly linked to artistic genres and movements such as classicism, realism, ephemeral installation and abstraction but are also encouraged to experiment with a range of adjectives to develop their repertoire of useful words. Some of the many examples may include words such as macabre, repugnant, sensational, strong, light, brutal, glamorised, picturesque and versatile. The teaching team recognise the value of high quality questioning and take every opportunity to delve a bit deeper with the most able encouraging them to articulate their thinking. During the summer term all students are given the opportunity to spend time evaluating the GCSE and A level exhibitions using a variety of worksheets designed to develop thinking. (See the examples in Figures 5.2 and 5.3.) This exercise then culminates in a plenary session where ideas and opinions are shared and discussed.

At Key Stage 4 and beyond, students have the opportunity to spend longer on a piece of work. A wide range of resources is available and students are encouraged to experiment with and mix their media. It is hoped that they will learn from their mistakes and exploit any interesting but unconventional outcomes. Over the last few years more and more students have become interested in some of the issues and movements characterised by the artists of the 1990s including installation art and every effort is made to accommodate them within the confines of the rather cramped conditions.

A range of extension and enrichment experiences are available for able students throughout the academic year and include:

- Challenge week – when the curriculum is suspended for a week and students are offered a range of options including a variety of art events.
- Masterclasses with artists from different movements and backgrounds, e.g. Japanese art, conceptual art, feminist art, etc.
- Regular visits to galleries and museums. (Tate Britain and Modern, MOMA Oxford, The National Gallery, etc.)
- Opportunities to visit art galleries during visits abroad. For example in Spain: Museo Picasso in Barcelona; Museo Dali in Figueras. In the USA The Museum of Fine Arts in Boston during an American exchange.

Checklist for able and talented pupils. Art department.
Does the pupil you have identified have some of the characteristics listed below?

Student name	Tutor/year group	Teacher	Date

(From Freeman 1998) **General characteristics**   *tick boxes*

Memory and knowledge – Excellent memory and use of information.	
Self regulation – They know how they learn best and can monitor their learning.	
Dealing with problems – They add to information, spot what is irrelevant and get to the essentials quickly.	
Speed of thought – They may spend longer planning but then reach decisions speedily.	
Flexibility – Although their thinking is usually more organised than other children's, they can see and adopt alternative solutions to learning and problem solving.	
Preference for complexity – They tend to make games and tasks more complex to increase interest.	
Concentration– They have an exceptional ability to concentrate at will and for long periods of time.	

Specific art and design skills

High observational drawing ability.	
High level of planning, compositions, layouts, constructions, structures and ceramics.	
High level of dexterity with tools.	
Understanding and following instructions, then expanding on them by extending a task, making artefacts, researching, and planning outcomes.	
Developing new techniques successfully, by exploration of media.	
High level of competence in all media and areas.	
High level of competence in the following media.	

drawing sculpture	painting printing	graphics collage	ceramics CAD

Mature and cognitive understanding of art and design concepts demonstrated in discussion and an ability to relate them to their own practical work in an intelligent manner.	
Highly organised, sequential working towards outcome.	
Good/Excellent organisation of materials, work ideas, homework.	
Excellent standard of presentation and care of work.	
High ability to research and write personally, using specialist vocabulary on art/design.	
Excellent grades in exam.	
Consistently gaining A1 grades for homework.	

*If a student demonstrates the majority of these qualities and stands out as **excellent against their peer group**, they may be identified as gifted and talented.*
Inform the coordinator.
Discuss with the pupil and aim to ensure you differentiate effectively in your planning, teaching, provision of resources, equipment and materials.
If you have concerns that a pupil is able and talented but is disguising their ability or underachieving, inform coordinator and HOD.

Figure 5.1 Departmental checklist

Exhibition Evaluation

Tick exhibition you view – GCSE Art ☐
A Level Art ☐

1. How many students are showing work in this exhibition? _____

2. Tick all the mediums/techniques you observe.

Painting		Photography		Installation	
Drawing		Textiles		Mixed media	
Printing		Ceramics			
Collage		Construction			
Computer		Sculpture			

3. Select one piece of 2D work that interests you.
Describe it.

> Pictorial notes

Say why it interests you.

Does it remind you of any other artwork?

Can you think of ways it could be developed further?

Name .... Form ....

Date ....

Figure 5.2 Exhibition evaluation sheet

Exhibition Evaluation

Tick exhibition you view – GCSE Art ☐
A Level Art ☐

1. How many students are showing work in this exhibition? _____

2. Select one piece of 2D work that interests you. Describe it.

   | Pictorial notes |

   Say why it interests you.

   Does it remind you of any other more famous artwork?

   Can you think of ways it could be developed further?

---

3. Select one piece of 3D work that interests you. Describe it.

   | Pictorial notes |

   Say why it interests you.

   Does it remind you of any other more famous artwork?

   Can you think of ways it could be developed further?

Figure 5.3 Exhibition evaluation sheet

The key characteristics of Art department A include:

- a strategy for identifying the able artists linked to the whole school register of able students;
- a member of staff who has particular responsibility for the able artists;
- a young teaching team who can offer a wide range of specialisms;
- a team approach to planning and delivering the art curriculum;
- flexibility of approach with regard to student grouping including opportunities for mixed age classes;
- an interest in developing the technical language of the visual arts;
- interest in all aspects of art history including the art of the 1990s with its recurring themes of identity politics and gender, the province of space and multimedia installation;
- a comprehensive library of books, slides and CD-ROMs;
- high quality displays.

Art department B

This department provides art education for approximately 1,400 pupils in an industrial town in the Midlands. It consists of three main buildings about 100 metres apart with a cluster of temporary classrooms grouped around the newest and central building built in the 1980s. This school has been interested in supporting the most able students for some time and has had an effective whole school policy for the able since the early 1990s. GCSE results as a whole are well above the national average and the art results are significantly above average. There are the equivalent of five full-time members of staff. One of the teaching team is a head of year and has a reduced timetable and there are two other part-time teachers. Another member of the team has sole responsibility for graphics, which is taught to GCSE and A level. There are three purpose built studios in the main building including a large ceramics area with spacious storage facilities and kiln. The graphics studio is housed in another building adjacent to the darkroom. It contains eight Apple Mac computers with specialist software and two PCs linked to the school network.

The main feature of this department is its focus on fine art with particular attention to drawing and painting. All the students follow an intense programme of drawing from Year 7 and as a result develop high levels of skill. This approach fosters confidence and enthusiasm, which in turn has a very beneficial effect on the departmental ethos of high expectation and excellence. Within this environment those who are technically able flourish and produce work of a very high standard, while those with the potential to be able to be artists have the opportunity to develop their skills. All students are encouraged to put in extra time and the studios are open at lunchtime and after school most days so students can continue with their work. These after hours sessions enable students of different ages to observe and discuss their work thus facilitating a rich exchange of ideas. GCSE art is taught as a twilight subject for able artists who wish to take an additional subject. The department owns a huge collection of inspiring objects and artefacts which are used for still life drawing classes. Staff take delight in creating quite extraordinary visual effects within the medium of still life which are both exciting to view and challenging to draw. Art history plays an important part in this department's work and constant reference is made to the work of established artists from every movement. Slide shows and other forms of visual reference are made available in most lessons.

Alongside the regular curriculum are what can be best described as special projects or commissions. From time to time students are offered the additional challenge of creating large pieces of artwork for exhibition in the school or beyond. In many cases the teaching staff manage to gain financial backing from local industry to offset some of the costs.

Examples of special projects

1. In association with National Power, who provided the materials and transport, a group of sixth form students created a free standing sculpted relief wall made up of individual building blocks, each block being approximately four feet high by four feet wide with a depth of one foot which on completion were cemented together. The overall theme celebrated the dignity of labour, and inspiration was drawn from an eclectic range of sources. These included the Elgin Marbles, the Russian Contructivist Movement and the early reliefs of Ben Nicholson. The focus was on the interacting forms of circles, squares and rectangles with even some consideration of primitive Inuit soapstone sculpture.

2. As part of the Summer Challenge Week, with financial and technical support from Southern Arts, 180 Year 8 pupils took part in an installation art event at a local beauty spot – an area of open hillside. Each pupil was provided with a piece of hardboard 2 foot square on which they painted part of a huge design. Each piece of hardboard was numbered so the students would know where their piece should fit. All one hundred and eighty pupils were then transported by coach to the hillside and marshalled into a large square where upon receiving the signal they raised the boards above their heads, creating the gigantic image. A helicopter crew from the local RAF station flew overhead at the appropriate moment and recorded the event on film.

3. Every year all departments contribute to a cross-curricular theme, which is coordinated by the head of art. All students in Key Stage 3 are involved. Some of the themes examined include the art and culture of the Aborigines, the South Americans, Japan and Asia.

4. A variety of commissions were received to produce large paintings (8 feet by 4 feet) for display in the welcome hall of the local industrial estate, the boardroom of a hydraulics company (featuring an environmental issue) and the main school assembly hall. The work was completed on sheets of reinforced hardboard.

5. Commissions for the A level graphics students to produce flyers, brochures and posters for local companies and academic institutions.

6. Special project with the St Ives Tate Gallery in Cornwall involving masterclasses with experts, culminating in a grand exhibition at the Tate of all artwork produced.

7. Annual excursions abroad to paint and draw in the field.
8. Life drawing classes at weekends for sixth form students with professional models (with written parental permission obtained in advance).

The key characteristics of Art department B include:
- a focus on the development of the skills of painting and drawing;
- particular interest in creating still life arrangements;
- a comprehensive collection of interesting and stimulating objects and artefacts;
- a great deal of access for students to the art studios outside the regular curriculum time;
- involvement in a wide range of special extra curricular projects and commissions;
- interest in high quality display and publicity of special events and commissions; and
- strong links with the local community and industry.

Art department C

Art department C forms an integral part of an inner city mixed comprehensive school with 1,600 students. The building was considered to be state of the art when it was first built in the early 1960s. However, now it is recognised as having serious design defects, which include long, dark and rather narrow corridors with an excess of windows in the classrooms, which makes it exceedingly hot in the summer months. Visitors to the school are inspired by the wealth of outstanding artwork on display. Until the Excellence in Cities initiative in 1999 this school had not got a particularly well established policy with regard to the most able pupils, although it had been making significant progress in raising standards across the whole curriculum with exam results improving steadily year after year.

The department consists of a suite of six art studios on the fourth floor with good views of the metropolis below. All are very light and spacious. The ceramics room is well equipped with specialist storage, drainage and kiln. Pupils rotate between studios when necessary to access the specialist materials and equipment.

This department has the equivalent of six full-time art teachers, four full-time and four part-time teachers who are also practising artists, producing, exhibiting and selling their own work. This dimension is seen as extremely valuable and provides useful links with the commercial art world. Each year pupils in the sixth form are taken to the annual Contemporary Art Fair in London which provides an opportunity to see how current artists are influencing our perception of the visual arts and how this art is exhibited. The department achieves excellent exam results and a good proportion of students go on to study art at university or art school.

The main feature of this team is their shared interest in the cognitive process in art, the thinking behind and around art and how it relates to the rest of the curriculum. They are passionate about their subject and see art as the central pivot on which all other aspects of the curriculum should depend. Even before the development of the QCA schemes of work they believed that knowledge of the whole curriculum was important for art teaching because it provided opportunities for students to make connections between issues raised in different subjects and so extend thinking. Over the years a network of connections have been built up linking the various curriculum areas to art.

For example, students studied Islamic art, which in itself is a modern notion generated not by Islamic culture but by outsiders who can contribute to and deepen pupils' understanding of the study of Islam in religious education. Such studies help students to realise some of the differences between the arts from Islamic lands and those from the West, where for centuries the Christian church was the major patron of, and inspiration for, the arts. Islam never developed institutions comparable to those that played such an important role in the making of Christian art. Further connections can be made when studying the geometric aspects of some of the two- and three-dimensional Islamic art and geometry in the maths curriculum. Another good example of this connecting curriculum approach can be seen with the study in history of the French Revolution which resulted in political and social upheavals and the work of artists such as David (1748–1825) and Goya (1746–1828). This in turn leads to further consideration of art as a tool for propagandists.

Simply providing opportunities to see the links between the various curriculum areas is not in itself enough to develop the cognitive skills in the able. The teaching staff believe that students need to practise using the technical language appropriate to articulate their thinking. They also need to understand that meaning in art is often conveyed through its metaphorical content. For example, Picasso's famous painting of Guernica shows little evidence that it is a painting about war. Yet we know that Picasso painted it in response to the nationalist bombing of Guernica in 1937. The sombre colour scheme has been interpreted as having been used to reinforce the painting's mood of despair, while the angular shapes and the expressions and poses of the people and animals convey suffering. All Picasso would say was, 'The horse represents the people, and the bull brutality and darkness.'

One way of helping students to develop a capacity to make sense of the ambiguities and visual metaphors in art is to use the semantic differential technique devised by Osgood *et al.* (1957) cited in Cunliffe (1998). Osgood's research suggests that people align sensory analogies such as slow and fast or sweet and sour with visual and aural modes. By getting students to identify where they would place a concept on a seven-point scale, one enables them to begin to understand and make use of synaesthetic metaphors. The semantic differential can be used to analyse a variety of issues in art and currently department C is developing strategies to help students to develop this kind of thinking about art. Examples of how this semantic differential approach can be used to analyse technique, process or composition and formal organisation can be seen in Figures 5.4 and 5.5 taken from work by Leslie Cunliffe (1998).

Reproduction of art work here

TITLE OF WORK

ARTIST'S NAME

After spending some time looking carefully at this work of art, record your response to it on a 1–7 scale by circling a number.

For example, if you think the work has a smooth technique, give it a 1. If you think it is rough, give it a 7. If you think it is somewhere in between, choose a 2, 3, 4, 5 or 6.

Example **small**   **1   2   3   4   5   6   7**   **large**

It is very important that you think of good reasons to justify your response. Write them down after you have circled your response.

detailed   1   2   3   4   5   6   7   vague

Give your reasons for your score...
....

soft   1   2   3   4   5   6   7   hard

Give your reasons for your score...
....

fine   1   2   3   4   5   6   7   coarse

Give your reasons for your score...
....

thin   1   2   3   4   5   6   7   thick

Give your reasons for your score...
....

smooth   1   2   3   4   5   6   7   rough

Give your reasons for your score...
....

Figure 5.4 Example of a semantic differential to cue students to analyse the process and technique in a work of art (Cunliffe 1998)

Reproduction of art work here

TITLE OF WORK

ARTIST'S NAME

After spending some time looking carefully at this work of art, record your response to it on a 1–7 scale by circling a number.

For example, if you think the work has a smooth technique, give it a 1. If you think it is rough, give it a 7. If you think it is somewhere in between, choose a 2, 3, 4, 5 or 6.

Example **small**   **1   2   3   4   5   6   7**   **large**

It is very important that you think of good reasons to justify your response. Write them down after you have circled your response.

         symmetrical   1   2   3   4   5   6   7   asymmetrical

Give your reasons for your score...
....

         stable   1   2   3   4   5   6   7   unstable

Give your reasons for your score...
....

         formal   1   2   3   4   5   6   7   informal

Give your reasons for your score...
....

         sour   1   2   3   4   5   6   7   sweet

Give your reasons for your score...
....

         3D space   1   2   3   4   5   6   7   2D space

Give your reasons for your score...
....

Figure 5.5 Example of a semantic differential mediating the ability to analyse the composition and organisation in a work of art (Cunliffe 1998)

The key features of Art department C include:

- knowledge of the whole curriculum so that a network of connections can be made between art and other subject areas;
- great interest in the cognitive process in art;
- opportunities to develop and practise the language needed to articulate thinking about the visual arts;
- teachers of art who are practising artists producing, exhibiting and selling their own work;
- links with the commercial art world; and
- high quality displays.

Conclusion

The case study departments show that there is no one way of meeting the needs of the most able artists. Much depends on the individual circumstances of the school and the individual strengths of the teaching team. However all three departments share some of the same characteristics:

- flexibility of approach to all aspects of art teaching;
- interest in developing thinking skills; and
- a creative and inspirational teaching team.

Also in each case a whole school policy for able students exists and systems are in place to support the work of departments in raising standards.

Flexibility

The teaching teams in all three case study schools deliver the curriculum in a variety of ways. They may work with groups of mixed age students, or provide twilight sessions after school hours. They make themselves and the studios available for continued work beyond the regular day. They are not constrained by a lack of resources and find creative ways to supplement provision. Good provision for the most able is not dependent on exotic and glossy resources. The individual specialisms and contacts of each teacher are exploited for the benefit of students. Creative strategies are used to overcome obstacles.

Thinking skills

Thinking about the visual arts is seen as a vital component for success in art. Students are encouraged to plan, monitor and evaluate their own thinking and performance. They have opportunities to develop the language of art needed to articulate thinking. The teacher acts as mediator to develop with the student an awareness and analysis of the thinking process they use. Attention is also given to the transfer of these processes to different contexts.

Inspiring teachers

Art teachers play a vital role in providing suitably challenging opportunities for able artists. They must have high expectations and display a continual enthusiasm and hunger for art. They must provide the technical support needed to generate confidence in the students and be prepared to share personal ideas and provide opportunities for success and for failure.

Whole school issues

Schools with systems and policies in place for able students provide important support to departments. Such a structure can help to maintain the focus on ensuring appropriate challenge and on developing an ethos which values high attainment.

Successful art departments have a particularly influential impact on the school ethos. The visual impact of glorious examples of students' artwork displayed around the school will provide opportunities for the institution to proudly celebrate its students' achievements. One cannot underestimate the beneficial effect of these displays of art on all students, teaching staff, parents and other visitors. They not only celebrate success but also play a part in raising the self-esteem of both the individual students who were responsible for the work and of the school as a whole.

Acknowledgement

The author wishes to thank the following for case study contributions:

Lamorna Wadell and Marcia Petty, Art Department, Park House School, West Berkshire; Paul Leonard, Deputy Head teacher, Didcot Girls' School, Oxfordshire.

References

Clark, G., Day, M. and Greer, D. (1987) 'Discipline-based art education: becoming students of art', *Journal of Aesthetic Education*, **21**(2).
Csikszentmihalyi, M., Rathunde, K. and Whalen, S. (1993) *Talented Teenagers: The Roots of Success and Failure*. New York: Cambridge University Press.
Cunliffe, L. (1998) 'Art and Art Education as a Cognitive Process and the National Curriculum', in Burden, R. and Williams, M. (eds) *Thinking Through the Curriculum*. London: Routledge.
Dudley LEA (1998) *Meeting the Needs of the More Able Pupil*. Dudley: LEA Publications.
Eisner, E. (1982) *Cognition and Curriculum*. London: Longman.
Fisher, R. (1990) *Teaching Children to Think*. Cheltenham: Stanley Thornes.
Freeman, J. (1998) *Educating the Very Able: Current International Research*. London: HMSO.
Hampshire County Council (1998) *Challenging Able Pupils – Guidelines for Secondary Schools*. Hampshire Inspection and Advisory Service.
Montgomery, D. (1996) *Educating the Able*. London: Cassell.
Winner, E. (1996) *Gifted Children: Myths and Realities*. New York: Basic Books.

CHAPTER 6

Design and Technology

Trevor Davies

Introduction

Instantly I had this glaring flash of something so obvious a child of six could have thought of it. If a clockwork gramophone can produce that volume of sound, then why not apply the principle to building a spring-driven radio. That was the Alka-Seltzer moment, the moment the tablet hits the water and begins to fizz. I left the television set on, with the narrator still submerging viewers in a tidal wave of dismal statistics and, late as it was, went to my workshop. A good idea turns every cog in your mind, making you scared of bed in case the whole machine grinds to a halt. (Bayliss 2000: 244)

Design problems: their origin and nature

Designers engage in cognitive and practical activity in order to construct and respond to design briefs, resulting in the eventual solution of problems. Problem and solution identification and method implementation may rely heavily on analysis and/or may require creativity. Designers work both individually and in teams; they serve customers, clients and production processes at a commercial level. How do design problems arise? How do thought and action go together in the responses to design problems? Design problems and corresponding solutions are at the heart of technological capability. Dasgupta (1996) believes that 'the processes by which artefacts are invented and designed – which we may ultimately regard as the intellectual epicentre of technology – exhibit certain significant features or attributes that appear to be universal and timeless in their nature' (p. 6).

Successful design through invention and innovation involves high levels of risk and many new ideas end in failure: 'consensus suggests that for every ten ideas for new products, three will be developed, one-point-three will be launched and only one will make any profit' (Baxter 1995: 2).

At all stages of ideation, development and selection, decision making is important. Motivational and social determinants, and a deep understanding of the full circumstances of the problem, usually precede solution through conscious and unconscious reflection. To reduce the risks associated with solving a problem, maximum information is required. This involves a good understanding of the processes of information seeking. Procedures associated with technological problem solving and design are often evolutionary rather than revolutionary. They usually derive from existing knowledge and skill, but new artefacts, and hence new knowledge are created, which enter the public domain as a result. Elmer and Davies (2000) conclude that the 'failure' of designers in fields such as architecture is often identified historically because public values change. For example, in the 1960s, buildings were constructed with more emphasis on functionality than on aesthetics. This situation no longer exists, as the public demands more attention to aesthetics which in turn requires newer frameworks for designing and creating new knowledge. Creativity is a vehicle by which new knowledge and skill is created. Creative acts, represented by the products of creativity, are the means by which design and technology makes a contribution to the lives of individuals and societal development, which in turn fosters further human creativity.

An example of such creativity is given by the current rapidly increasing penetration of the marketplace by the revolutionary Dual Cyclone vacuum cleaner, the invention of James Dyson, reported by *The Times* to be:

> the most inspiring business story of the late 20th century. Knocked back at every turn by multi-national giants who ridiculed his [Dyson's] invention, plagiarised by international business villains, plagued by debt as he sought to pursue his vision in a country reluctant to fund and research development, he worked alone for 14 years, from the concept of the machine to its appearance in the shops, clinging relentlessly to his dream. (Coren 1996)

Educating in design and technology: a balancing act

The National Curriculum Design and Technology Working Group Report (Department of Education and Science 1989) was strongly influenced by the work of the Assessment of Performance Unit (APU 1981) that, innovatively at the time, identified the interaction of mind (mental modelling) and hand (concrete modelling) as critical to the development of capability in design and technology: 'It is our contention that this inter-relationship between modelling ideas in the mind, and modelling ideas in reality is the cornerstone of capability in design and technology. It is best described as "thought in action"' (Kimbell *et al.*, 1990: 21).

This implies learners holistically engaging with the processes of designing (ideas generation and selection, evaluation and investigation) and making (planning, mock-up generation, refining and detailing), but with embedded opportunities for creativity at any stage. Creativity is widely recognised to be a key feature of the most outstanding work in design and technology and something to concentrate on with gifted and talented students. OFSTED (2001a) note for example that:

Much of the outstanding work of students' main designing and making project is linked to industry or a community based project and nearly always involves a real client . . . in some cases highly creative solutions are adopted and developed.

Impact of the National Curriculum on educational provision

Schools and teachers, under the impact of the 1988 Education Reform Act, are currently over-constrained in some respects through attempting to work 'to the letter of the law' when delivering the curriculum to students. Or they are providing coaching to enable students to pass through 'examination hoops' at the expense of addressing wider DT objectives (Ofsted 2001a). The 'qualitative' aspects of learning often receive limited attention. The realities of schools are that there are many pressures: fixed curriculum requirements and constraints; assessment and examination approaches; strong external governance including political lobbies and parents; limited resource availability including time and teacher expertise. This can affect design and technology education adversely, given the particular model of 'design processing' adopted in the Order (as with all prescriptive models), where knowledge and skills are closely defined. Reviewing the Order and implementing changes has helped, but major difficulties still remain with respect to encouraging creative approaches. Amongst teachers, there is a widely recognised difficulty of balancing the teaching of 'skills' and the promotion of creative responses by most able learners. Kimbell (1996) states that: 'the centralising influence of a national curriculum runs the risk of placing a dead weight on innovation – discouraging imaginative teachers and schools from developing their curricula' (p. 99).

In recent literature, difficulties in implementing the vision of the Working Group are indicated in articles such as: 'Problem-solving and the tyranny of product outcomes' (McCormick and Davidson 1996: 230–41) and 'Young children's problem-solving in design and technology: a taxonomy of strategies' (Roden 1997: 14–19). They indicate the complexity of the demands of teaching design, linked to manufacture. Consequently, in most schools, working with materials such as paper, wood, plastics, food and textiles serves as a vehicle to teach knowledge, material preparation and finishing skills. Through manufacturing products, learners can gain a feeling of achievement and have something to take home to parents. Teachers also feel that learners have then produced tangible, valued outcomes, within the closely defined, often minimal time and resource allocation. But this often plays to students' enjoyment of the subject and does not challenge the most able appropriately. Creativity in teaching and learning is elusive and rarely prioritised. When it is prioritised, its nature is not defined or closely considered and is often conflated with problem solving. Bloom (1956: 33) postulates that in fields of knowledge that are changing, knowledge should be presented as a transitory medium that enables users to solve relevant problems. It should not be presented as absolute truth. McCormick and Davidson (1996) report from their classroom based research that:

. . . these outcomes (product) undermine some of the design process and problem-solving activity that teachers are concerned to foster. Each of the teachers has different objectives and different views of the design process and problem-solving (and their inter-relationship), yet do not support either in ways that might be expected. (p. 240)

Kimbell (2000) says that while the cornerstones for creativity to be fostered in design and technology in school are the motivation to improve, and the capability to create, neither the Office for Standards in Education (OFSTED) nor the Teacher Training Agency (TTA) actively encourage it. He argues that their requirements and procedures do not give teachers the essential support for dealing with learners, of whom the most able suffer most: 'Teachers must be given emotional and intellectual support and space to foster their creativity, allow them to trust and take risks and learn from their mistakes' (p. 124).

Meeting the needs of the most able in design and technology

In education, all learners need to be introduced to the range of experiences, knowledge, skills, processes and values that allow them to prepare for their responsibilities in professional and/or citizenship roles. Eyre (1997) identifies three separate components which together lead to outstanding educational achievement:

- innate ability;
- opportunity/support; and
- motivation/hard work.

Gagné (in Eyre p. 6) proposes a model for dealing with more able and exceptionally able learners, which when applied to the field of design and technology emphasises the following:

Giftedness (innate ability/aptitude)

- Intellectual (powers of reasoning and judgement making);
- creativity (originality, inventiveness, humour);
- personal and social (leadership, empathy, self-awareness); and
- others.

Talents

- Technological (skill-based e.g. mechanics, electronics, computers);
- social action (teamwork, leadership); and
- games of strategy (logical thinking, e.g. puzzles).

Motivation and appropriate temperament/personality factors are necessary to ensure that development occurs through learning, training and practice. Important environmental factors include: the influence of home; significant others (for example, parents and teachers); the nature of the undertakings/events engaged in; chance. All play a part in the progress and achievement of our most able students.

Barak and Doppelt (1998) propose that thinking skills need to be explicitly developed as part of a technology curriculum based on recognition that higher order competencies do not happen spontaneously. The promotion of such skills should also occur through adopted assessment procedures in order to maximise learning. Hill (1998) recognises the need for students to interpret design activities in technological problem solving as an opportunity to explore which: 'encourages student confidence in the freedom to explore and take risks. This confidence becomes critical when we understand that in creation and invention, there are always states of order and disorder' (p. 3).

In learning situations, learners should have the potential to act creatively in the way in which they behave and interact with their world in the process of gaining experience and understanding.

Some possible qualities of gifted and talented students in design and technology include:

- readily taking on board novel ideas and effectively discussing them;
- relating novel ideas to familiar ideas and using their knowledge and skill to act on them with 2D and/or 3D modelling;
- moving beyond the information given, recognised through the nature and quality of their questioning;
- transferring their ideas and understanding from familiar to unfamiliar contexts, e.g. with product development;
- moving between the specific and the general and identifying simple, elegant problems or solutions from complex, disorganised information;
- representing their ideas in a variety of ways to reflect a sense of audience in one or more of visual, spatial, verbal, mathematical, aesthetic, etc. forms;
- giving clear evidence of metacognition, reflecting on own thinking and learning and being self-critical in a constructive manner;
- working effectively within a group as a leader and/or team member.

Possible issues

- Children with exceptional potential are relatively more affected than the average if obliged to work in areas in which they are unlikely to fulfil their potential;
- many exceptional achievers are unsociable and can fulfil their potential as an individual;
- many exceptional achievers have strong values and beliefs even from very young, i.e. are driven; and
- girls and boys have different rates of intellectual (as well as physical) development. To make full use of their intellectual abilities, exceptional girls need to be more psychologically independent than the average girl – have a self-confident, cheerful attitude to life. Underachievement in boys is far more likely to be labelled than underachievement in girls (DfEE 1996).

In making provision for the educational development of most able learners in design and technology we must take into account: cognition; emotion; available opportunities for development; culture.

To enable high achievers to flourish they must gain benefits from:

- the materials they work with;
- good teaching;
- encouragement;
- opportunities to practise;
- examples to follow; and
- an appropriate climate and ethos.

Characteristics of good practice at each key stage

In the main findings of the OFSTED (2001b) 1999–2000 Secondary Design and Technology Subject Report it was noted that 'achievement in making continues to be better than in designing, where students often spend too much time on superficial work. This situation leads to more able students underachieving at Key Stage 3. At Key Stage 4 the highest achieving students plan their time and resources, use their existing knowledge, skills and experience and work with independence and initiative to solve the problems they encounter. A small selection (six) of recent (1998–2001) OFSTED reports (2001a) for grammar schools were examined in order to identify common characteristics for schools with the best records of attainment and achievement. With the schools selected, subject attainment and achievement for design and technology was judged to be above average for similar schools, hence these institutions are achieving amongst the best results with some of the most able students in our schools.

The following sections summarise features of the work associated with the highest levels of achievement:

At Key Stage 3:

- very good graphical skills, research, analysis;
- good communication skills to explain their ideas, evaluate and improve their work as it develops; and
- ease and self-assurance in their approach to work.

In one of the best schools:

The highest attainers (Year 7) construct architectural models of adventure playgrounds in card, imaginatively and creatively. They show attention to detail and their ideas are based on productive, focused research.

At Key Stage 4:

- depth of research, evaluation and analysis are evident;
- flair for design incorporating innovative features that include function as well as

form, for example an innovative mechanism for catching and releasing boats on a boat-hook;

- ICT is increasingly being used in imaginative and creative ways, particularly with CAD/CAM;
- exceptionally high personal expectations on the part of students;
- extremely high motivation levels, trust in teachers' judgements, concern for detail and the ability to engage with teachers and peers through effective questioning; and
- high levels of independence.

At Advanced Level:

- The best work invariably links to industrial or community based projects and students work for 'real' clients;
- student expectations and project challenges are very high;
- the highest order design with a flair for creativity, for example where a student designed and manufactured an innovative 'flat-pack' garden seat designed to circumvent a garden tree and allow for its steady growth through incorporating expanding joints.

In these schools, characteristics of teaching that lead to the highest attainment and achievement include:

- teachers having a very good command of their subject and a diverse range of personal backgrounds but with relevant experiences;
- teaching throughout having good pace, clear objectives and the use of effective rigorous, penetrating questioning which stimulates effective responses from students;
- high quality visual aids used effectively to challenge students' thinking to provoke student responses and discussion;
- teachers marking consistently and giving continuous feedback to students;
- a positive ethos and teachers building close positive relationships with students;
- expectations being very high;
- schemes of work providing sequences to learning patterns and planning for full student participation;
- teaching showing progression through each stage of the National Curriculum; and
- appropriate challenges for gifted and talented students often being provided through extra-curricular activities which sometimes generate better quality work than through the mainstream curriculum.

Delivering creativity in the design and technology curriculum

A model for developing creativity with teachers and learners in design and technology

To achieve a creative act, the potential for creativity must exist. In order for this potential to be realised, the stage at which a problem is formulated often presents the greatest opportunity for creativity. The individual tackling the problem needs to possess the confidence, interest, or mandate to attend to the problem. Often they are supported through some form of mentorship, based on a relationship with a 'significant other' whom the individual trusts. Learners construe problems through bringing personal resources to bear on the weighing of risks and the exercise of judgement making about perceived benefits. For teachers, their constructs derive from their experiences of working within design and technology related fields, mediated by their experiences of education and the legislative requirements placed upon them. Teachers are additionally influenced by the personal empathy they have with individual learners.

The graphical model presented in Figure 6.1 is an organising frame and sets out some of the issues and factors for consideration in the contexts of teaching and learning design and technology in secondary schools but with particular reference to the needs of the most able students.

Cognitive and affective issues are identified and methodological questions associated with teaching and learning and the relationships between them, are raised in this organising frame. As creativity is a very human construct, explanations for its manifestations and consequences are thought to lie firmly in the social and cultural circumstances that pervade life and living. Issues raised associated with the form and nature of design and technology education and its development, are pertinent to aiding or blocking the realisation of creative potential, its application to creative acts and their subsequent recognition.

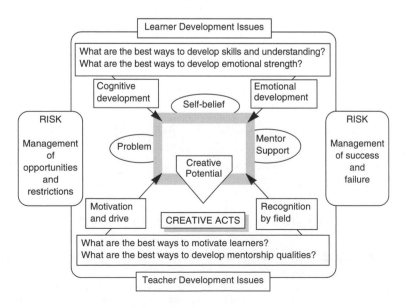

Figure 6.1 Issues in teaching and learning

A 'case study' research project examining the links between creative teaching and creative learning with gifted and talented learners

Considerable effort was put into selecting a school for an 'in-depth' research project that had a reputation for 'success' in creative teaching and learning within design and technology. The school selected was a girls' independent school in the home counties. The research was structured as an ethnographic (phenomenological) case study. A group of three teachers representing resistant materials (Ray), food technology (Sheila) and textiles (Helen) and six eleven- to fifteen-year-old students (Ann, Brenda, Carey, Dianne, Ewan and Fay) were involved in in-depth interviews (all names used are fictitious). Research tools from Personal Construct Psychology (repertory grids) (Kelly 1955; Fransella 1978) enabled rapid access to deeply held constructs (personal meanings) held by the respondents. Examination of school documentation and an interview with a deputy head teacher helped to set the school context for the research. Prior to the interviews with each teacher, they were invited to select around six pieces of student work that they felt were associated with student creativity. Following the interview a small selection of the most creative students for interviewing was jointly agreed upon. Subsequently, these students were invited to an interview bringing with them the work already seen plus around five other pieces which they chose themselves (created in school

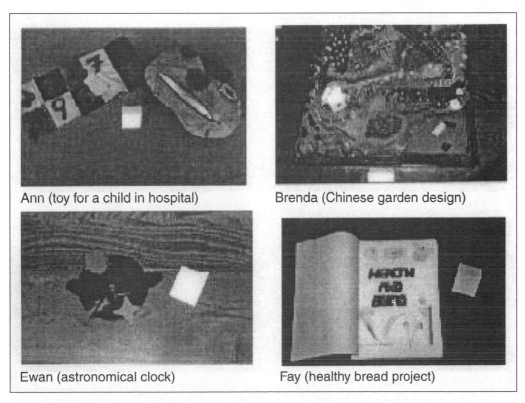

Ann (toy for a child in hospital)   Brenda (Chinese garden design)

Ewan (astronomical clock)   Fay (healthy bread project)

Figure 6.2 Work brought to interviews

or elsewhere). A small selection of the work brought to interviews is given in Figure 6.2. The responses of the teachers were carefully cross-checked against the responses of the students.

The analysis from this research generated interesting conclusions about the educational climate and conditions prevailing in workrooms and their role in promoting or inhibiting the environment for creativity. Additionally, it provided conclusions about the learner responses and attributes with respect to creative behaviour.

Results of the analysis

The following two tables (Tables 6.1 and 6.2) summarise families of 'creativity attributes' that were elicited from some or all of the respondents as being relevant to the development of creativity. In the first table (Table 6.1) are those attributes that are concerned with promoting an environment that encourages creativity. In Table 6.2, the nature of the learner responses that result in creativity are identified. Against each attribute is noted the responses of both teachers and students as to whether they believed the attribute was well addressed (+), neither positive or negative (0) or whether they were negative (−) about its treatment in their circumstances. Where no response was instigated about the importance of an attribute by any student the cell is left blank.

Areas of agreement and disagreement can be easily observed from the match between the positive and negative responses of both teachers and students. There are also examples where the non-registry of an attribute is both surprising and significant. For example: that teachers do not recognise the importance of parents' roles as mentors; that students do not relate to the personal creativity of the teacher in the subject area. Attributes for which there are significant differences in the responses of teachers and learners include the following:

Attribute summaries

Teaching (attribute families):

- the promotion of secure trusting relationships;
- the creation of variety in contexts for learning; and
- the promotion of an interactive exchange of knowledge and ideas.

Learning (attribute families):

- natural curiosity and reflectiveness of approach;
- motivation and single-mindedness to improve.

For individual attributes, there are issues of disagreement, concern and insecurity in each of the following areas:

Teaching (individual attributes):

- learners' risk-taking is encouraged;
- teachers help to manage learners' emotions;
- risks taken with learners' learning;

Table 6.1 Promoting the environment for creativity (teaching attributes)

Conditions for creativity	Teacher response	Student response
Promoting secure trusting relationships		
A non-threatening environment	+	0
Individual differences recognised in learners	+	0
Teachers help to manage learners' emotions	0	0
Risks taken with learners' learning	–	–
Learners are trusted	+++	+
Learners' risk-taking is encouraged	– –	0
Teacher is self-critical	++	
Teacher takes risks with personal work	+	
Teacher shows an appreciation of creativity	++	++
Net response	*7+*	*3+*
Encouraging freedom of action		
Learners' originality is valued	++	+
Learners' originality and innovation is encouraged	– –	++
Learners are encouraged to take initiatives	+	–
Teaching styles encourage learner decision-making	+	+
Net response	*2+*	*3+*
Creating variations in contexts for learning		
Directed and non-directed approaches are balanced	0	0
Open and closed activities are balanced	–	0
Net response	*1 –*	*0*
Balancing skills development and personal challenge		
Having high expectations of learners	+++	+++
Selection of teaching 'content' reflects learners' needs	++	–
Learners' mental modelling is scaffolded	+	+
Rigorous critical testing of work and ideas encouraged	– – –	+++
Net response	*9+*	*6+*
Interactive exchange of knowledge and ideas		
Has relevant up-to-date knowledge of subject	+++	
Has relevant up-to-date skills in subject	++	
Teacher is personally creative	+	
Scepticism promoted	– – –	– –
Self-expression encouraged	–	–
Questioning prompted and encouraged	+	
Stimulates ideation and hypothesising	++	+
Net response	*5+*	*2–*
Real-world outcomes encouraged – making an impact		
Interest and excitement prompted through meaningful activity	+	0
Ensures relevance of work to learners' interests	0	– –
Net response	*1+*	*2–*

Table 6.2 Learner responses: features of creative behaviour (learning attributes)

Conditions for creativity	Teacher response	Student response
Rigour and discipline applied to learning subject		
Integration of cognitive and practical activity	++	0
Effective exploration of ideas prior to action	−	++
Moves outside recognisable boundaries	− −	− −
Effectiveness of goal-setting	+++	+
Deals with problems objectively	+	−
Net response	*2+*	*1 −*
Natural curiosity and reflectiveness of approach		
Self-monitoring and reflexivity embedded in the learning	− −	+++
Challenges assumptions about tasks	− −	+
Responds to situations with great interest and curiosity	− −	− −
Net response	*7 −*	*1+*
Motivation and single-mindedness to improve		
Determination/strategies to build confidence	0	+
Inner confidence exhibited/determination to build confidence	+	−
Ownership of task	0	+
Motivation	− −	− −
Degree of self-directed learning	+	+++
Perseverance with work in DT	0	−
Net response	*1 −*	*1+*
Responses to critical support and mentorship		
Accommodation of support from within the school		++
Accommodation of support from external agencies	++	
Challenges assumptions about people	−	+
Net response	*1+*	*2+*

- teacher takes risks with personal work;
- learners' originality and innovation is encouraged;
- teacher is self-critical;
- directed and non-directed approaches are balanced;
- selection of teaching 'content' reflects learners' needs;
- learners' mental modelling is scaffolded;
- has relevant up-to-date knowledge of subject;
- has relevant up-to-date skills in subject;
- teacher is personally creative;
- scepticism promoted;
- self-expression encouraged;
- questioning promoted and encouraged;
- self-monitoring and reflexivity embedded in learning;
- challenges assumptions about tasks.

Learning (individual attributes):

- effective exploration of ideas prior to action;
- self-monitoring and reflexivity embedded in learning;
- accommodation of support from within school;
- accommodation of support from external agents.

A teacher's ability to make an impact on students and their learning is therefore inhibited by:

- the quality of the relationships they build dealing with cognitive and affective matters;
- their ability to use their personal experiences and understanding of creativity to benefit students;
- the way that they deal with risk which does not build confidence enabling students to cope with uncertainty;
- lack of recognition of and the ability to accommodate the impact that external agencies and experiences have on learners;
- adopting approaches to dealing with knowledge, skill, understanding and capability that students cannot sometimes follow;
- teaching in ways that does not encourage modelling. Modelling accommodates and utilises social and cultural contexts encouraging the relationship between thought and action to be further developed.

Tensions in the creative teaching and learning of design and technology

Personal and professional experience is the foundation for decision making in the management of teaching in design and technology. Teachers weigh up the impact of activities on students, the range of potential outcomes, and the associated problems likely to arise. These are complex matters and likely subjective responses from students are an important factor when planning. Unlike subjects with a clearly definable content, little reliance can be placed on sharing a universal language to reflect upon thoughts and ideas which tend to exist only within subsections of the field in design and technology. The research findings highlight some of the misconceptions and assumptions held by teachers about learners and learning and also the particular emphases in teaching that reflect the current climate and culture in design and technology classrooms.

Limited role of the learner designer

For very young children, it is easier to perceive the nature of, and promote, creative activity. Younger children have lower levels of knowledge, skill and understanding and often rely more on imagination. Furthermore, original acts which have personal value are easier to mentor, resulting in confidence building tempered with realism about the quality of the work produced. As children grow and mature intellectually, challenging opportunities which stretch individuals are more difficult to plan, reflecting more sophisticated logistical and expertise requirements. In secondary education, the 'learner designer' may work with limited and superficial problems, resulting in a dulled sense of purpose and little meaningful action if the student feels that the objects and purposes of their work are contrived and/or trivial. On the other hand, if the work is construed by the student to be meaningful, students then illustrate their creative potential more clearly. Students do not, under the conditions that often prevail in schools, value the personal creativity of teachers who do not relate their own creativity to classroom situations.

Student responses to teacher expectations

Rhetoric promoting student empowerment and the need for students to take ownership of a problem is easily articulated but difficult to achieve in practice. Teachers feel that students expect them to be the fount of all knowledge. However, the respect that many students have for their teachers' abilities centres on their competence to support them through examinations, not necessarily on their respect for mastery of the subject matter or its delivery.

When students develop their own ideas and express them orally, or in 2D or 3D form, it is not a simple matter to identify whose work it really represents. Students are eager to satisfy the teacher and attempt to meet their expectations by 'reading' signals based on the ways teachers communicate meaning and their interpretations of the teacher's actions. Additionally, teachers might subtly or otherwise attempt to influence the direction a student takes to achieve guaranteed success. This does not necessarily invalidate the actions of the teacher or the student, but shapes 'realistic expectations' of teacher and student achievement for given situations.

Good mentorship in the subject appears to exist when teachers take responsibility for students' emotional development, as well as their cognition, as part of a planned strategy.

Student expectations

Learning is a very personal process and can be severely hampered or enhanced by:

- the teachers they have and have had previously;
- the views and actions of their parents and family;
- their interpretation of the outside world;
- their perceived needs to prepare their path to future goals.

Creative students are motivated by a very diverse range of approaches, themes, activities and sets of circumstances when designing and making. Equally so, their failure to experience one or more of these factors, or 'giving up on the challenge', can result in serious demotivation and negative attitudes.

Values are recognised to be important in the teaching of design and technology. To introduce a firm social dimension, in addition to teaching designing and making skills, knowledge and understanding, demands extensive planning. The teacher needs a flexibility of response to the personal needs of students, manifest through sensitive intervention. Students become easily bored with many of the routines associated with preparing and finishing materials such as plastics and wood. Many question the worth of the work, as they are aware that when using power machinery for example, jobs are completed more efficiently and accurately in industry, often accompanied by the use of computers.

The influence of parents on student responses

Relevant home-based design and technology is sometimes enjoyed more by students than school-based work. Here, time is less of a constraint and their enjoyment enhanced through the activities undertaken not being formally, rigidly, assessed in ways that are sometimes perceived by the students to be irrelevant and unnecessary. The social basis of their work is often readily consolidated at home. As a teacher, it is easy to underestimate the role parents play in the way students react to the problems set. When parents have spent time with them encouraging practical activities and endorsing their value in early childhood, it is likely that students will trust their judgement, and will often be influenced by their opinions and reactions. When this comes into conflict with the opinions of the teacher, losses are often more likely to be suffered in subject and teacher credibility.

Parents and teachers both influence how each student develops a world view about design and technology, also how they should react to it and prepare to cope with it in their lives. Girls in this study collaborate closely with mothers when uncertainty prevails. Parents, even those who claim to lack technological capability, are respected by their children through the way they live their lives at home, solving 'technological problems' on a day by day basis. To the students, they are seen to be solving 'real world' problems, unlike teachers who are perceived to be introducing contrived model-based problems with 'set piece' solutions. Female teachers (textiles/food) can gain their authority in their respective material areas through being perceived as 'mums' in the classroom, not necessarily as subject specialists.

Peer pressure

The acceptability of personal achievement to peers is an important consideration for individual students, particularly as they mature, and can act as a constraint to the realisation of creative acts. In design and technology teaching environments, where there is a culture of sharing ideas and working together towards collaborative goals, students recognise the benefits. However, complex relationships between peers can block the development of understanding, interest and motivation. The relationships are 'emotive' and must be understood, faced and harnessed by teachers in order to create an appropriate climate that will encourage a culture for learning.

Factors affecting the responses of learners

Students retrospectively recognise the experiences that have been of most value, often when they have succeeded where they expected to fail. High attainment is often achieved through the sensitive support, belief and patience of the teacher. Quality relationships between teachers and students are fundamental. Students are often reluctant to believe that the teacher working closely with them will be helpful until the teacher has gained the student's trust.

Expectations of students and teachers are often in conflict, or are at least not mutually re-enforcing, reflecting diverse value systems about the worth and purposes of design and technology. Teachers can react inappropriately to the conflicting demands of students because they do not understand the significance of what the students request and the ways in which they request it. Early in their experience, students enjoy working with a wide range of materials, building up a personal knowledge bank to cope with future situations. Often that knowledge bank is shallow because implications of experiences are not fully developed and/or explored. 'Handling' the teacher becomes an art form, with more mature students reflecting their likes, dislikes and prejudices about school and the subject. Teachers are often locked into their own 'professional' mode of thinking and do not recognise in a 'human' way the distortions in the relationship framed by the students' rejection of the subject.

Risk taking by teachers

There are many areas where a teacher takes risks in order to plan and implement meaningful experiences for students, including creating a climate for them to take risks. There is evidence to suggest that successful risk taking results in confident, analytical, positive students able to take decisions for themselves, even able to make judgements about the appropriateness of their teacher's advice.

In responding to design problems, students need to evaluate their choices, select solutions and reduce the risks associated with each stage of their work. Their judgements will sometimes need to take into account conflicting advice from different sources, including understanding based on the student's prior experience. This might result in a direct challenge to the teacher. Whether or not the credibility of the teacher remains intact depends upon the quality of the relationship and the mutual trust existing between teacher and student. In order for the teacher to respond to such situations adequately, risks need to be assessed, managed and the impact of the teaching monitored, in order to plan further interventions with the student.

Creativity: building the foundation

For gifted and talented students to achieve their creative potential, an appropriate climate needs to be created and the curriculum and teaching designed to match. Torrance and Myers (1970) discuss in detail the importance of 'incompleteness or openness' in encouraging creative people. This could be in school and/or at home. From their research they identify that this can be the single factor that maintains interest in a problem or issue (p. 53). A major tool of teaching is questioning:

> fundamental to the development of better questioning skills is the teacher's ability to be respectful of the questions children ask and to help them achieve the skills for finding the answers. Nothing is more rewarding to the child who asks a question than to find the answer. This does not mean that the teacher must answer the question immediately or answer it at all. (p. 61)

But the challenge is to maintain the degree of openness that creative learners will be stimulated by. The task of the teacher is to make good professional judgements about their students' needs. Sefton-Green (2000):

> . . . would suggest that those teachers and arts educators who ascribe value to creative activities are, in effect, valuing their students as people who have something to say. On the other hand, an exclusive attention to what students are learning suggests that young people have not quite attained that status – they are 'intermediate beings', on their way to becoming proper people. (p. 227)

But it results in new knowledge and output. It is widely recognised that there is nothing new in an absolute sense, only reformulations and transformations of existing knowledge. Access to learners' cognition in the subject may be achieved through examining the products and work that they generate.

Recommendations for action in secondary schools

Design and technology teachers:

- evaluate students' prior experience and attempt to build upon it actively;
- build effective parental links – involve parents more formally in teaching and learning situations;
- express their own creativity through their teaching. Create space, time and opportunity to reflect upon their work;
- create an appropriate climate for learning. Balance competition and collaboration between children;
- teach values through design and technology and design and technology through values. Consider carefully how values are dealt with. Start from where the students are at;
- emphasise the building of relationships and trust with individual students;
- encourage children to use their imagination. Emphasise problem solving; reward experimentation, in addition to teaching practical skills working with materials;
- develop teaching strategies that promote reflection and analysis;
- emphasise increasingly the application of knowledge and skill;
- actively encourage creative thinking;
- reward initiative and risk-taking;
- support children working with complexity;
- celebrate students' performance;
- introduce students to the use of equipment and tools with great sensitivity and appropriate support;
- teach problem solving, critical and lateral thinking at an appropriate level. Build the confidence of children in their own decision-making;
- support students in investigating and understanding the creativity of others in the fields associated with design and technology (case studies based on the invention and innovation of others);
- 'teach' creativity and teach 'creatively';
- consider and incorporate in teaching strategies the role of the knowledge and skill in a changing, challenging information society;
- emphasise formative assessment and feedback from teacher to child. Minimise the impact of summative feedback, particularly that linked to assessing 'finished decorative products'. Assess 'processes' more rigorously and imaginatively;
- give worthwhile feedback to students that is challenging.

School managers:

- encourage teachers to build their own creativity in their fields of interest. Create space, time and opportunity for teachers to reflect upon their personal work and their teaching;
- create the climate for teachers to:
  - take risks in their own teaching;
  - reward initiative and risk taking by students;
  - celebrate both individual and collaborative achievement appropriately;
- encourage industrial and other links as contexts for curriculum activity;
- use qualitative as well as quantitative indicators to measure the success of design and technology departments;
- encourage and support extracurricular design and technology in appropriate ways which can offer enhanced environments for creative work;
- emphasise and support ongoing pedagogical training for teachers as a key part of professional development;
- involve more technologists in senior teaching positions. Develop more role models for 'new millennium' design and technology teaching.

References

Assessment of Performance Unit (APU) (1981) *Understanding Design and Technology.* London: HMSO.

Barak, M. and Doppelt, Y. (1998) 'Promoting creative thinking within technology education'. Paper presented at the International Workshop Seminar for Scholars in Technology Education, Washington DC.

Baxter, M. (1995) *Product Design.* London: Chapman & Hall.

Bayliss, T. (2000) *Clock This: My Life as an Inventor.* London: Headline Book Publishing.

Bloom, B. S. (ed.) (1956) *Taxonomy of Educational Objectives: Book 1 Cognitive Domain.* New York: David McKay Company Inc.

Coren, C. (1996) 'How one man inspires others to "Do a Dyson" '. *The Times,* 28 October.

Dasgupta, S. (1996) *Technology and Creativity.* New York: Oxford University Press.

Department for Education and Employment (DfEE) (1996) *Highly Able Girls and Boys.* London: DfEE Publications Centre.

DES (Department of Education and Science) (1989) *Technology for Ages 5–16: Final Report.* London: HMSO.

Elmer, R. and Davies, T. (2000) 'Modelling and creativity in design and technology education', in Gilbert, J. and Boulter, C. (eds) *Developing Models in Science Education,* pp. 137–56. The Netherlands: Kluwer Academic Publishers.

Eyre, D. (1997) *Able Children in Ordinary Schools.* London: David Fulton Publishers Ltd.

Fransella, F. (ed.) (1977) *Personal Construct Psychology.* London: Academic Press.

Hargreaves, A. (1994) *Changing Teachers, Changing Times: Teachers' Work and Culture in the Post-modern Age.* London: Cassell.

Hill, A. (1998) 'Community-based Projects in Technology Education: An Approach for Relevant Learning'. Paper presented at the International Workshop Seminar for Scholars in Technology Education, Washington DC.

Kelly, G. (1955) *A Theory of Personality.* New York: The Norton Library.

Kimbell, R. (1996) 'The role of the state in your classroom', *The Journal of Design and Technology Education* 1(2), 99–100. Cardiff: Trentham Print Design Ltd.

Kimbell, R. (2000) 'Millennium conference – a once in a lifetime experience', *The Journal of Design and Technology Education* 5(2), 119–25. Cardiff: Trentham Print Design Ltd.

Kimbell, R., Stables, K., Wheeler, T., Wosniak, A. and Kelly, V. (1990) *The Assessment of Performance in Design and Technology.* London: School Examinations and Assessment Authority.

McCormick, R. and Davidson, M. (1996) 'Problem solving and the tyranny of product outcomes', *The Journal of Design and Technology Education* 1(3), 230–41. Cardiff: Trentham Print Design Ltd.

Office for Standards in Education (OFSTED) (2001a) *Annual Report of Her Majesty's Chief Inspector of Schools 1999–2000: Standards and Quality in Education (Feb 2001), http://www.ofsted.gov.uk/public/index.htm* (accessed 12th August 2001).

Office for Standards in Education (OFSTED) (2001b) Subject reports, *OFSTED Subject Reports 1999–2000, http://www.ofsted.gov.uk/inspect/index.htm* (accessed 12th August 2001).

Sefton-Green, J. and Sinker, R. (2000) *Evaluating Creativity.* London & New York: Routledge.

Torrance, E. P. and Myers, R. E. (1970) *Creative Teaching and Learning.* New York: Dodd, Mead & Co.

CHAPTER 7

History

Sue Mordecai

Introduction

History has courted controversy by its very nature and maybe therein lies the fascination with the subject. It is perhaps ironic that while schools are directed to a more inclusive and accessible curriculum for all, the demands of the teaching and learning of history have never been greater because of the knowledge, skills and understanding that pupils are expected to acquire. For some schools history is also seen as vulnerable in the secondary curriculum in terms of time, competing priorities and access to specialist teachers. However, it could be argued that the broadening of the curriculum and access not to 'a history' but to 'histories' which embrace our multicultural society offer opportunities for history to flourish. History is also enhanced by the expanding use of ICT and the links at KS3 and KS4 to statutory citizenship (August 2002 onwards).

The perception amongst some secondary school pupils is that history is not relevant to them and that it is a 'hard' subject – in fact one well suited to and associated with the more able. The 1996 Dearing Review of Qualifications for the 16–19 years age group categorised history, physics and mathematics as being 'more difficult than average' thus perpetuating the myth. Indeed the requirements in history at KS3 are that pupils are expected to acquire and apply knowledge, skills and understanding in the areas of:

- chronological understanding;
- knowledge and understanding of events, people and changes in the past;
- historical interpretation (and indeed historical significance);
- historical enquiry; and
- organisation and communication.

The reality that these are to be developed through three British studies, a European study and two world studies is in itself demanding and challenging within a very crowded curriculum with constraints of timetable and organisational issues. Within this context it is incumbent upon the teacher to ensure that all pupils, including the most able, are learning effectively.

Why study history?

'How do you know who you are unless you know where you've come from? How can you tell what's going to happen unless you know what's happened before? History isn't just about the past. It's about why we are who we are – and about what's next' (Tony Robinson (1999) *The National Curriculum Handbook*).

In addition, John H. Arnold suggests the following reasons. Firstly is simply enjoyment. 'There is a pleasure in studying the past, just as there is in studying music or art or films or botany or the stars. Some of us gain pleasure from looking at old documents, gazing at old paintings and seeing something of the world that is not entirely our own' (Arnold 2001). Secondly, history is a vehicle for developing our thinking inasmuch as it takes us out of our present context and makes us consider how other people behaved thus leading to the mind questioning why and how we do the things we do. Finally, history should make us think differently about ourselves. History shows that there are many courses of action for us to consider. Arnold concludes that, 'History provides us with the tools to dissent'. Just what the gifted and talented need!

Recognising gifted and talented historians

History tends not to produce the child prodigy, unlike say, mathematics or music. It is unusual for a pupil to be identified by a primary school on transfer to secondary school as a gifted historian because the nature of the subject requires a degree of maturation and experience. It is more likely that a child who is considered 'good at history' is seen as a good all rounder or has particular strengths in the verbal linguistic domain of abilities. The demands of the primary curriculum and statutory testing may also be contributory reasons why the potential able historian is not easily identified.

It is important that history departments start the identification process early and employ a range of identification methods. For pupils starting in Year 7 departments will often rely initially on data such as the Key Stage 2 SAT scores particularly for English and Cognitive Abilities Tests (CATs). In both cases these are only starting points. Identification methods used need to include subject specific criteria. Pupils with ability in history are likely to display certain characteristics. However these characteristics cannot be seen in isolation and the value of articulating such a list lies in the discussion: 'What does it mean to be good at history?'; 'What constitutes excellence in history at KS3, KS4 and post-16?'; 'Does the teaching of history in the school allow excellence to flourish?' If not, why not?

The following list, adapted from the history section of the QCA 'Curriculum guidelines for gifted and talented pupils', acts as a useful starting point in the identification process. Pupils who are considered gifted and talented in history are likely to have many of the following characteristics:

Literacy

- Skilled at inference and deduction when reading texts;
- able to synthesise information to present a cogent summary;
- use subject specific vocabulary with confidence;
- able to follow a line of argument, make effective contributions backed up by evidence;
- access complex source materials.

Historical knowledge

- Extensive general and historical knowledge;
- locate existing and new knowledge easily within a chronological framework; and
- demonstrate a strong sense of period as a result of the study.

Historical understanding

- Understand and apply historical concepts;
- draw generalisations and conclusions from a range of information and evidential sources;
- identify patterns and processes;
- appreciate the relationship between questions and answers;
- recognise the relationship of other disciplines.

Enquiry

- Apply discrimination in the selection of facts and evaluation of historical evidence;
- can manipulate historical evidence and information;
- appreciate the nature of historical enquiry and the pivotal role of historical evidence;
- ask frequent and challenging questions;
- intrigued by the similarities and differences between different people's experiences, times and places and other features of the past; and
- thrive on controversy, mystery, problems of evidence and show resourcefulness and determination in pursuing an avenue of enquiry.

The gifted and talented historian is not expected to display all these characteristics!

It is important for departments to share their lists of nominated pupils who are considered gifted and talented as there is often a correlation between certain subjects. For example, if pupils are identified as gifted in English or religious studies or geography but not identified in history this may result in the history department reconsidering their identified list of gifted and talented. The reverse was true in the case of one mixed comprehensive school where all departments were asked to identify their gifted and talented in Years 7 to 9 by the first half term in preparation for an INSET day. The lists of nominated pupils were circulated to all staff for comment and consideration as part of their INSET on the education of the gifted and talented. The resulting debate was interesting. The history department had nominated a girl in Year 7 who did not feature on any other list. She was a very quiet empathetic girl lacking in confidence who had gone unnoticed in class except by her history teacher who discovered her fascination with history.

Some issues related to the teaching of history

Literacy and history

The teaching and learning of history relies very much on the language skills of the pupil. 'At any level, speaking, listening, reading, reference skills and writing frequently all play a part in the process of historical enquiry, the uses of sources, historical thought and understanding and in the communication of historical findings. Indeed it would be difficult to develop in children the process skills of history without the extensive use of this entire range of language skills' (Hoodless 1998).

Pupil progression and development in historical knowledge, understanding and skills is essentially related to the ability to use language. If gifted and talented pupils are to make progress at Key Stage 3 and GCSE, analytical and discursive writing is essential. In order to be successful at Level 8 or to have their work classified as 'exceptional performance', pupils must be able to produce consistently well structured narratives, descriptions and explanations. It is often perceived that if pupils cannot write extended prose and read the standard texts, then almost by definition they are deemed to be 'low attainers' or 'no good' at history. However, if a pupil's profile of abilities includes good oral ability, strong logical and visual domains of abilities then there should be aspects of history teaching which give pupils the opportunities to reveal ability in the subject. Indeed, it is quite possible for the more able historian to be analytical in thought and verbal expression but fail to articulate these successfully in written form. The careful and selective use of ICT may be a liberating tool for such pupils who may indeed be gifted and talented historians. With the emphasis on inclusive education in schools this indeed will pose a challenge for the teacher not least because of the increasing diversity of the school population.

ICT and history

Information and communications technology in the history classroom is an important issue, but many history teachers would acknowledge that there is a gap between the potential and the reality. While the video recorder/television has had a considerable impact with the majority of history teachers using it as part of their regular practice, computers in the classroom have not yet had a transformative effect on the teaching and learning of history. However, OFSTED reports indicate an increase in the use of ICT. In *Inspecting History 11–16* (2001) Ofsted gives an example of work in Year 9 with more able pupils where 'effective use is made of information technology (IT) to describe, explain and analyse, including using word processing which incorporates advanced layouts and scanned illustrations. Some data analysis on 18th/19th century trade statistics also uses IT, with use of software (Powerpoint) to make short presentations relating to the abolition of slavery. Software (Excel) was also used for graphs.'

National Curriculum 2000 specifies that ICT is to be used across the curriculum and that pupils are to be given opportunities to use ICT to 'support their learning in all subjects'. However Wheeler (2001) contends that many websites, including those commissioned by the government, are simply electronic books, offering little that could not be gained from using a textbook. Nevertheless, she does concede that most pupils who are asked to find out about a topic are motivated to use the internet to research information in preference to visiting the library or using a textbook. Wheeler gives an interesting insight into an internet based lesson on the Middle Ages presented in the form of a game which resulted in those pupils who were deemed to be of low ability becoming the highest achievers, leading her to conclude that 'A pupil's ability to learn online may not necessarily equate to his or her ability to learn in the classroom setting.' As computers become more embedded in everyday practice there is still much to be learnt regarding sustained pupil motivation and the impact on achievement.

The use of ICT to support learning in history presents teachers and students with access to a variety of resources that can considerably enhance understanding of and enthusiasm for the subject. The caveat to this is that access to the web does not guarantee the quality or the quantity of materials found there. For example, at the time of writing there are over 20,000 sites for the First World War. Furthermore, these sites are scattered across the internet.

Effective teaching and learning in history – OFSTED overview

The OFSTED booklet *Inspecting History 11–16* is intended not only for inspectors, but also to help teachers evaluate the teaching and learning of history in their school. It is useful as a starting point for history departments to discuss the features and how it applies to them. The generic qualities of good subject knowledge and high expectations are the most important factors for effective teaching and learning to take place for more able pupils. OFSTED identifies specific factors of effective history teaching. These factors are essential for all pupils, including the most able, who need this foundation in order to gain mastery of their subject:

- a knowledge of and enthusiasm for the subject, which results in the pupils not only seeing the fascination of history but what it means to be an historian;
- pupils are encouraged to think about historical issues, especially those which court controversy, with both sensitivity and objectivity;
- pupils are given opportunities to see and use first hand evidence;
- there is a balance between the imparting of information and independent enquiry and research; and
- pupils are provided with a range of opportunities to present their findings.

In evaluating pupils' learning, OFSTED puts the focus on how effectively they acquire knowledge, skills and understanding in history and in particular learn to:

- respect historical evidence;
- use historical vocabulary;
- ask historical questions;

- evaluate the usefulness and reliability of different sources;
- recognise that there can be different interpretations;
- realise that conclusions may be tentative and need to be substantiated by evidence;
- respond with understanding to historical material; and
- relate one event or period in history to another.

Extending thinking and learning

In his book *Effective Resources for Able and Talented Children*, Barry Teare poses the question: 'What makes a piece of work challenging?' This is a useful discussion for a history department to keep in mind when planning work. Indeed adapting the question provides a useful evaluative tool: 'Did you find this piece of work challenging? Why?' Teare has produced a number of resources that can be used with gifted and talented secondary pupils. The activities are motivating and challenging and can be used in a variety of contexts – both within and beyond the classroom, for example, as differentiated homework tasks, in summer schools, in history clubs and as competitions. Teare's 'Peace Treaty' is an excellent activity. It is based loosely upon the Treaty of Versailles. There are parallels with the First World War but it is not an exact duplication. It is useful for exploring the difficulties of peace settlements in general. Most importantly the activity challenges the higher order thinking skills of analysis, synthesis and evaluation.

The following are some ideas that can be used to extend the gifted and talented from Year 7 through to Year 13.

Questions

- The answer is . . . What is the question? For example: the answer is primary source, what is the question? Other examples of answers are radical, revolution, empire, anachronism, etc. This can be used to ensure clarity and understanding about terminology. This can be extended with longer answers.
- Provoking debate: Why is there an absence of women in history?; Did Neil Armstrong land on the moon, or was it all an elaborate Hollywood hoax? Was the death of Princess Diana a tragic accident or something more sinister?
- Increasing the complexity: Is historical objectivity ever attainable?; Is there any point in considering what might have happened? How far does the success of a successful revolution depend on popular support? Is there anything to be said for Carlyle's view of history as 'the biography of great men'?

Subject-specific vocabulary

- Ask the most able to write three definitions of a word of which only one is true. For example write three definitions of chronology, era, colonisation, slavery.
- What if . . . questions are an important part of the repertoire of asking questions. For example, what if you could travel back in time to Tudor England. Who would you want to interview? Why? What questions would you ask him/her?

Different text types to explore and present information

- Imagine you are an historical figure from the 1850s. Write to another person of that time using pen and paper or email or text messaging, giving their most important recent news.
- Devise a crossword on medieval life as a challenge for others.

An historian at work

- The year is 2020 and you are asked to mount a small exhibition to show what life was like in your school in 2002. You have a maximum of eight objects and you have to write a short explanation of what the object is and why you have chosen it. How does your choice as curator differ from that of your colleagues?

Fiction

Exciting historical novels introduced in the primary school are often the hook of engagement for children (see Table 7.1). Giving pupils a suggested book list of historical novels enriches the subject and can offer useful extension work. For example Hans-Peter Richter's *I Was There* has the narrator and his friend Heinz eagerly joining the Hitler Youth Movement, while their friend Gunther joins only in response to pressure. This book gives a remarkable insight into the attitudes of young people and their responses to the events of the Third Reich. Some of the books by the popular author Philip Pullman are set in Victorian London and combine a gripping story with absorbing historical background. Pupils should be challenged to think of the pros and cons of historical fiction and whether the writer has a duty to present the 'truth' of the chosen period. It is worth exploring the contribution of such fiction to the understanding of historical events.

ICT

An increasing number of sites offer quality resources with topics linked to the National Curriculum:

www.historyonthenet.co.uk – 'History on the Net' is an excellent starting point and gives a list of other sites, with a brief description and evaluative comments. For example: *www.SchoolHistory.co.uk* is described as 'An excellent site produced by a history teacher with lots of information on KS3 and KS4 topics and an extensive range of links to other sites offering further information.'

Some additional sites worth considering are:

www.history.org.uk
www.historytoday.com
www.bbc.co.uk/webguide
www.learn.co.uk/glearning/secondary
www.philosophers.co.uk
www.historyworld.net

Table 7.1 Possible activities related to fiction texts

Does this novel accurately portray the era in which it is written or set?	

Specific references in QCA Schemes of Work KS3:
  History: 15 Black peoples of America; 18 Twentieth century conflicts
  Art and Design: 9A Life events	

Prompts to support the process of researching the 'big question' asked in a QCA history unit of study	
Enquiry	How are people, places, events, artefacts, circumstances evoked by this novel? Do you think that the novel is portraying an honest picture of the life of the time? What are your questions about one of these aspects?
Interpretation	Keep a reading log to chart: • the mystery of life as described in the novel; • life as inferred by the novel; and • life as deduced from another source of evidence.
Organisation	Could you present your findings as a written conclusion substantiated with an analysis of the value, usefulness and significance of a/the novel as a source?

Pupils could be posed the challenge of creating a school interactive website along the lines of the one developed at Wolverhampton Grammar School: *www.wgshistory.com*

Extra-curricular activity

Use older students to:

• set up a history club;
• a philosophy club;
• an archaeologist club;
• compile a newsletter;
• devise quizzes; and
• enter competitions.

Visual resources

A stamp of history

In 1996 the Royal Mail issued a new set of stamps entitled: 'Great twentieth century women of achievement'. Living women had to be excluded, as only members of the royal family can feature on stamps while still alive. The Stamp Advisory Committee, made up of Post Office representatives, politicians, philatelists and designers, chose the five women achievers. A member of the committee explained their choice: 'While there were many brilliant women to choose from, what was exceptional about the five selected is that their achievements were outstanding throughout their lives. These great women have all died within the past decade. They were an inspiration to their contemporaries and remain inspirational'. The five chosen were:

Marea Hartman – Sports Administrator   Dorothy Hodgkin   – Scientist
Margot Fonteyn – Ballerina   Daphne Du Maurier – Writer
Elisabeth Frink – Sculptor

Such a list excludes these women: Enid Blyton, Amy Johnson, Agatha Christie, Virginia Woolf, Edith Cavell, Laura Ashley, Marie Stopes, Barbara Hepworth and Emmeline Pankhurst.

The task:

- Find out more about each woman.
- Having researched the named women, do you agree with the choice of the Stamp Advisory Committee? Why? Is there anyone who is not mentioned who you think should have been chosen? Why?
- If you were a member of the Stamp Advisory Committee, who or what would you choose and why, to feature on a set of five stamps for the following:
    'The greatest Victorians'
    'The greatest Tudors'
    'The greatest scientists and inventors'
    'The greatest political leaders'
    'The greatest social reformers'

Visits to historical sites, galleries and museums

Learning in this context can bring history alive with interactive approaches and imaginative use of images, artefacts and people (see Table 7.2). It is most effective when:

- it is an integral part of the study rather than a 'bolt on';
- the learning outcomes are clear to the pupils;
- pupils can use evidence provided in handling collections; and
- they can place the evidence in the appropriate historical context.

The British Museum and the National Portrait Gallery are examples of highly active education departments for learners of all ages (see Table 7.3).

Resources

Subscribe to:

- *History Today*
- *BBC History magazine*
- *Teaching History*
- *Teaching Thinking*

Table 7.2 A possible activity related to visual resources

Is a portrait a reliable source of evidence?	

Specific references in QCA Schemes of Work KS3:
    History: 7   Looking at portraits
    Art and Design: 7A Self Image; 9B Change Your Style	

Prompts to support the process of researching the 'big question' asked in a QCA history unit of study	
Enquiry	What do you know or assume about the person? What questions would you like to ask the person/artist? How might a closer look at the portrait help you to answer your questions?

Interpretation	What can you see in the portrait? – describe the details shown in the foreground and background by annotating 'the facts as seen' with labels on a copy or quick sketch.
	
	What do you infer as the 'story' in the portrait? If a portrait shows a moment in time:
	    What do you think might have happened a moment before?
	    What do you think might happen next?
	
	What are the feelings evoked by the portrait? Look at:
	    the 'temperature' shown by colours used, how they are applied;
	    the attitudes shown in facial expressions;
	    the status shown in the body language of the pose;
	    the drama in relationships between people, objects, space; and
	    the signs and symbols given as clues.
	
	How and why do you think the portrait was made? Write your first thoughts then find out by listening to the tape, asking a guide, reading information.

Organisation	Could you present your findings as a poem?

A level students could take responsibility for organising and classifying a resource bank/archive for other pupils.

Create links to:

• a university history department;
• a local historian;
• local museum/archive/library;
• a school in another country; or
• The Young Historian Scheme run by The Historical Society.

Table 7.3 Possible activities related to a visit

Can a visit to a site, museum or gallery provide valuable, useful and significant evidence to support the enquiry?	

Specific references in QCA Schemes of Work KS3:
  History: 11 Industrial Changes
  Geography: 12 Images of a Country
  Art and Design: General Unit; 7C Recreating Landscapes; 8A Shared View; 9C
                        Personal Places, Public Spaces	

Prompts to support the process of researching the 'big question' asked in a QCA history unit of study	
Enquiry	What do you know already – chronology, landmark changes? What are your questions about this? What do other people think? How do you intend to find out? How will the visit, amongst other things, help your enquiry?
Interpretation	What are the main features of this exhibit? What are the main features of this other exhibit/contemporary source/your own assumptions? What are the similarities and differences between this and the other?
Organisation	How could you present your findings? ● as a mind-map? ● a Venn diagram? ● a writing frame?

School-based case studies

The following case studies are from the Priory School, Orpington, which is a large mixed comprehensive with a wide ability intake. They have been written by Cathy Bridges, head of history at the school.

Case study 1 Key Stage 3 Year 7

Extending gifted students in mixed ability classes

In Year 7, students are currently taught in mixed ability groups. To enable all students to work at their own pace and maintain a challenging atmosphere within the classroom, the history department trialled splitting the year group into three distinct groups: gold, silver and bronze. Students were aware that the groups, and the tasks they were set, were differentiated. However, all activities centred on the same content and this had no adverse effects. The bronze group were the most able.

The topic was Thomas Becket and the task, spread over three weeks, was an investigation of his murder using historical sources. Decision making and problem solving activities dominated the overall activity as students built up a picture of the past. Using differentiated materials, students had to piece together the events leading to Becket's murder. Additional and contradictory information was 'leaked' to the bronze group at various times throughout the three weeks in order to challenge the decisions they had originally made and make them re-assess their original choices. The final piece of work was a piece of extended writing giving the facts of and the reasons for Becket's death.

Case study 2 Key Stage 3 Year 9

Enthusing students with agricultural change through role play!

An able Year 9 group were made members of a small rural village c. 1750 called Pottage Croft. Each student adopted a role in the village, e.g. squire, vicar, cottager, small tenant farmer, squatter, etc. A display of the open field system was put on the display board – the students were told that this was subject to change at any time. The activities began with research into their character and the role each played in the community. Key words were introduced and researched and the open field system was adopted, despite its disadvantages, as the way of life.

The next activity saw the visit of a representative of parliament promoting the virtues of enclosure. A speech was delivered to which all villagers were invited. They were then asked to consider the implications for them and their families. This was led by class discussion. The consequences of enclosure were discussed in depth. Most of the village were swayed by the speech and eager to experiment with new farming ideas and make some money.

When the students arrived at the next lesson, the display had been changed, the common land had gone and many villagers found themselves with the dilemma of losing their land. Commissioners were in the village and asking for proof of ownership! An urgent village meeting was called and decisions about individual futures had to be made. After the meeting each student prepared, with additional source information, a case for or against enclosure, tending to focus on their own situation and therefore from their point of view.

The role of the characters then changed and this was recorded in their books. Many were now working for others, the village had changed dramatically and some were even considering a move to the towns! At various times, students were asked to present their current situation in brief bulletins, by oral presentation to the class.

Throughout the lessons, new machinery and farming methods were introduced and students were able to appreciate the pace and consequences of change at this time, while developing their knowledge of the agricultural revolution. This activity allowed students to feel part of a historical situation, albeit on a small scale. They were individually affected by changes, whether positively or negatively. They had to make decisions about their future, within the constraints of the time period. Their research became personal and as a result more depth was achieved. They were self-motivated and interested about what was going to happen next.

Case study 3 Key Stage 3 Year 9

Exploring ways of presenting historical events

At the end of their Year 9 unit an able group of students were asked to design and create a memorial to the victims of the Holocaust. The aim of the activity was to enable students to consolidate their learning and explore different ways of presenting historical information. The criterion was to incorporate accurate historical detail into their finished piece of work and to be creative. No other requirements were specified and this was deliberately left an open ended and broad ranging task. It was made clear to the group that not everyone is necessarily artistic – but everyone can be creative.

A lesson was spent discussing the main features that could be included in their work and their initial ideas. Students were encouraged to visit other departments in the school to help them complete this activity.

Students were initially eager to present the horror of the concentration camps and focus predominantly on the physical aspects of experiences within camps. However, students were encouraged to reflect on the more global consequences and effects and began to explore a more holistic approach to the activity. Each student was asked to write a brief explanation of their final piece of work.

The results overall were of a high quality, but some pieces were surprising in their depth of understanding and presentation. One student produced a box filled with soil and placed a featureless *papier-mâché* face on top of the soil. This, he claimed, represented the millions of faceless people who had suffered and died. Simple but effective.

An action plan for history departments

The following checklist for action (see Table 7.4) has been designed for history departments, to be used as a basis of reviewing the current provision for gifted and talented pupils. It is intended to complement and feed into generic guidance.

Conclusion

So, in conclusion, what do we mean by 'effective learning' for the most able in history? Perhaps this can be answered by stating the hoped-for outcomes to be achieved by the time the pupil leaves school. Without wishing to be glib, the first outcome should be that the learning would leave the pupil wanting more!

They should be equipped with an understanding of the complexities of history, but should have the necessary knowledge, skills and understanding to unravel those complexities. They should know that history is a discipline that is guided by particular rules of evidence. They should understand the problematic nature of

Table 7.4 Checklist for action

Comment	
	Agreement within the department on what constitutes a gifted and talented pupil in history at KS3, KS4 and post-16
	Subject specific criteria agreed
	In addition to the above, other identification procedures are in place
	A register of gifted and talented pupils is in place for each year group
	There is agreement which is articulated in departmental policy as to what constitutes effective teaching of the gifted and talented in history
	An audit has been carried out into the preferred learning styles of pupils
	Schemes of work are audited to ensure there is coverage of the higher order thinking skills, e.g. at Key Stage 3 are they given opportunities to analyse and explain different historical interpretations and evaluate them? At Advanced Level are they able to demonstrate a critical awareness of a range of differing perspectives on the past, making clear connections, comparisons and contrasts and placing them in context?
	There is an audit of resources to ascertain the level of challenge. Take textbooks as an example – catalogues are beginning to specify resources that are aimed at the gifted and talented
	Written work is analysed and there is a portfolio of work by the gifted and talented to demonstrate progression in history
	Monitoring and evaluation include a focus on the gifted and talented
	Self-assessment by pupils is encouraged, together with interviews to ascertain their views on the amount of challenge they receive
	Review of extra-curricular activities
	Up to date with national initiatives, such as subject specific guidance on gifted and talented from QCA, the development of the Advanced Extension Awards in history and the development of websites

historical interpretation. They should have the confidence and capacity to analyse, evaluate and make judgements regarding the sources used. They should possess a curiosity about the past and the present and an enquiring mind that questions, questions, questions.

References

Arnold, J. H. (2000) *History: A Very Short Introduction*. Oxford: Oxford University Press.

Arthur, J. and R. Phillips (2000) *Issues in History Teaching*. London: Routledge.

BECTa (2001) Information Sheet: 'Gifted and Talented Children and ICT' (Available from *www.becta.org.uk*).

Hoodless, P. (1998) *History and English in the Primary School: Exploiting the Links*. London: Routledge.

Jenkins, K. (1991) *Re-Thinking History*. London: Routledge.

OFSTED (2001) *Inspecting History 11–16*. London: HMSO.

Teare, B. (1999) *Effective Resources for Able and Talented Children*. Stafford: Network Educational Press Ltd.

Teare, B. (2001) *More Effective Resources for Able and Talented Children*. Stafford: Network Educational Press Ltd.

Wheeler, H. (2001) 'Designing a History Website to Supplement National Curriculum Teaching at Key Stage 3' (Available from *www.historyonthenet.co.uk*).

CHAPTER 8

Geography

David Leat

Geography is a boundary crossing subject. The downside to this is that it has periods of identity crisis, when its advocates struggle to justify its contribution to the curriculum or education. The upside, however, is that it provides a wonderful range of learning experiences. It is not just that it is topical; it is very catholic, in that it draws upon information in many forms – text, image, moving image, symbols, graphics, spoken word, models, sound etc. Thus it can appeal to all the senses and use the spectrum of cognitive and emotional processes that help make sense of rich information.

If geography teachers look in the 'The National Curriculum – Handbook for secondary teachers in England' (1999) (available at www.nc.uk.net) they should be impressed and reassured by the ease with which the subject can address the values, aims and purposes of the National Curriculum. However this chapter will particularly highlight the contribution that geography can make to Key Skills and Thinking Skills. These strands offer tremendous opportunities for geography teachers to demonstrate how much the subject has to offer very able pupils and indeed all pupils.

The National Curriculum Handbook provides a little more detail on Key Skills:

- Working with others . . . includes the ability to contribute to small group and whole class discussion, and to work with others to meet a challenge . . . to appreciate the experience of others and consider different perspectives, and to benefit from what others think, say and do.
- Improving own learning and performance – involves pupils reflecting on and critically evaluating their work and what they have learnt, and identifying ways to improve their learning and performance. (They need to be able to identify the purposes of learning, to reflect on the processes of learning, to identify obstacles or problems in learning).

Thinking skills are described thus:

- Information processing skills – these enable pupils to locate and collect relevant information, to sort, classify, sequence, compare and contrast, and to analyse part/ whole relationships.

- Reasoning skills – these enable pupils to give reasons for opinions and actions, to draw inferences and make deductions, to use precise language to explain what they think, and to make judgements and decisions informed by reasons and evidence.
- Enquiry skills – these enable pupils to ask relevant questions, to pose and define problems, to plan what to do and how to research, to predict outcomes and anticipate consequences, and to test conclusions and improve ideas.
- Creative thinking skills – these enable pupils to generate and extend ideas, to suggest hypotheses, to apply imagination, and to look for alternative innovative outcomes.
- Evaluation skills – these enable pupils to evaluate information, to judge the value of what they read, hear and do, to develop criteria for judging the value of their own and others' work or ideas, and to have confidence in their judgements.

Teaching Thinking is one of the components of the Teaching and Learning in Foundation (TLF) subjects strand of the DfES KS3 strategy which impacted all schools in 2002.

Definition and identification

Research on expert problem solvers (Chi *et al.* 1982) suggests that they have both excellent subject (declarative) knowledge and cognitive skills (procedural knowledge). They know a lot of 'what' but also a lot of 'how' and they know how to integrate them. Wood (1988) describes research on chess grand masters, which demonstrates that if they are shown a board in a state of play for only a few seconds they can reproduce their positions on another board. By contrast, chess novices can only recall a few pieces and positions. What the expert sees is not individual pieces but configurations of pieces; meaningful patterns that are recalled to reconstruct the board. The grand masters do not have a bigger memory, but the chunks that they remember are not individual pieces but configurations or groups of pieces. The experts make more sense of what they see.

One of the most influential analyses of academic attainment is the SOLO (Structure of Learning Outcomes) taxonomy (Biggs and Collis 1982). This taxonomy was based on the analysis of a large sample of Australian pupils' work across the spectrum of subjects and sought to establish criteria to describe superior performance. Five levels of performance were described, with the top three being:

- Multistructural: students select two or more relevant points from the data available but ignore inconsistencies and make no integration (i.e. do not link the points together in explanation).
- Relational: students use all or most of the relevant information and integrate it (i.e. link the data into an explanatory sequence), reconciling any conflict but remaining within the given context.
- Extended abstract: students use abstract principles and often generate more than one explanation; they use information and examples not given in the task.

Whilst the taxonomy is an intriguing qualitative description of attainment, Peter Davies (1999) makes the point that the taxonomy was based on data response tasks in order to reduce the risk of children relying on rehearsed answers. However, it also reduces the need for subject specific knowledge. He also points out that it is very difficult to translate the generality of the levels into subject specific levels that apply to a variety of contexts. Davies analysed pupil performance in trial NC tests in geography, which were eventually shelved. He arrived at three overarching criteria (1995), which help differentiate performance in geography.

- Specificity: this essentially describes the ability of pupils to handle variables. Science deals with variables by controlling them in experiments, but geography deals with 'messy' contexts in which multiple variables interplay. This provides difficulty for low achieving pupils. They tend to be limited to describe places as high or low with nothing in between and whole areas are inappropriately considered as being homogeneous – Africa is hot and dry. High achieving pupils handle variables with greater dexterity. A place can be relatively high with a specific altitude and Africa becomes a jigsaw of climatic regions. High achievers can also handle complex variables such as accessibility and use them to explain other patterns.
- Completeness: completeness relates strongly to the quality of explanations of links between variables. Low achieving pupils tend to suggest links between two extreme or bi-polar variables – e.g. more doctors leads to low death rate. High achieving pupils present explanations as sequences connecting several variables, which can take on a variety of values. They connect several variables in a variety of more explicit ways.
- Judgement: low achieving pupils see the world in very simple and stark black and white terms. Generally, they use one criterion to judge quality or viewpoint. High achieving pupils not only use several criteria, they can perceive and unpack endemic conflicts of interest between groups and they are more able to avoid sweeping judgements and see nuances, such as apparently hostile groups forming common cause over an issue.

Lastly some mention should be made of metacognition, which in simple terms means thinking about thinking. A number of studies relate superior academic performance to metacognitive ability, which allows pupils to monitor and self-regulate their performance in tackling problems. Metacognition is also implicated in the prized ability to transfer learning. Interestingly research also shows that pupils tend to use metacognitive ability when they are faced with tasks that challenge them, rather than in doing routine tasks (Veenman and Elshout 1999). As one would expect able pupils to be pushed to the limits of their expertise, metacognition is of great significance to them.

In summary, therefore, one can begin to characterise high achievement in geography as being associated with:

1. a rich general knowledge, both local and global, about the world;
2. good information processing skills; and
3. the ability to see pattern in situations and similarities between contexts through those patterns (geographers would tend to call this conceptual knowledge);
4. the capacity to be specific about the value of variables and to use a variety of variables to describe and explain.
5. the ability to see a variety of viewpoints and in some sense to see the world and its complexity through the eyes of different people.
6. to have a capacity for self-monitoring, self-regulation and metacognition, so that work is not impulsive and a full range of knowledge and ability is brought to bear on tough problems; and
7. the ability to work with others and to learn from them.

There are many similarities between this list and the general abilities list of able pupils provided by Clark and Callow (1998).

Effective provision

On the basis of the foregoing, effective provision should be underpinned by some important pedagogical principles:

1. challenge
2. high quality talk
3. transforming information
4. purpose
5. metacognition

1. It almost goes without saying that effective provision should provide challenge (see Eyre 1997), but it is less clear what this always means. Within the context of the introduction to the chapter it does imply that able pupils should be given adequate opportunity to develop the key skills and thinking skills. Particular emphasis should be given to the key skills of Working with Others and Improving Own Learning and Performance. The former is justified on the grounds that beyond compulsory education, employment is increasingly a social and cultural activity rather than an individual one. The latter is justified on the grounds that it is largely virgin territory for pupils. Without challenge metacognitive awareness is much less likely to occur.
2. Talk is vital to learning. Through the giving and elaboration of reasons pupils are likely to develop 'inner speech' (see Wegerif 2000), the ability to slow down and think one's way through problems. Furthermore, there is much evidence that pupils feel that they draw upon more knowledge and generate better ideas where they engage in collaborative talk. These ideas are referred to as distributed cognition (Bruer 1994). The vital criteria are that pupils should work as groups rather than just in groups.

3. Teaching thinking in geography offers many opportunities for deep processing of information. A simple but effective way of thinking about this is to give pupils information in one format and require them to translate it into another medium (see Maps from Text example below). Eyre (1997) makes a similar point in suggesting that pupils are allowed to record information in unusual ways.

4. Few pupils see the point of what they do at school, beyond the utilitarian need to gain qualifications. There is a real need to connect learning outcomes, particularly in relation to pattern and metacognition, to life outside the classroom. What pupils learn, for example, about resolving conflicts in national parks and rainforests should have some relevance for their experience of conflict between gangs, friends and family members. Keep asking yourself how doing geography can help pupils make sense of their experience of life.

5. Teachers need to learn to debrief pupils to encourage metacognition and transfer (see below). Thus reflection and the use of a technical language related to the subject (Eyre 1997) are important building blocks for outstanding performance.

Classroom provision

Teaching thinking, as exemplified in the work of the Thinking Through Geography (TTG) group, adopts an approach that encourages infusion into schemes of work. You can import some of the strategies without throwing away whole schemes of work. You can start tinkering and therefore change can be gradual.

The examples chosen here are selected because they help exemplify the principles of effective provision. Further pedagogic strategies and exemplar lessons can be found in *Thinking Through Geography* (Leat 1998) and *More Thinking Through Geography* (Nichols and Kinninment 2001).

Maps from text

So much work is text based in schools and often requires little more than finding the right chunk and copying it, with a few words altered. This does not demand much of the brain. Symbols, images and drawings as an expression of ideas are seen as the terrain of art. However preliterate societies used symbols to represent ideas and to scotch the idea that this is therefore an inferior form of representation, it is worth recalling that advertising spends billions on imagery to communicate. The terrific books by Edward Tufte (1990, 1997) highlight the case for the power and importance of visual representation.

So in Maps from Text, pupils are presented with text. It may be printed or spoken and they are asked to represent their understanding through the drawing of visual images (combinations of maps, symbols, and sketches). The use of words should be limited to annotation. The advantage of delivering the information through the spoken word is that you can control the pace of proceedings so much better. It is worth pointing out that some pupils can feel very exposed and uncomfortable with this task, but in our experience they don't complain as much as most adults. It puts them in unfamiliar territory. In the reading of the text you can give brief pauses. The particular text (Figure 8.1) is taken from a novel, *The Infinite Plan*, by Isabel Allende (niece of the murdered president of Chile).

Tell the pupils that you are going to read them a piece of text and they have to draw symbols, stick figures, sketches etc. to represent their interpretation of the meaning, so that they can recall and reconstruct it. Stress that artistic ability is of no relevance at all. As you read, judge whether you need to give pauses, but don't let the pace slacken too much.

As immigrants from Mexico arrived, they descended on friends and relatives, where often several families were already crowded together. The laws of hospitality were inviolable; no one was denied a roof and food during the first days, but after a while each person was to fend for himself. They streamed in from towns south of the border, looking for work, with nothing to their names but the clothes on their backs, a bundle over their shoulders, and the will to get ahead in that Promised Land where, they had been told, money grew on trees and a clever man could become an impresario with his own Cadillac and a blonde on his arm. What they had not been told, however, was that for each success, fifty were left by the wayside and another fifty went back home defeated, nor did they realise that they themselves would not benefit but were destined to open the way to the children and grandchildren born on that hostile soil. They had no idea of the hardships of exile, how they would be abused by their employers and persecuted by authorities, how much effort it would take to reunite their family, to bring their children and old people, or how great would be the pain of telling their friends goodbye and of leaving their dead behind. Neither were they warned that they would quickly lose their traditions, or that recollections would corrode and leave them without memories. There was no way they could have foreseen that they would be the lowest of the low. Immaculada and Pedro Morales called themselves 'wire-cuttin' wetbacks' and, rocking with laughter, liked to tell how many times they had crossed the border, sometimes swimming the Rio Grande and other times cutting wire fences. They had returned to their native land several times on vacation, entering and leaving with children of all ages and even grandmother, whom they had brought from her village after she was widowed and her mind had begun to fade. After several years they obtained legal papers, and their children were born as American citizens. There was always room at the Morales table for new arrivals, and the second generation grew up hearing stories of poor devils who crossed the border hidden like contraband in the false bottom of a truck, or who jumped from moving trains or crawled underground through old sewer pipes, always with the terror of being caught by the immigration officers. . . .

Pedro reported to his betrothed 'The gringos are all crazy: they put peaches on meat and jam on fried eggs; they take their dogs to the beauty parlour and don't believe in the Virgin Mary; men wash the dishes inside the house and women wash the cars outside on the street, wearing a bra and short shorts that show everything. But if we don't have anything to do with them, we can live the good life.'

Figure 8.1 Text from *The Infinite Plan*

General guidelines on follow up:

1. Working in pairs, ask one pupil to retell the story or reconstruct the description to the other. This can be reciprocated and/or the partner can be asked to explain what each feature of their 'map' represents. Invite them to amend and improve their map as they talk.
2. If it is a story or analytical passage ask them what it is all about.
3. Now ask how the task was done. You will probably need to provide some prompts to support their reflections, such as
   - did you draw all the time or wait?
   - what was difficult?
   - did you have any pictures in your head from hearing the words?
   - did you refine your drawing at all?
4. Extend this discussion into the area of their feelings about the task and its utility. Is this a useful way to process information, does it help understanding, is it made more memorable?
5. Finally one can ask what questions they would want to ask about this passage – what are they curious about?

Variations

1. You can make the task more cooperative by making the ultimate map a group product, with groups having two or three members. How they produce the composite can be left to them.
2. You can ask pupils to stop writing during part of the reading, so that you can explore with them what they remember of this passage without having drawn anything (usually very little).
3. Ask pupils to highlight or circle causes of migration in one colour and effects in another.

Adapting the approach

The principle is that you provide a written or spoken text and ask pupils to draw. So they could be asked to transform this description of coastal erosion: 'The force of a wave against a rock face creates a great deal of pressure within the air spaces in fractures and joints or between rock strata. The approach of water compresses air within fractures, which then explodes as water recedes and is released. The repetition of this explosive effect causes further fracture of the rock, which then falls away from the cliff.'

Evaluating the strategy

Go back to the introduction and read through the NC Key Skills and Thinking Skills and consider the extent to which these are being addressed. The match is not perfect but it is impressive. If we also consider the principles of provision it is evident that this is a demanding strategy, it requires constructive and exploratory talk and information is deeply processed. The extent to which pupils see a purpose and start to think about their thinking will depend on the extent to which the activity is discussed and unpacked in the debriefing.

Classification

Classification is one of the strategies included in the first TTG book (Leat 1998). The exemplars presented there are relatively straightforward. The potential is much greater. The advantage of classification is that it forces concept formation. By having to put phenomena into groups, students are struggling to find characteristics which unite them. The example presented here comes from a unit on environmental management. In essence there are a limited number of ways in which planning tries to resolve competing demands.

Instructions

Pupils should work in groups of three or four. The possible methods for dealing with footpath erosion are given to them, cut up, in an envelope (Figure 8.2). They are asked to put them into 3–5 groups that reflect the different ways in which the problem can be tackled. As they begin to settle upon a classification, ask them to think hard and produce a name for each group, which reflects the aim of such measures. Emphasise the importance of the name.

1. Put in stone steps on the steep bits of path.	9. Make the car park smaller.
2. Make other car parks near other footpaths.	10. Stop all advertising of the national park.
3. Remove the picnic tables, litter bins, information boards and signs from the car park area.	11. Develop the local farm into an attraction with a farm walk, a farm shop, and a milking parlour viewing platform.
4. Develop a country park just outside the national park.	12. Plant new grass, which is very tough and can stand up to trampling.
5. Close all roads in the valley to cars and only allow buses and bikes.	13. Do an advertising campaign explaining the problem.
6. Increase the car parking charge from £1 to £5 a day.	14. Fence off the path to allow the vegetation to recover.
7. Level the path and lay an artificial surface such as concrete or tartan track.	15. Put in signs asking people not to walk on the path to the mountain tops.
8. Make new routes up the mountain.	16. Remove all sheep from the mountain.

Figure 8.2 Resource for classification of methods of tackling footpath erosion

Follow up

1. Ask one group to send a representative to the neighbouring group to find out the nature and labelling of their categories. The visitor should listen and ask questions for clarification, but their task is not to argue their case (although this may happen). The hosts should explain/justify their reasoning. On their return to their group, the visitor should explain what they have heard and seen.
2. Each group should consider whether, in the light of what they have heard about other classifications, they wish to make any changes to their categories or the labels. It seems to be the minority who adjust their categories.
3. Now comes a big jump by providing a transfer context. Present another environmental management scenario where demand for the environmental resource outstrips the supply of that resource with some damaging consequences. Ask them to consider their 'footpath' headings to the new context to see if they fit the new context. Invite them to edit the names of the categories as necessary and for each heading create one management method that could be used in the new context. An example is given below in Figure 8.3.

Your task

Use the same headings as you developed in the footpath activity and use them to make predictions about what could be done in Croydon to tackle their traffic problem. If you need to, change your headings a bit.

A bit of assistance: say that you are working on a heading called 'Encouraging use of other paths'. What is the equivalent of paths in the Croydon situation? – be a flexible thinker. Secondly the 5Ws (Who? What? Where? When? Why?) will help to generate ideas. If you are thinking about how other forms of travel can be encouraged, you can ask yourself:

- Who could use other forms of transport?
- What other forms of transport are there?
- Where could this transport be found or located?
- When or at what time would it be most popular?
- Why or how could people be encouraged to use it?

Croydon is a borough in London with a serious traffic problem. The problem is similar in a way to the problem of footpath erosion in national parks. There are too many people using a limited resource with bad effects being produced.

Croydon Council produced a consultation document on a 'Sustainable Transport Strategy'. The introduction from the leader of the council said:

The costs of unchecked traffic congestion can be measured in terms of loss of work time, missed meetings, increased stress, higher risk of accidents, reduced investment in public transport, deteriorating environmental conditions and increases in asthma and other respiratory diseases.

Figure 8.3 Croydon's traffic

Progression

Whilst powerful pedagogical strategies provide a flexible toolkit for addressing the needs of more able pupils, one needs to develop a framework for planning progression. In some senses this is a daunting task because with such stimulating and powerful learning activities it is far more difficult to predict and control learning outcomes.

One partial solution is to plan for progression in the use of the strategy and place responsibility for progression in learning with the students. So you could plan to use the Maps from Text three times during a year. On the second and third occasions you make the task progressively more challenging, either through the text or by the follow up tasks. After each instance the pupils can be asked to reflect on what they have learned with a written version going into a planner or exercise book. This can be added to or amended over the year. This also provides important insights for you into any growing awareness of learning and how it can be improved. This process is greatly strengthened if you remind the pupils on appropriate occasions that they might be able to draw on these insights.

Debriefing

One of the key skills in the NC for KS3 is Improve One's Own Performance. Note that it is the pupil, not the teacher, who has responsibility here. This assumes that pupils can analyse their own performance so that they might improve it. Metacognition is the important concept to be confronted here.

Our educational system, both in Britain and the Western world generally, has the effect of inculcating in pupils some very narrow views of what learning is about. In concrete terms this may be encountered in the classroom when pupils express a preference for:

- doing routine tasks, which do not demand much thought or risk;
- having a lot of written work in their books; and
- tasks having a right answer.

One researcher who has studied these phenomena extensively in the US is Carol Dweck (1999). She distinguishes between pupils who have an entity theory of intelligence and those who subscribe to an incremental theory. Entity theorists believe that one is born with a fixed amount of ability and that's it. This conception leads to a fear of challenge because you have everything to lose as you may not succeed, thus undermining one's self-concept. There is some evidence that this conception is built up through low level tasks reinforced with lavish praise for neat smudge-free work. It is thought to afflict bright, conscientious girls in particular. Incremental theory characterises a belief that intelligence is not a fixed commodity, it can be developed. Incrementalists like challenge in the shape of open, demanding tasks because they believe that they can learn from the experience. This would explain why some able pupils are suspicious of teaching thinking, especially if it is different from their normal experience. Pupils are socialised into being pupils, those that hold to an entity theory of intelligence have learned it from their experience of being taught.

So on a number of grounds, debriefing is very important. It can open up learning as an issue to be talked about and made visible, without which pupils will have little prospect of meaningfully improving their own performance. This is vital if lifelong learning is to become a reality. Secondly, debriefing can begin to persuade doubting pupils that challenging tasks and teaching thinking are worthwhile activities. Finally, there is little chance of 'doing' metacognition if you don't engage in the debriefing process.

A study by four teachers in the Thinking Through Geography group has provided a framework within which one can start to develop this practice. In the space available it is impossible to go into great detail (see Leat and Kinninment 2000 for further help), however some starting points will be helpful. They described ten roles that teachers perform which contribute to developing metacognitive awareness.

It is worth highlighting four of them:

1. Collating pupils' ideas. One of the goals in TT is to make the best thinking available to all. In debriefing, one is collecting together methods of working and reasoning so that it is on view. Many pupils are shy or unaware of the merit of their ideas, so it is incumbent on the teacher to trawl the class for good thinking while the pupils are working. Listen to them, look over their shoulders, sneak around the room and make a note of good thinking. Then you are in a position to invite pupils to share their thinking. 'Cheryl, I heard you say something really important. Can you share it with us . . . you were saying about . . . ' or 'Ashraf, you drew something really interesting, a dollar sign, what was that to represent?'
2. Providing feedback. TT is not floppy stuff in which anything goes; it has a hard edge. Any pupil contribution (and yours) is open to critique and comment by others. Therefore, you should practise reflecting back pupil contributions instead of automatically evaluating them. 'Debbie just said that not being able to use words was really difficult. What about the rest of you, do you agree?' Evidence collected by TTG members strongly suggests that pupils welcome constructive critical feedback as it helps them improve their work and thinking. Feedback was one of the very important principles in the review of the effect on pupil performance of formative assessment by Black and Wiliam (1998). Such practices can contribute to raising GCSE results by between one and two grades.
3. Asking pupils to explain themselves. Most pupil answers are a couple of seconds. You should be aiming to get them to speak for 10, 20, even 30, seconds so that they fully explain themselves and justify their reasons. Use phrases like 'Go on', 'Why do you think that?', 'Tell us some more', etc.
4. Making connections. You need to develop analogies, examples, stories etc. which help connect their learning to other contexts. You can connect the Maps from Text exercise to the symbols that are used in holiday brochures to describe hotels and

holidays, road signs that, regardless of nationality, communicate a visual message or even designer labels that carry a message. You can connect the classification exercise to how they organise their CD collection or what drawers they put their clothes in. Remember that one characteristic of superior performance in geography is to go beyond given information and make connections.

References

Biggs, J. and Collis, K. (1982) *Evaluating the Quality of Learning: The Structure of Learning Outcomes.* New York: Academic Press.

Black, P. and Wiliam, D. (1998) *Inside the Black Box: Raising Standards through Classroom Assessment.* London: King's College.

Bruer, J. (1994) 'Classroom problems, school culture and cognitive research', in McGilly, K. (ed.) *Classroom Lessons: Integrating Cognitive Theory and Classroom Practice.* Cambridge, Mass.: MIT Press.

Chi, M., Glaser, R. and Rees, E. (1982) 'Experience and problem solving', in Sternberg, R. J. (ed.) *Advances in the Psychology of Human Intelligence* (Vol. 1), Hillsdale, NJ: Lawrence Erlbaum Associates.

Clark, C. and Callow, R. (1998) *Educating Able Children: Resource Issues and Processes for Teachers.* London: David Fulton Publishers.

Davies, P. (1995) 'An Inductive Approach to Levels of Attainment', *International Research in Geographical and Environmental Education,* 4, 47–65.

Davies, P. (1999) *Assessment of Geographical Attainment in the First Three Years of Secondary Schools.* Unpublished PhD thesis, University of Manchester.

Department for Education and Employment/Qualifications and Curriculum Authority (1999) *The National Curriculum: Handbook for Secondary Teachers in England Key Stages 3 and 4.* London: DfEE/QCA.

Dweck, C. (1999) *Self-Theories.* Philadelphia, PA: Psychology Press.

Eyre, D. (1997) *Able Children in Ordinary Classrooms.* London: David Fulton Publishers.

Leat, D. (1998) *Thinking Through Geography.* Cambridge: Chris Kington Publishing.

Leat, D. and Kinninment, D. (2000) 'Learn to debrief', in Fisher, C. and Binns, T. (eds) *Issues in Geography Teaching.* London: RoutledgeFalmer.

Nichols, A. and Kinninment, D. (2001) *More Thinking Through Geography.* Cambridge: Chris Kington Publishing.

Tufte, E. (1990) *Envisioning Information.* Cheshire, Connecticut: Graphics Press.

Tufte, E. (1997) *Visual Explanations.* Cheshire, Connecticut: Graphics Press.

Veenman, M. and Elshout, J. (1999) 'Changes in the relation between cognitive and metacognitive skills during the acquisition of expertise', *European Journal of Psychology of Education (Special Issue on Metacognitive Experiences and Their Role in Cognition),* pp. 509–24.

Wegerif, R. (2000) 'Learning to talk, talking to learn', *Teaching Thinking,* **1** (spring), 42–6.

Wood, D. (1988) *How Children Think and Learn.* Oxford: Blackwell.

CHAPTER 9

Modern Foreign Languages

Hilary Lowe

Introduction

Modern languages teaching in this country is at a crossroads. In the light of concerns such as levels of achievement, poor recruitment to modern foreign language (MFL) courses and to teaching posts and the conclusions of the Nuffield enquiry (2000), modern foreign language teaching is taking a hard look at itself. This involves reflecting on the place of language teaching in the school curriculum, a critical examination of aspects of current methodologies, and a consideration of the long-term survival of modern foreign language study in the education sector at all levels. Coinciding with this is a renewed interest in the needs of able pupils and in effective teaching and learning generally, both of which are fuelling a range of curriculum developments. While recognising the enormous benefits which have accrued through the 'languages for all' agenda and the significant role which modern language teachers have had in enabling learners of all abilities to experience success in their language learning, we now need to consider with equal energy the needs of those pupils who show a particular aptitude in language learning. There is a strong case to be argued that *all* able learners should experience success and a high level of competence in one or more foreign languages. There may be an equally strong case to be argued that by looking again at the needs of the smaller group of very able language learners, we may also raise achievement for the many.

Although many pupils demonstrate high levels of attainment in MFL at GCSE (OFSTED Subject Reports 99/2000), there is evidence of significant variations in achievement (OFSTED 1998/1999), including a continuing disparity between boys' and girls' attainment. Many able pupils are neither as successful nor as motivated as they might be in their language learning (SCRE [Scottish Council for Research in Education] 1999). The reasons for this are many and complex, but numerous commentators, including teachers themselves, have cited uninspiring course content and undemanding teaching and learning approaches as major reasons (e.g. Chambers 2001), along with a lack of awareness of the long-term benefits of language study (Marshall 2001). Studies such as that by Milton and

Meara (1998) have concluded that the least able and the most able were being failed by current provision. This may be the reason for poor recruitment to advanced study of MFL, with only 10 per cent of high attainers at GCSE (with some increase through A/S) proceeding to further study post-16. This is a significant loss, not only in personal and educational terms, but also in terms of national language competence and cross-cultural understanding.

The needs of able learners may not have been best served by aspects of communicative approaches which have given an uncertain place to explicit understanding of language systems and an increasing emphasis on MFL largely as a 'skill' – sometimes for the most banal of transactional and situational language. While the National Curriculum Programmes of Study highlight the importance of 'knowledge of language' and 'cultural awareness', many courses and coursebooks in KS3 and 4 have in reality shied away from giving students deeper insights into the culture of the foreign country or the study of language in its own right – influenced to some degree by the nature of GCSE syllabuses. This state of affairs is not to argue for a return to so-called traditional MFL methodologies but rather to a move to a pedagogical approach which develops communicative competence within motivating and challenging contexts, with a focus on Canale's (1983) categories of:

- grammatical competence;
- sociolinguistic competence;
- discourse competence; and
- strategic competence.

Against this backdrop, how can we improve provision for those learners who are capable of high attainment in one or more foreign languages? Firstly, by understanding their particular needs and, secondly, by designing programmes and approaches which will give them the requisite skills, knowledge, enjoyment and motivation.

The able language learner

Defining an able or 'gifted' language learner is particularly problematic in a school setting. In this country the learning of another language usually takes place at a later stage of a child's education and, in most cases, progress is dependent on teacher input and on opportunity. The nature of language learning through instruction means that the relationship between ability and performance is often less clear cut than in some other curriculum areas. The full picture of linguistic ability emerges only after a relatively long developmental period. Cummins (1984) (in Graham 1997) describes the concepts of BICS (Basic Interpersonal Communication Skills) and CALP (Cognitive/Academic Language Proficiency), with the latter taking a long time to develop and maturity being a critical factor.

Although many people are clearly able to learn and use a foreign language competently, including many who function in at least two on a daily basis, we know that some children and adults do seem to have greater aptitude than others for learning languages. Second language acquisition research has sought to explain this linguistic 'aptitude' and the ability to proceed to expert levels of performance (as demonstrated by, for example, the UN conference interpreter). The reasons are complex and probably due to a combination of innate ability and environmental factors. Research focusing on 'good' language learners has identified a range of characteristics as significant:

- general 'intelligence';
- aptitude: e.g. grammatical, discourse, sociolinguistic competence; memory; aural assimilation and discrimination; rapid learning;
- personality: e.g. risk-taking, lack of inhibition;
- age of acquisition: 'critical period hypothesis' is well supported by research (including current brain research);
- motivation and attitude: positive attitudes and intrinsic and instrumental motivation (perhaps advantaging older learners);
- learner preferences/styles: e.g. field dependence and independence may have some impact on successful second language learning;
- learner beliefs: e.g. in the value of language learning and in their ability to succeed; and
- learner strategies: the good language learner appears to be conscious of what works best for them and consciously applies successful strategies (cognitive, metacognitive and social). (Lightbown and Spada 1993)

The research of Naiman *et al.* (in Cook 1997) concluded that successful learners employed six broad 'good language learning' strategies:

- finding a learning style that suits;
- involvement in the language learning process;
- awareness of language both as system and as communication;
- attention to language expansion;
- developing L2 as a separate system; and
- recognition of the demands of language learning.

Other research has linked success in learning a foreign language to ability in phonological and syntactical decoding in the first one, to rapid executive and linguistic processing and to the role of working memory (Gaonac'h and Larigauderie 2000). Further developments in neurobiology may well yield interesting findings about the language learning processes.

On the basis of research evidence and the experience and observations of MFL teachers, a number of schools and individual LEAs have evolved their own working definitions and checklists of characteristics of able language learners. The QCA's (www.qca.gov.uk) guidance on the teaching of able language learners includes a checklist of characteristics and identification methods.

The following checklist summarising the main characteristics of an able language learner has been developed with teachers and MFL PGCE students:

- interest in 'difference'; openness and empathy to foreign cultures;
- curiosity about how language works and interest in form for its own sake;
- recognition of grammatical patterns and the function of words in sentences;
- use of technical vocabulary to discuss language;
- use of linguistic and non-linguistic clues to infer meaning;
- ability to identify and memorise new sounds; good listening discrimination skills;
- ability to reproduce the sounds of the language;
- flexible thinking;
- good memory;
- ability to extrapolate general rules from samples;
- ability to apply principles from known languages to the learning of new ones;
- effective communication strategies: uses paraphrase; borrows from L1; circumlocutes; identifies with hearer;
- intuitive feel and 'flair' for the language;
- ability to make connections between items, between what is known and what is new, to make jumps in understanding;
- curiosity about meanings and the 'why' factor;
- ability to assimilate 'chunks' of language meaningfully;
- attention to detail; keen to produce accurate language;
- liking to do things with language; putting things together in creative and imaginative ways;
- independence, concentration, perseverance, risk taking;
- awareness and use of a range of strategies to learn; and
- mastery of first language.

What about learners who may be bilingual – are they 'gifted' in languages? They often pose a particular challenge as they are in advance in many ways but often also need support in some skills. Bilingual children will need particular provision in school but may or may not, ultimately, have the potential to become highly proficient linguists.

Able language learners do not constitute a homogeneous group – experienced teachers know that some of their pupils have greater competence in some areas of language skills than others. Several factors may contribute to pupils showing a particular aptitude for learning foreign languages. Some students, for example, may demonstrate a very analytical approach to the process whilst others approach it more intuitively.

In the early stages of language learning it is difficult to make firm assumptions about learners' abilities. Providing opportunities for learners to demonstrate potential and high achievement is the most important method of identification but it should be substantiated by a range of information about pupil potential, performance and motivation. It should include performance in other subjects, English levels, prior language learning experience (including home or additional languages) and assessment against checklists. Comparative information is particularly important with pupils who may be underachieving.

Effective provision for able language learners

In planning effective provision for able language learners we can learn from both the generic research into the needs of able learners as well as the evidence of effective second language learning and teaching. Provision should take account of pupils' affective and social needs, as well as intellectual ones, and be part of a school-wide approach to supporting gifted and talented pupils. What then constitutes effective provision by an individual department?

An effective curriculum for able learners has been described as one in which modifications are made to:

- context for learning;
- content, e.g. teaching and learning processes; and
- methods, e.g. modification of task, pace and support increased pace. (Maker and Nielson 1995)

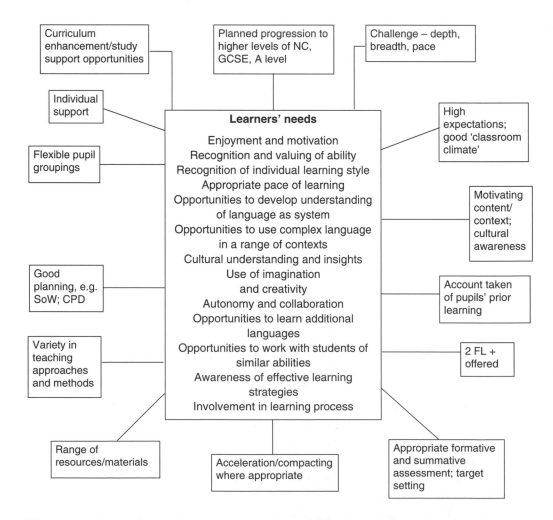

Figure 9.1 Example of effective provision in an MFL department

An MFL department making effective provision for its able pupils will address these aspects of curriculum through a range of strategies, as indicated in Figure 9.1.

Departments will recognise many of the elements of good planning for all learners; a department which is effective with its most able learners is likely to be one which has a focus on good teaching and learning generally. The extent to which a department draws on the range of strategies within and beyond the classroom will depend on the needs and abilities of its pupils and the resources available.

Planning for progression

In MFL there is a tension between 'vertical' and 'horizontal' provision, between a need to balance pace and new learning with deepening and extending the language learning experience. Planning the learning experience and being clear about objectives for pupils' learning, are critical in ensuring progression in:

- content;
- knowledge and use of language;
- language learning skills; and
- cultural understanding.

The nature of a challenging programme for able language learners will depend on the stage of learning but involves an understanding by teachers and students about what should and can be expected of able students at different stages. Able language learners aiming for level 6/7 at the end of Key Stage 3 and A* at GCSE need exposure to specific learning processes and experiences if they are to:

. . . show that they understand a wide range of material that contains some complex sentences and unfamiliar language, understand language spoken at near normal speed, including brief news items and non-factual material taken from radio or television, and need little repetition. (National Curriculum Attainment level 7)

. . . give information and narrate events both factually and imaginatively. They express and justify ideas and points of view. They produce longer sentences using a range of vocabulary, structure and verb tenses. Their spelling and grammar are generally accurate, and the style is appropriate to the response. (GCSE grade A criteria)

The QCA guidance for developing KS3 Schemes of Work (QCA 2000) describes those features of progression which underpin effective MFL provision, and exemplar material shows the characteristics of particular levels ('KS3 Optional Tests and Tasks'). The GCSE and A level assessment objectives can also provide a broad basis for planning.

Example 1

An MFL department's planning documents give a detailed guide to expected NC levels of all teaching groups at different key stages, with appropriate learning outcomes, production and assessment tasks.

Effective teaching and learning

Progression and differentiation are two sides of the same coin; provision for able language learners, therefore, lies in planning opportunities and activities with sufficient breadth and depth to develop the linguistic and cognitive skills required for:

E.g. NC levels 6/7	E.g. GCSE A/A*	E.g. A level & AEA distinction
Understanding and applying familiar language in unfamiliar contexts; understanding main points, specific details and points of view; some independence in reading; applying strategies for comprehension; using descriptive language in short, structured writing; recognising and using past, present, future tenses Understanding wide range of factual and non-factual material with some complexities; initiating and sustaining conversations; improvising and paraphrasing; extended, more complex writing for different purposes and audiences Accuracy/fluency in language use and pronunciation	Giving and asking for information, feelings, views and opinions; explaining; narrating; identifying attitudes and emotions; drawing conclusions Reporting speech Detailed and extended narration Summarising and reporting views and opinions Suggesting and hypothesising Discussing advantages/ disadvantages (evaluating) Comparing and contrasting Accuracy and fluency in syntax and lexis	Understanding in depth and critical awareness of aspects of contemporary TL society; using the language to analyse, hypothesise, evaluate, argue, justify, persuade, develop viewpoints in speech and writing; critical thinking and recognition of relationships between the subject and broader context; understanding and applying grammatical system and a wide range of structures and idioms *'An in-depth understanding of a wide range of complex texts in a variety of registers; a high level of awareness of structure, style and register; applying understanding in effective, critical analysis and evaluation; using a very wide and varied range of syntax and lexis, including idiom and specialised vocabulary; demonstrating independent judgement using appropriate evidence in well-structured, coherent essays synthesising different aspects or points of view'* *(Advanced Extension Award Syllabus)*

Figure 9.2

The targets described are ambitious targets for language learners. Effective teaching for high attainment at different key stages therefore needs to have an increasing and progressive focus on:

- pupils learning and using a range of vocabulary, expressions and grammatical structures;
- accurate use of verbs and tenses, gender, word order, relative clauses, linking words, adverbs, adjectives;
- understanding a wide range of written and spoken texts, of varying length and complexity;
- recycling 'known language' in different contexts and in creative ways;
- extended and freer writing and speaking;
- creative and imaginative use of language;
- pupils' ability to initiate and sustain an oral exchange/presentation;
- reacting confidently to unpredictable elements;
- expressing personal views and seeking those of others;
- 'higher order' skills of deduction, inference, analysis, synthesis, evaluation;
- improving pronunciation and intonation;
- developing good language-learning skills;
- knowledge and understanding of different topics, ideas, concepts (from concrete to abstract and controversial); and
- an increasing awareness of culture of target language country.

The implications for continuity and progression for able learners are clear. Many MFL teachers bemoan, for example, the so-called 'gap' in students' knowledge between GCSE and A level. The issue of transition should not be underestimated – a sturdy foundation needs to be built early for the development of those skills needed in advanced language study. Neither should GCSE be an artificial barrier for those students who are already capable of going beyond – or at least of aiming for real mastery in all elements of the syllabus.

The recent OFSTED MFL Subject Report (OFSTED 2001b) highlights the following good practice:

> Expectations were built up effectively through Key Stage 3, for example, with the teacher reminding pupils, 'remember your linking words, *d'abord, ensuite*' etc. Pupils' sights were set on gradually extending their writing; half a page in Year 7, a page and a half in Year 9, two pages in Year 10 . . . They enriched their compositions with a mental 'cut and paste', researching earlier work on different topics for authentic expressions. By Year 10 pupils were expected to work into their writing in French and German a range of structures such as a range of negatives, reflexives, *il faut, wenn* and *weil* clauses . . . (p. 3)

The role of the teacher in pupils' learning in MFL is critical, as they provide the main target language resource; set the pace for learning; play a key role in encouraging and promoting target language use by pupils. Providing motivating contexts for learning, setting high expectations and promoting high attainment is achieved through the conscious use of a range of techniques and methods. In short, 'modelling' and 'scaffolding' are vital ingredients in the language lesson for all learners.

Teaching approaches and differentiation strategies

Giving depth, breadth and pace to the MFL programme involves drawing on a wide range of differentiation techniques and teaching approaches familiar to many MFL teachers, as well as introducing additional elements or contexts for learning. In one way or another, differentiation strategies involve a combination of modifying the task, text/resource, pace, level of independence and outcome expected, as shown in the examples (Figure 9.3) below.

This is how one teacher used a range of strategies to challenge her Year 11 pupils (and pep up a familiar GCSE topic):

Pupils were revisiting a familiar role-play topic in German, checking in at a youth hostel. The high standards resulted from a series of sound, simple decisions by the teacher. The pupils were given some choice, but the role-play had to include pursuing, through questions, individual needs or interests, such

Differentiation strategy by:	Encourages challenge through:
Task	• Open ended activities • More complex demands and responses • Use and application
Outcome	• Amount of work expected • Different assessment criteria • More complex responses
Level of independence/support	• Removing scaffolding/support to help meaning • Doing own research • Use of reference materials/resources
Pace/time	• Less time to complete tasks • Some material 'compacted'/accelerated
Resource	• Access to a range of material • Resources/texts at different levels of complexity • Access to other adults
Interest	• Prioritising skill to be developed • Self-selected activities

Figure 9.3 Differentiation strategies

as a health problem or sports or cultural facilities. There had to be at least a dozen exchanges each way. Pupils were required to switch partners several times so that they couldn't rely on a memorised script, and then they had to reverse roles, recycling language again. All this took place at pace, with changes every two minutes. (OFSTED 2001b: 3)

and how one department achieved high standards:

Listening and speaking skills are developed through plenty of opportunities to communicate with the teacher and with other pupils in a wide range of games, surveys and role plays. Short sessions, when pupils say as much as they can on a chosen subject, extend abler pupils . . . Reading skills are developed through matching tasks and later by skimming more complex and authentic texts for detail and gist . . . (Dobson 1998: 6)

How differentiation is used and organised will depend on the needs and interest of the pupils, but departments making effective provision will take account of pupils' individual needs in departmental and lesson planning. Many departments already use an approach which sets out 'core' and 'extension' objectives for pupils; the QCA exemplar KS3 Schemes of Work take a 'must, should, could' approach to differentiating learning objectives and outcomes. This kind of approach means that differentiation is integrated into everyday classroom activities – whether mixed ability or setted – and prevents extension becoming a case of the same for everyone with more in quantity rather than quality for the most able.

Planning should also take account of the role of formative assessment in gauging pupils' prior learning, planning future learning and setting targets. Feedback and marking which focuses very clearly on evaluating and improving learning are effective in helping all pupils to progress, including the most able, who need to understand what is expected for high attainment (in particular those who may be underachieving). Able learners also need to be actively involved in looking objectively at their own standards. Summative assessments also need to be pitched at the right level. Departments need to look critically at coursebook materials to ensure that they are adequate and may need to adapt or create their own assessment materials.

Autonomy and independence

Producing autonomous language learners is the ultimate aim of language courses and is clearly to be encouraged with able learners, but as a differentiation strategy it needs to be handled carefully. All learners, including very able ones, need a structure, a model and a clear idea of the criteria for high performance (beware too many 'open-ended' tasks!). Autonomy and independence will also mean different things at different stages of learning, e.g.

- the Year 7 pupil taking responsibility for learning new language items;

- Year 8 pupils working in pairs on a role play and writing a script;
- the Year 9 pupil selecting reading material and working independently on activities;
- Year 10 pupils working in a group using cue cards and a tape recorder; and
- the A level student selecting a multimedia listening activity and setting their own learning targets.

Independent learning is often a means of enriching in and beyond the classroom. It is important that teaching approaches and resources enable able learners to move along at their own pace and to have access to a wide range of materials and different activities. The use of ICT and flexible resources is a motivating way, not only of differentiating, but also of encouraging responsibility for learning and the means to achieve it.

Example 2

- The MFL department is using an 'extension and enrichment' monitoring sheet to track opportunities within their current course and coursebook. The results are shared and discussed at a department meeting and integrated into schemes of work, linked to appropriate resources
- An MFL department is tracking opportunities for higher level thinking in MFL as part of a whole-school approach to developing critical and higher order thinking opportunities
- A school offers after-school provision for extension work for pupils working at A* with a group of neighbouring schools
- A school has a bank of flexible learning resources for its pupils; with resources clearly marked at different levels of difficulty

Content and context

Teaching and learning in MFL does not take place in a vacuum. Learning is affected by motivation and matching the interests, maturity and abilities of the learners is, therefore, an important aspect of good MFL provision – particularly as able language learners are dealing with complex and interesting ideas in their own language. A number of schools have introduced innovative and interesting ways of making the learning context and content more motivating and challenging.

Example 3

- The MFL faculty successfully offers a cross-curricular course in KS3 and 4 which integrates the learning of a foreign language with, e.g., art, business studies, religious studies, with very positive outcomes for its most able linguists
- A school integrates the teaching of ICT skills with French in Year 7

Enhancing pupils' learning

Enriching pupils' learning is part of classroom differentiation but for able language learners should also involve experiences beyond the classroom, since that is where the most authentic use of language occurs. MFL have always offered extra-curricular and study support programmes – many of them enriching other subject areas (e.g. design and technology, art, drama). There exists an increasingly wide range of practice in enrichment opportunities and curriculum enhancement. Those which have particular appeal for able language learners are:

- cross-curricular opportunities;
- summer schools with a specific focus/theme;
- joint projects with counterparts abroad;
- drama/musical performances;
- study trips/work experience;
- mentoring/tutoring other pupils; and
- masterclasses.

Many enrichment activities are valuable experiences in themselves, and pupils undoubtedly gain from them. Many of the most effective and rewarding enrichment activities are well thought through, having a clear rationale and, in many cases, a link back to the school curriculum.

Example 4

- A 'Gifted and Talented Summer School' includes able language learners working with a local higher education institution on improving accuracy and fluency in speaking and writing, another links a Design Technology project with the production of a play in the foreign language.
- An MFL department puts on a show at the end of the year, incorporating work done in all classes by all pupils throughout the year; the most able have opportunities for extended and high level language performance.
- An LEA identified for a summer school able Year 8 language learners from across its schools followed by an accelerated course to GCSE with input from external masterclasses.
- A school provides translation and interpretation services by its community language speakers.

Acceleration

Pace is an important aspect of differentiation for able language learners and often means pupils moving to more advanced levels at a faster rate or the organisational acceleration of pupils who 'grade-skip' or are entered for public examinations earlier than the norm. A combination of the nature of foreign language learning, the rapid rate of learning of many able language learners and the organisational difficulties of making space for another language in any other way means that acceleration can be an effective way of providing for pupils' needs. An increasing number of schools have introduced acceleration in MFL but it does not constitute effective provision in itself. At its best it is based on:

- careful selection of pupils (not only for perceived ability but also for motivation and suitability for fast paced work);
- a carefully planned curriculum (which does not sacrifice depth and breadth and mastery of basic concepts);
- a clear educational rationale, e.g. freeing time to undertake an additional language, starting an A/S course of study, planned language enrichment.

Example 5

- A school identifies its very able language learners in Year 7 for an accelerated programme, to include planned exposure to more advanced grammatical concepts to GCSE in Year 9, thus enabling them to take up additional languages to GCSE.
- An MFL department identifies its able language learners in Year 9 for early entry GCSE in Year 10; the programme includes an enriched programme of culture and links to the TL country. Pupils are selected with great care (from sets 1 and 2) on the basis of a range of information about aptitude and emotional suitability. Next year the department will introduce an enriched A/S programme in Year 11.

Language provision

Enriching the curriculum for able language learners should include the possibility of learning more than one foreign language. Diversification of the number and range of languages on offer is common to many language colleges and to other schools able to recruit suitable staff and to make the necessary organisational adjustments – not always easy in the current climate. Some departments are taking advantage of the flexibility allowed by revisions to the statutory curriculum, the possibility of working with specialist Language Colleges and Beacon schools, collaborating with other schools (on the Excellence in Cities 'cluster' model) and working in partnership, for example, with higher education institutions.

Example 6

- A school offers Japanese to all its Year 7 pupils, as a short course in Years 10 and 12, a subsidiary at International Baccalaureate level and at a local primary school.
- A school has a compulsory second European language in Year 9 and Urdu after school.
- A group of Excellence in Cities schools collaborate to offer a second FL to able pupils, including an intensive residential weekend.

Developing classroom provision

Able language learners need access to the opportunities and skills which will enable them to achieve highly, yet there is evidence that many pupils with potential are still not being challenged appropriately. The 1999/2000 Secondary Modern Foreign Languages Report (OFSTED 20001b) finds (amongst many positive features and improvements in pupils' achievements):

> . . . insufficient challenge in the tasks set, and a failure to cover the range of opportunities in the Programmes of Study

> teachers' expectations are often not sufficiently raised through the Key Stage . . . pupils have an insufficient basis for progression

> Students often struggle with the transition from GCSE to the greater demands of GCE A level . . .

Developing provision for able language learners involves teachers looking at existing practice and programmes and considering whether the learning objectives, opportunities and routes for progression are suitably challenging. Fortunately, curriculum planning rarely takes place in a vacuum. Many departments already have in their schemes of work or planning the potential to adapt approaches and activities for able language learners. Effective teaching and learning for all is a starting point for considering what distinctive and different provision should be made for the most able.

Provision for able language learners can be developed (sometimes relatively economically and efficiently) through:

- ensuring that pupils have access to the 'tools of the trade', i.e. understanding and applying language which makes a difference to meaning and has 'transferability' value, e.g. discourse markers (e.g. 'connectors' and time expressions); a range of verbs and tenses, adverbs and adjectives;
- explicit knowledge of language analysis tools (à la National Literacy Strategy) e.g. metaphor, irony and familiarity with grammatical terminology;
- a range of differentiation strategies to include adjusting text, task and pace: tasks can often be modified to prompt higher order responses by e.g. adjustments in wording (à la Bloom's taxonomy), e.g. *pourquoi, wie, justifiez votre reponse*, or a single question used to evince a complex response, e.g. *was ist Ihre Meinung?*; using one text for more intensive work on language and meaning;
- increasing challenge and enjoyment by using authentic materials and materials intended for older/more advanced learners; textbooks for target language learners; video/CD-ROMs;
- extensive reading to extend linguistic and cultural understanding: using GCSE/post-GCSE texts; simplified/abridged versions of target language literature; factual texts, e.g. to include magazines;
- creative and imaginative use of language in class activities and enrichment, e.g. producing publications; displays; reading material and exercises for younger pupils;

- encouraging greater independence through the use of ICT and internet to enrich and extend and provide interesting content; flexible access to a wide range of resources;
- explicit development of language learning skills and strategies to include conscious highlighting in the learning of the first and second FL of knowledge and strategies to enable faster and more effective learning in the latter;
- considering how general cognitive challenge can be enhanced alongside linguistic challenge through 'problem solving' tasks or more conceptually demanding content, e.g. a move to broad themes such as youth culture and self-expression; communication; global concerns; wider cultural/social aspects;
- setting targets for learning and involving learners in the process; and
- enrichment beyond the classroom.

Knowledge and understanding

Table 9.4 contains suggestions for progression in some of the building blocks in knowledge and understanding, as suggested by the National Curriculum programmes of study.

Developing language skills

Able language learners need to have the opportunity to develop language skills – singly or, more naturally, in combination – to a high level. The strategies in Table 9.5 can increase challenge for pupils through responses to stimuli or as self-contained practice activities.

All of these activities can be located at the higher levels of the NC, GCSE and A level, in a range of topic areas and contexts such as, for example, games, competitions, imaginative, information-gap activities – including many which can be ICT based. They can also be exploited in short or long activity sequences, remembering that able pupils need to develop the extended use of mixed skills perhaps in a project (e.g. on citizenship), or in a task based learning activity.

The following are examples which develop some of the above suggestions:

Listening: Pupils are given one picture of a family/town/room and listen to a text to note the changes (prior learning: comparisons/adjectives/specific vocab.); pupils listen to tape then through a jigsaw activity to find written description to match recording (with a number of red herrings); they listen to a recording and spot inconsistencies with written text, with written/oral follow up

Speaking: Pupils talk about a topic for one minute; pupils in hot-seat give two bits of topical information; role-play 'in the manner of' to show awareness of register; give presentations; predict content of article from outline/headline; discuss reactions to images (photos/paintings/music); use statistics/diagrams/surveys for a report synthesising information, e.g. magazine/internet survey on smoking.

Table 9.4 Building knowledge and understanding

Learning focus	Outcome	Suggested activity
Word/sound		
Interrelationships of spoken/written word	Recognition of aural and written form	Spot the difference/odd one out; vocabulary games
Homophones	Recognition and use in reading and listening	Multiple choice activity to complete sentence; plays on words/jokes/puzzles
	Discrimination between off different word functions in reading and listening	
Grammar		
Basic syntactical rules and application (e.g. adjectives/pronouns)	Ability to analyse 'chunks' of language, to show syntactical structure and value	Pattern recognition and practice in lessons (including creative activities); infer rules
Syntactical relationships (e.g. adjective – noun – verb); lexical patterns, prefixes/suffixes	Recognition of grammatical function of words and connections; deducing meanings of unknown words	Language manipulation exercises and use, e.g. *triste/tristesse*; comprehension
Features of discourse	Use of text coherence and cohesion markers	Writing/speaking using 'connectors': for time, cause/consequence
Range of vocabulary and structures		
Complex structures, e.g. in French, 'qu'est-ce que . . .'	Active use of more complex structures	Use in role-play/interview
Synonyms/antonyms/polysemy	Active and accurate use to enrich writing and text cohesion	Mind maps/semantic maps
Register and its linguistic/paralinguistic features	Recognition and use of varieties of TL, including use of metaphor	Write texts for different audiences: publicity, complaints, formal invitations

Table 9.5 Developing language skills

Focus on listening	Focus on speaking

Correct sentences which are not true
Put synonyms/similar phrases in order heard
Answer questions in TL
Complete diagram/flowchart
Listen for overall gist/key points
Listen for specific detail/greater number of items
Report responses in different person in TL
Write message from aural stimulus
Identify views/opinions/emotions
Give own opinion and justify
Note discrepancies between spoken and written version
Listen in restricted time
Report from memory
Intensive pronunciation/intonation practice
Vary length, difficulty of audio texts
	Longer/more complex response
	Ask the questions
	Respond to the unpredictable
	Oral presentation from memory
	Discuss/debate/present a case
	Exchange complex information
	Simple interpretation
	Role-play:
	    Adapt a dialogue
	    Make up a dialogue
	    Change role/play more complex role
	    Imitate a dialogue heard
	    Act out a dialogue to pictures/video
	Speaking activity with 'constraints' ('include' . . .)
	Summarise/report
	Meet targets for accuracy, quality of language

Focus on reading	**Focus on writing**
Find TL equivalents, synonyms/antonyms/ definitions Track vocabulary ('lexical friends') Make up questions/exercises Put events in order/rank Make notes Summarise Use clues to solve problem Anticipate/predict Identify key points Identify opinions/emotions Give examples of . . . Note how many times . . . Explain why/how . . . Give own opinion Single question to elicit, e.g. decision/conclusion Report orally Reading for pleasure Varying length/difficulty of text	Adapt/edit a story/article/letter Draft/redraft own writing Adapt for different audiences Creative writing – songs, poems Translation Express ideas/views Complete/begin text Write extended piece Write to an open stimulus e.g. photo; headlines E-mail Mind map Using a range of tenses, structure, vocabulary, clauses, connectors Use different register/conventions/style Minimum sentence length; complex sentences; sentences to include how, why etc. Minimum text length Write to a time limit Collaborative writing

Reading/mixed skills: Pupils undertake a range of language and comprehension activities on an interesting text (e.g. the biography of Zidane Zidanie!)

Writing: Pupils write a series of 'consequences' statements on a given topic, each one increasingly longer with an additional complexity

Mixed skill with ICT: pupils plan a journey using German railways website, to include fastest/cheapest route (this includes several steps as well as synthesising and information skills)

Language skills–thinking skills

All language learning activities beyond mimicry and copying are intellectually challenging although the distinction between 'linguistic' and 'cognitive' demands is ill defined.

> Learning a language in itself is a complex, cognitive task of working out structural rules, norms of use and appropriateness, how to sequence utterances (discourse) as well as cultural constraints. Bilingual children who have learnt a second language have accomplished a sophisticated feat involving a wide range of problem-solving skills and strategies such as selective attention, forming hypotheses, putting rules into use and monitoring their effectiveness, as well as considerable skills in memorising. (Williams 1998: 85–6)

The guidance for the MFL NC (DfEE/QCA 2000a) defines 'thinking skills' in MFL principally as pupils reflecting and clarifying on their own thinking processes and problem solving strategies. By this definition activities which both promote and use thinking skills include:

- identifying and understanding links between languages, in lexis, syntax and grammar;
- drawing inferences from unfamiliar language and unexpected responses;
- using knowledge of grammar to deduce meaning;
- applying knowledge for communication purposes;
- inferring rules/uses from language patterns;
- making connections; hypothesising;
- using language creatively to express ideas, attitudes and opinions;
- evaluating; checking; and
- knowing where to look for information.

It is worth considering in more depth, though, the range of cognitive and linguistic skills which are inherent in and developed through the language learning process. A number of researchers (e.g. Cummins and Swain (1986), O'Malley and Chamot (1989)) developed the description of a hierarchy of cognitive and metacognitive processes in language learning, which include directed attention, self-monitoring, grouping, elaboration, transfer, evaluation. As we have seen, the assessment objectives for higher levels of NC, GCSE and the A and AEA level draw on these strategies. Language learning at advanced levels involves understanding of complex semantic and syntactical concepts ('competence'), as well as the application of language to complex situations and ideas ('performance'), i.e. thinking for language learning as well as language for thinking and problem-solving. The MFL curriculum should seek to promote opportunities for both types.

The *Framework for Teaching English Years 7–9* (DfES/QCA 2001) indicates a wide range of activities which involve or develop thinking skills in one way or another and many of which could be applied to the MFL teaching context, for example:

Information processing: put ideas in a different format (e.g. flowchart/star chart); compare different points of view

Reasoning: identify how meanings are implied; using evidence (e.g. statistical) to support argument; giving structured talk

Enquiry: locate resources for a task; make notes for later retrieval

Creative thinking: active reading approaches, e.g. predict/question; mental mapping; speculate, role-play

Evaluation: develop critical reflection; refine/redraft work; modify views

Many of the examples given earlier of activities to promote knowledge and understanding of language and language skills fall into these categories. A similar 'thinking skills' framework could be used to select ready made activities from textbooks and to devise others to challenge and motivate learners, from Year 7 to Year 13.

Examples

1. *Guessing game: e.g. in French* mon premier/mon tout
2. *Logic and grammar puzzles: e.g.* In Kirchestrasse gibt es sechs Häuser . . ., Vier Haustiere . . .; Die Türen sind verschiedener Farben: . . .; *Who lives where, which pet . . .?*

   > *Il n'y a rien dans le verre*
   > *Il n'y a personne dans le verre*
   > *Il n'y a ni vin ni bière dans le verre*
   > *Le verre n'est pas vert!*

3. *Comprehension and imaginative activities,* e.g. using e-mail 'smilies' to hide a message; deciphering a text message; deciding if a text is describing, predicting, telling; explaining, persuading
4. At a more advanced level the majority of activities should involve students in higher level thinking, e.g.

   A level students working on aspects of the world of the future; the most able are given opportunities in class to hypothesise/speculate on a series of predictions about science/technology/communication/health using complex ideas and structures.

A level students working on stylistic devices; some students are working on examples in one text; the most able are comparing three different texts and will transform another using a range of stylistic/rhetorical strategies

A level students working in groups using a range of resources (video, audio and internet material, on which some prior language exploitation work has been done) on a topical theme and evaluating their usefulness in supporting a simulated TV debate on a controversial aspect of violence. Students may choose a complex text from a newspaper giving a psychological viewpoint with complex language. Students role play opinions in the debate to which they are personally opposed. They write their chosen views for homework, with supporting evidence.

Enrichment beyond the classroom

As we have seen, enriching the FL curriculum can mean extending the range of language to be learnt and used, the range and variety of contexts, extended reading and listening opportunities and longer term projects in and beyond the classroom. Additional examples of activities beyond the classroom are:

• intensive language days in school and elsewhere (for example with a 'theme');
• e-mail/videoconferencing links;
• links with post-16 and higher education institutions;
• special projects, e.g. with Lingua/Comenius focus;
• competitions (e.g. song writing);
• newspaper/magazine/radio/video/website production;
• current events board;
• links with local foreign firms;
• 'bring a language to school'; and
• twilight sessions for new languages/intensive language teaching.

Managing MFL in the curriculum

It is important that departments consider what organisational arrangements will enable them to make effective provision for their most able pupils. School managers can support them in this by ensuring that curriculum provision, pupil grouping and timetabling and option arrangements are flexible enough to meet the needs of all pupils. The question of the place of the MFL curriculum is an important but currently vexed one. In multilingual and multicultural Britain, and in an increasingly globalised world, the importance of a school's role in ensuring national language capability and cross-cultural understanding cannot be overstated.

Taking things forward

If provision for able language learners is to be of consistently high quality and not reliant on individual teachers' efforts, departments will want to consider what steps to take in planning and development. Departments may wish to think big and start small or may wish to give a particular focus to their development planning and professional development over a period of time. Many schools will already have a representative in the MFL faculty who works with other staff or the able pupils gifted and talented coordinator in developing provision for able pupils. Some departments have begun with identification checklists, identify pupils and developing schemes of work and activities to challenge them. Some have found it helpful to audit their students' needs (perhaps focusing on specific pupils) and identify where and how their needs are being met. Others have audited resources and reviewed syllabus options. Peer observation with a clear focus and trusted colleagues can be a very powerful way of reviewing and reflecting on practice. The checklist in Figure 9.6 could be used to review and plan provision.

Action	Discussed	Implemented
Definitions of high ability		
Characteristics		
Analysis of pupil data		
Identification		
Organisational strategies, e.g. grouping		
Opportunities for challenge/extension/ progression in schemes of work		
Range of teaching and learning styles		
Audit of students' learning styles		
Audit of skills/processes used in teaching/learning		
Audit of resources, including ICT		
Classroom routines and expectations		
Assessment/target setting		
Differentiated homework		
Portfolio of exemplary work		
Enrichment activities		
Staff development		
Departmental policy		

Figure 9.6 Able pupils – MFL departmental self-review

Conclusion

We need a nation of competent speakers of other languages and of expert linguists who have been switched on by their studies at school and university and teachers who feel satisfied with their own efforts. Recognising the needs of able learners is firmly on the educational agenda and is already having an impact. The advent of greater flexibility in the 14–19 curriculum, the fruits of the Literacy Strategy, the promise of a particular focus on effective teaching and learning in MFL in the National Strategy, should all contribute to meeting the needs of able language learners. We might also begin to consider more innovative solutions such as distance learning and intensive courses. Much will depend also on recruiting high quality language teachers and assuring a stable and key place for MFL in the curriculum – and on developing language learning before Key Stage 3. Perhaps one of the most persuasive arguments for nurturing our able language learners comes from Daniela Boston (1985): 'Our very survival depends on intelligent leadership that understands other cultures and speaks their languages.'

References

Government reports

DfEE/QCA (1999) *National Curriculum for MFL*. HMSO.
DfEE/QCA (1999) *National Curriculum Handbook for Secondary Teachers in England & Wales*. HMSO.
DfEE/QCA (2000a) *Guidance for MFL KS3 Schemes of Work*. HMSO.
DfEE/QCA (2000b) *National Literacy Strategy*. DfEE/QCA.
DfES/QCA (2001) *Framework for Teaching English Years 7–9*. QCA.
Development Education Association (2001) *Global Perspectives in the NC: Guidance for KS 3 and 4 MFL*.
OCR (2000) *A MFL syllabus 2001*. OCR.
OCR (2000) *AEA MFL syllabus 2001*. OCR.
OCR (2000) *GCSE MFL syllabus 2001*. OCR.
OFSTED (2000a) *Annual Report of Her Majesty's Chief Inspector of Schools 1989/1999*. OFSTED.
OFSTED (2000b) *Inspecting Subjects 11–16 MFL*. OFSTED.
OFSTED (2001a) *Annual Report of Her Majesty's Chief Inspector of Schools 1999/2000*. OFSTED.
OFSTED (2001b) *Subject Reports: Secondary Modern Foreign Languages*. OFSTED.
QCA (1997) *Modern Foreign Languages in the National Curriculum: Managing the Programmes of Study Part I: learning and using the target language*. QCA publications.
QCA (1998) *Modern Foreign Languages in the National Curriculum: Managing the Areas of Experience Programmes of Study Part II: areas of experience*. QCA publications.
QCA (2000) http//www.standards.dfee.gov.uk/schemes/mflindex/htm
QCA (2001) *Optional Tests and Tasks MFL (update)*. QCA.

SCAA (1996) *MFL: Consistency in Teacher Assessment Exemplification of Standards KS3*. SCAA publications.

Scottish Council for Research in Education (McPake, J. and Johnstone, R.) (1999) *Foreign Languages in the Upper School: A Study of the Causes of Decline*. Edinburgh: SCRE.

Research references

Canale, M. (1983) 'From communicative competence to communicative language pedagogy' in Richards, J. and Schmidt, R. (eds) *Language and Communication*. Harlow: Longman.

Chambers, G. (ed.) (2001) *Reflections on Motivation London: CILT Reflections on Practice series*. CTC Survey, P. Downes.

Cook, V. (1997) *Second Language Learning and Teaching*. London: Arnold.

Cummins, J. and Swain, M. (1986) *Bilingualism in Education*. London: Longman.

Dobson, A. (1998) *MFL Inspected: Reflections on Inspection Findings 1996/97*. London: CILT.

Gaonac'h, D. and Larigauderie, P. (2000) *Memoire et Fonctionnement Cognitif*. Paris: Armand Colin.

Graham, S. (1997) *Effective Language Learning*. London: Multilingual Matters (ML in Practice 6).

Lawes, S. (2000) 'Why learn a foreign language?' in *Issues in Modern Foreign Languages Teaching*. London: RoutledgeFalmer.

Lawes, S. (2000) 'The unique contribution of MFL to the curriculum' in Issues in *Modern Foreign Languages Teaching*. London: RoutledgeFalmer.

Lightbown, P. M. and Spada, N. (1993) *How Languages are Learned*. Cambridge: CUP.

Maker, J. and Nielson, A. (1995) *Curriculum Development in the Education of the Gifted*. Texas: Pro-Ed.

Marshall, K. (2001) 'What turns them on, what turns them off' in Chambers, G. (ed.) *Reflections on Motivation*. CILT.

Milton, J. and Meara, P. (1998) 'Are the British really bad at learning foreign languages?' *Language Learning Journal* **18** (December), Rugby: Association for Language Learning.

Nuffield Languages Enquiry (2000) *Where Are We Going With Languages?* NLE PO Box 2671, London W1A 3SH.

Oxford, R. (1990) *Language Learning Strategies*. Boston, Mass.: Heinle & Heinle.

O'Malley, J. M. and Chamot, A. U. (1989) *Learning Strategies in Second Language Acquisition*. Cambridge: CUP.

Reflections on Motivation. London: CILT Reflections on Practice series.

Williams, M. (1998) 'Teaching Thinking through a Foreign Language' in *Thinking Through the Curriculum*. London: Routledge.

Sources of further information and resources

There is a plethora of resources and useful organisations available for language teachers, many of which can be used or adapted for able language learners. The following organisations are a good starting point:

Centre for Information on Language Teaching
Association for Language Learning
Becta
National Grid for Learning
Xcalibre website (resources for able students in all subjects)
QCA website
Technology Colleges Trust
Foreign embassies and consulates
Goethe Institute
French Institute
Canning House (Spanish and Portuguese)
Organisations for teachers of foreign languages abroad, e.g. CNDP; Sevres; foreign ministries
Museums and tourist organisations
Specialist organisations, e.g. United Nations
Association for Science Education
Local Higher Education Institutions

Resources

In addition to KS4 and materials intended for A level and advanced level GNVQ, the following could be considered:

Cross-curricular materials from target language countries, e.g. history/geography/science
Guidance for KS3 and 4 Modern Foreign Languages: Global Perspectives in the National Curriculum (Development Education Association)
Textbooks for teaching the foreign language from target language country
TL magazines
TEFL/TESOL teaching books
Books in English with target language problem solving/thinking skills activities
Video/audio recordings, including music
Collections of photographs
Publications for teachers in TL country, e.g. in France *Textes et Documents pour la Classe* (CNDP)
Self-study materials

CHAPTER 10

Music

Frankie Williams

Introduction

> Of all the gifts with which individuals may be endowed none emerges earlier than musical talent. (Gardner 1993)

Musical intelligence is a dimension recognised by Howard Gardner (1993) as one of the seven intelligences, the others being:

- linguistic intelligence;
- spatial intelligence;
- logico-mathematical (scientific) intelligence;
- bodily-kinaesthetic intelligence;
- intra-personal intelligence; and
- inter-personal intelligence.

He states that a pupil with musical intelligence:

- can hear music 'in the head';
- is sensitive to melody, tones, rhythms and patterns;
- is intuitively aware of forms and movements;
- can respond emotionally to sounds;
- has a strong musical memory; and
- can play with musical patterns.

'Music has a history of providing, or attempting to provide, for more able pupils who display a musical talent' (Wallace 2000: p. 36).

Musical aptitude often shows itself early, but only if opportunities are created for this to happen. The National Curriculum provides that opportunity but there is often limited expertise or finance to nurture it. All primary schools can report on a pupil's ability in reading, writing and number but not necessarily their ability to sing or create music.

Definition and identification

The OFSTED Update 32 of Spring 2000 offers a definition of 'gifted' and 'talented' as follows:

> Although an accurate definition is elusive, 'gifted' is usually taken to mean a broad range of achievement at a very high level, accompanied by very well developed learning skills. 'Talented' is usually taken to refer to one or more specific talents, such as sport or music, and not necessarily across all areas of a pupil's learning.

OFSTED's inspection of strategies to promote educational inclusion includes meeting the needs of the gifted and talented. They will address two main questions:

- How well are pupils, variously defined as gifted and talented, achieving in terms of their personal development?
- How well are the needs of these pupils being met by the school?

These questions are linked closely to the focus which inspectors are required to give to the achievement and experience of different groups of pupils and the effectiveness of the school's provision in promoting and protecting their interests (OFSTED Update 34 Winter 2000 p. 39).

How do we define musical talent for this purpose? We are not looking for those who have been taught well, or have the most experience but those who have musical talent. However, we may be looking for a mix of skills that not only include a 'good ear', ability to sing and play in tune, a good musical memory, a secure sense of rhythm, a motivation or love of this area and strong opinions, but also a commitment and 'stickability'.

There may be a number of pupils in a school who show a proficiency in an instrument or the voice. Performing is an easily observed skill and pupils will show varying levels of skills. Some will be more technically proficient than others; some will show greater sensitivity and understanding of the music. The observer needs to be experienced to identify the talent.

Frieda Painter in *Who Are the Gifted?* (1980, p. 19) suggests:

> . . . a distinction must be made between a musically gifted child and one who is merely a competent performer. An essential characteristic of true musicality is that the individual feels and hears music within (her) himself. He has an overriding inner urge to express himself through the medium of sound and these internal pressures will lead him to choose to spend most of his time listening to and playing music. His own striving after perfection will make him willing to practise endless hours to gain the technical skills which will enable him to give a performance sufficiently excellent in quality to satisfy (her) himself.

We need to come to an agreement on what makes a talented musician in school terms.

Judit Pasku (1998) has been researching the transfer effects of music activities inside and outside school and reminds us that

> in intellectual fields a cognitive role in an expert level of performance is more obvious than in the field of sports and arts. It is because there is no physical activity in intellectual fields. Performance in the fields of arts is usually characterised by skilfulness, rather than cleverness. But a cognitive role, the above mentioned mental representations, which are mediators between the seemingly monotonous drills or practice and the superior performance, are essential in these fields too. (Paper given at S. Catherine's College Oxford 1998)

It seems we are in need of gifted and talented definitions for musical talent.

These definitions are some of a number that give music a special place. Child prodigies are known to have existed; Mozart comes to mind as probably the most well known example. What was Mozart's giftedness or talent – precocious performance perhaps. This would probably be the result of practice and training, of hard work and commitment. Wolfgang Amadeus Mozart was born into a musical family. His father, Leopold, a violinist and composer, encouraged his son Wolfgang and his daughter Anna (Nannerl) to play and compose, and paraded them around Europe. Bach, Beethoven, Johann Strauss and indeed many names of today: Lloyd Webber, Tortelier, Jackson and Laine-Dankworth are all families of musicians where tradition, opportunity and commitment are 'built in'.

Family or parent/carer involvement has a large implication for the teacher and in the loco parentis role. Can musical talent be identified? If so, can it be nurtured? Can the best teacher be found so that the correct technique, posture, breathing or whatever be imparted so that no bad habits form? How should a young composer be encouraged and developed? When should a young singer begin lessons? There will be many different views in the answers to the above but what it does is remind us how really crucial the role of teacher is, particularly if the pupil does not come from a family of Mozarts, Bachs, or Lloyd Webbers. So we are already far into the process, relying on other requirements such as commitment and a quality we might term 'stickability'. There is also the underrated element of motivation. Self-confidence is another factor for which the teacher holds an enormous responsibility. The cooperation between all those involved around the pupil is all-important. How many able musicians do we miss?

Pupils who have a musical aptitude fall into the categories of prodigy, exceptional ability and talented. The latter category may be the one upon which schools may need to concentrate. Pupils may be able to hide their talent; it may not be obvious for a number of reasons that may be socially or culturally based. If the talent is to show itself through jazz, folk, non-western, rock and pop style, which may be a more natural musical habitat for many talented musicians, the opportunity has to be provided. The National Curriculum, if interpreted well and broadly, should provide these opportunities, which will allow music teachers to identify such talent. Composition in the classroom often misses the composer who outside school is writing songs, pieces for friends in bands and ensembles, or composing soundscapes with computers.

Musical aptitude can be seen through responses in listening and performing and through creating music.

How do we recognise effective provision?

Very few schools have effective transfer information for musically able pupils, even if they have been learning an instrument. It is an important area to develop as many pupils drop out of commitment to music given the excuse of a change of school. The provision of both in school and out of hours opportunities should add up to a coherent programme. Opportunities can be made available through local education authority networks, school networks, higher education, further education, and arts organisations. These networks may provide the progression for pupils and see them across the primary/secondary bridge.

All secondary schools will have a coordinator for gifted and talented children and some will have identified a gifted and talented cohort which will receive a distinct teaching and learning programme. In music there will, no doubt, be individuals who have exceptional abilities, are easily identified, and may already have been involved in special procedures in their previous school. Let us take the example of Michael.

When Michael was eight-and-a-half years old, his primary school head teacher rang the local music inspector to ask for advice. It appeared to the staff of the primary school that Michael not only loved music but appeared to be talented. He could sing well in tune and learned songs quickly and memorised them well. He had begun to learn the piano earlier in the year and was already playing in assembly. Michael's parents were not musical themselves but enjoyed listening to music. Michael enjoyed making up pieces and he was encouraged with composition. Arrangements were made for Michael to learn the clarinet with a visiting music teacher, and a close eye was kept on his progress. On transfer to secondary school special arrangements were made for him to visit a music college once a week, to take GCSE music early and to take a performance diploma. He was also introduced to music technology and encouragement in his composition continued. Over time opportunities were provided for performance ranging from assemblies to playing the first piano concerto of Shostakovitch, and to have his own compositions performed in public. The responsibility for progression was taken jointly by parents, music teachers, senior managers, and the LEA. It is a partnership that is needed across phases of education if pupils are not to be let down.

The role of the music department

What are the qualities of a good music department, which will be able to deal with all the various needs of a wide range of pupils, styles and genres? It is probably beyond policies, differentiation, and curriculum and lies more in responsibility; development of the individual, activities that provide relevant opportunities; creative personal challenge and having access to expertise in a wide range of styles and genres. Teachers have a number of roles: ensemble director, theory trainer, instrumental tutor, developer of repertoire; motivator; improvisation tutor and IT composing mentor; vocal tutor; recording engineer; band manager – the list is endless. Even if one teacher manages to be that versatile it is impossible to do it all unaided. The head of department role, or director of music, which could be seen as a more appropriate title, is partly one of managing a team of full- and part-time teachers providing a wide ranging musical diet. Time needs to be made for this. Providing a professional environment is also crucial, with good quality instruments, recording and playback equipment, computers and appropriate software and peripherals, and access to expertise. If staff and pupils are given access to this kind of environment music flourishes.

Terms such as acceleration, fast tracking or enrichment may be misleading in this context. What is needed is a match to the need of the pupil with regard to musical experience. Reorganising the use of time for both pupils and teachers may be the only way of providing what is required. Using resources from outside the school in a creative way is also important for managing resources for a larger number of pupils who may not be as easy to identify. Flexibility within the individual's timetable may also be necessary.

Recent developments in funding mechanisms allow for flexibility and creative approaches to the music curriculum. Involvement of a number of part-time staff to cover the wide variety of styles and range of opportunities now needed is a good strategy to employ. The one person department cannot be expected to deliver a sufficiently varied curriculum.

In the classroom context, pupils who are competent instrumentalists may not find composition easy and may need to spend extra time on this. A fine instrumentalist may be invited to use their instrument in a different way. Pupils may need to use synthesisers and computers to express their musical ideas, while some pupils have an exceptional ability to memorise music.

Consider a lesson in which a teacher spent ten minutes setting up microphones and instruments. He was assisted by pupils, and after this, the pupils grouped to create the most effective calypso which was recorded by others – in the can by the end of the 50 minute lesson. Ask yourself, was that a good lesson? Did it provide opportunities for talented pupils while meeting the requirements of the National Curriculum? Musical memory featured heavily in the above example, and some pupils do exhibit the ability to memorise and recall musical information. The teacher had the expectation of a disciplined professional performance. Ways have to be found to allow pupils to show this talent, such as singing back, playing back, writing or explaining sequences or melodies and directing events and ensembles themselves.

Commitment and perseverance are essential ingredients for success. If a pupil is given an opportunity, it is how they deal with it that is important. An anecdote about Philip may help to illustrate this. Philip did not enjoy school but one day found a 'bashed in' tuba with what must be called 'metal fatigue' in the back of the music cupboard. He asked to take it home to clean. After two weeks of the tuba walking to school and back with Philip every day, its shine returned and it was only then that the teacher realised it had no mouthpiece. After much persuasion the music department budget was stretched to purchase not only a mouthpiece, but lessons for Philip. Within five years he owned his own instrument, joined an army band and made it his career. Was Philip talented?

Imagination and ability may well show itself when a pupil is given opportunities to compose. Creative, innovative ideas with interesting structure, instrumentation and patterning are some of the features to look for. More able pupils may well be extra-critical and impose very high standards on themselves, therefore one needs to be careful not to cramp original ideas, particularly if the style or genre is not a natural or favourite one for the teacher.

Many pupils may play an instrument, compose or improvise outside the school environment and may be very skilled. These pupils may have access to excellent teachers and opportunities and not need extra help, but some may not be aware of the help and access to equipment, groups and courses that may be available. Teachers also need to be aware of the musical expertise shown outside the school. There may be many pupils performing well beyond the general expectation for their age group but in an out of school context.

Aural cultures, jazz, folk, rock, pop and other contemporary genres are included alongside European and Indian classical music, and opera, in the current music curriculum. The first MA in folk music is now available in the North-east of England. In the past, perceptions of what makes a pupil musically talented may have been culturally based. Teachers need to be sensitive to pupils' situations and how they feel about being talented.

Nevadita would play her violin under her chin on a Saturday morning at music school in the first violin section, taking part in orchestral repertoire from Beethoven to Beatles arrangements and Indian film music. On Thursday evenings, Nevadita would play in the classical Indian music group with her violin resting on her lower arm with a flat left wrist. She straddled both aural worlds and pleased both teachers. Was she a talented pupil?

Annie passed Grade 8 violin with distinction, aged 15 and led the county youth orchestra – a well-taught and intelligent pupil. She was a born leader who took the job seriously and was conscientious in that position. Was Annie musically talented?

We need to challenge our own perceptions of talent continually. There are many talented musicians in special schools. Alan, a non-verbal fourteen-year-old pupil in a special school, had been given some time with a computer music system as he enjoyed sounds. A programme had been specially written for Alan so that he could choose which pieces he wanted to hear and he was able to control elements such as tempo and dynamics. The day after the system had been installed a member of the school rang to ask for it to be removed, as Alan was upset and flailing his arms in apparent pain and disgust. Alan was found at the computer looking miserable but seemingly pleased to see that something was happening. On listening it was noticed that the speakers had been set up incorrectly (i.e. the left speaker on the right side and vice versa). After the speakers were reversed, Alan burst into applause, smiling and laughing. The staff who had worked closely with him for some years were in tears. They had not noticed that the speakers were reversed, neither had they realised that Alan had such an ability with sound. An opportunity presented itself that opened a new world of possibilities for Alan. He possessed an acute ear, or at least one that was more acute than that of the teachers. Was Alan talented musically?

There are many issues across the key stages as pupils develop musicality at different rates. Encouragement is all important, as is acceptance of creative ideas and high expectations.

What you need to know

- Does data you have from the feeder school, music services or other sources suggest musical talent?
- Do pupils have regular opportunities from which you can identify musical strengths?
- Do pupils who may not have access to musical opportunities outside the classroom have extra help to access musical activities through the school?
- Do all pupils have the opportunity to learn an instrument, including the voice, especially if their family cannot afford to pay?
- Do children who may underachieve, such as highly mobile groups including travellers, refugees, children in care and disaffected pupils, have opportunities to access appropriate musical resources, activities and support?
- Are teachers aware of musical ability shown outside school?

What you need to do

- Identify pupils, making sure processes are transparent, non-discriminatory, flexible and effective;
- develop an Individual Learning Plan (ILP) for talented pupils;
- provide appropriate musical opportunities;
- liaise closely with other music teachers and musical institutions associated with the pupil;
- liaise closely with the parents;
- match resource to pupil need, not to what will suit the department or the school;
- target groups of underachievers;
- establish a musical environment in which all pupils at whatever age or stage can feel comfortable, develop and enjoy music at an appropriate standard for their ability. This may, and probably will, include looking beyond the school itself to mentors, expert teachers, masterclasses, local ensembles and groups;

- show progression and link to performance events. For example, all class groups should have the opportunity to listen to others perform and have their compositions and performances played and recorded;
- all performances, whether in class, or on a more public stage, should be taken seriously and the standard of presentation should be high so that pupils are not embarrassed but see them as a source of achievement and a professional exercise;
- PA and electronic equipment needs to be of good quality;
- senior managers need to be in support of all events and aware of the progress of identified pupils and promote their interests; and
- training should be provided for staff and governors to be able to support parents, carers and pupils to plan their learning and practice and develop further their talents and expertise.

The above advice is in line with the OFSTED guidance on meeting the needs of gifted and talented pupils.

Parents/carers will have a wide range of views on how they wish their child's talent to be nurtured and developed. Parents'/carers' opinions and perceptions are an important part of the process and the steps taken by the school will be based on close liaison with them.

Mr and Mrs X approached the local authority asking for help with their daughter who was seen by themselves and the school (verified by the head teacher and director of music) as musically talented. Some local authorities have scholarships or grants available but the following list gives some alternative responses:

- audition to a national specialist music school;
- Saturday morning school at a music conservatoire; summer schools; other courses;
- special arrangements locally – e.g. half a day specialist music input;
- access to facilities/mentor in nearby specialist arts college; FE or HE or other establishment;
- extra teaching from private teacher or LEA music service;
- access to local/national orchestras, groups, bands, choirs, ensembles etc.;
- extra time for daily practice facilitated; and
- arrangements made to attend specialist events, competitions, masterclasses, festivals, concerts, recordings and gigs.

The list of possibilities is long and depends on individual pupil need and local resource. It is important for all music providers associated with the pupil to liaise closely.

The contribution of professional musicians is now a welcome and expanding ingredient in music education

– when one considers a school, college or university and the resources of skill, knowledge and experience it contains (itself only a tiny fraction of the community's store of skill and knowledge which is waiting to be drawn upon) one greatly regrets that only a tiny, arbitrarily chosen, sector is accessible to any individual student; the rest, if he is aware at all of its existence is put out of his reach by the demands of the syllabus and of examinations (Small 1997: 187 in Swanwick 1988: 118)

Swanwick goes on to add that, although the formal education system 'has a part to play in organising such specific elective activities such as choirs, brass bands, jazz, folk and "pop" groups, "musicals" and so on . . .' the school or college is only one opening providing music in the community, but it can give pupils and those in the community the possibilities that are available 'out there'. Once again, providing musical opportunities is all important. It is the responsibility of the schools and colleges to give enough direction and motivation to ensure that choice is available and therefore allow access and develop expertise. The range of possibilities from music services and private providers is expanding. Many opportunities at local and national levels are available, ranging from orchestras, choirs and bands, to rockschools, DJing, composer events and cross arts events.

Professional orchestras, ensembles and opera companies are a wonderfully rich resource of inspiration and expertise. They provide a multitude of educational projects and work experience opportunities. School instrumentalists can play alongside professionals or perform as a soloist at the appropriate stage. Young composers can meet professional composers and discuss shared musical problems. Artists in residence and relationships with venues are ways of building these opportunities.

Teachers with a deep understanding of their subject are the essential ingredient to successfully implementing high quality provision for more able pupils. They will accept that a number of their pupils may have a greater talent than they have, and will welcome that; they will set challenging tasks and provide appropriate opportunities. Inclusion in normal class lessons will be carefully planned to maintain a stimulating environment. The teacher is the key to many pupils having the opportunities they need and, by setting high expectations for all pupils within an active musical environment, the talented musician should be able to be identified and flourish and help to create that active musical environment.

References

Eyre, D. (1997) *Able Children in Ordinary Schools.* London: David Fulton Publishers.

Freeman, J. (1998) *OFSTED Reviews of Research – Educating the Very Able – Current International Research.* London: The Stationery Office HMSO.

Gardner, H. (1993) *Frames of Mind – The Theory of Multiple Intelligences* (2nd edition). London: Fontana Press.

George, D. (1992) *The Challenge of the Able Child.* London: David Fulton Publishers.

George, D. (1997) *The Challenge of the Able Child.* (2nd edition). London: David Fulton Publishers.

Hargreaves, D. J. (1986) *The Developmental Psychology of Music.* Cambridge: Cambridge University Press.

Heal, M. and Wigram, T. (eds) (1993) *Music Therapy in Health and Education.* London: Jessica Kingsley Publishers.

HMSO (1979) *Gifted Children in Middle and Comprehensive Secondary Schools.* London: Her Majesty's Stationery Office.

Institute of Education, Music Department (1990) *The Tower Hamlets String Teaching Project – a Research Report March 1990.* London: Music Department, University of London.

Koshy, V. and Casey, R. (1997) *Effective Provision for Able and Exceptionally Able Children.* London: Hodder & Stoughton.

Leyden, S. (1998) *Supporting the Child of Exceptional Ability.* London: David Fulton.

Mills, J. (1993) *Music in the Primary School* (revised edition). Cambridge: Cambridge University Press.

Montgomery, D. (2000) *Able Underachievers.* London: Routledge.

Painter, F. (1980) *Who Are the Gifted? Definition and Identification.* Knebworth: Pullen.

Pasku, J. (1998) 'Transfer effects of the outside school activities'. Occasional paper, NACE European Conference, St Catherine's College, Cambridge, 16–19 July.

Paynter, J. (1982) *Music in the Secondary School Curriculum.* Cambridge: Cambridge Educational.

Spruce, G. (ed.) (1996) *Teaching Music.* London: Routledge.

RSA (2000) *Arts Education in Secondary Schools – Effects and Effectiveness – the NFER Study – Summary and Commentary* (London: RSA).

Sloboda, J. A. (ed.) (1988) *Generative Processes in Music – The Psychology of Performance, Improvisation, and Composition.* Oxford: Clarendon Press.

Sternberg, R. J and Davidson, J. E. (1986) *Conceptions of Giftedness.* Cambridge: Cambridge University Press.

Storr, A. (1992) *Music and the Mind.* London: Harper Collins.

Swanwick, K. (1988) *Music, Mind, and Education.* London: Routledge.

Swanwick, K. (1999) *Teaching Music Musically.* London: Routledge.

Teare, B. (1997) *Effective Resources for Able and Talented Children.* Stafford: Network Press.

Wallace, Belle (2000) *Teaching the Very Able Child.* London: David Fulton Publishers/ NACE.

White, J. (1998) *Do Howard Gardner's multiple intelligences add up?.* London: Institute of Education, University of London.

Williams, P. (1986) *Chetham's – old and new in harmony.* Manchester: Manchester University Press.

Resources

Asian Music Circle, London

Associated Board of the Royal Schools of Music, 14 Bedford Square, London WC1B 3JG.

Tel. 020 7636 5400 Fax. 020 7436 4520 Email: *abrsm@abrsm.ac.uk*

Website: *www.abrsm.ac.uk*

Bhavan Centre Website: *http://www.bhavan.net*

Birmingham Conservatoire, University of Central England, Paradise Place, Birmingham B3 3HG.

Tel. 0121 331 5901, Fax. 0121 331 5906 Email: *george.caird@uce.ac.uk*

Website: *www.uce.ac.uk*

British Association of Symphonic and Wind Band Ensembles, Wayfaring, Smithers Lane, Hale Street, Tonbridge, Kent TN12 5HT.

Tel. 01622 872758 Fax. 01622 872758 Email: *basbwe@winds.org.uk*

British Federation of Youth Choirs, Devonshire House, Devonshire Square, Loughborough, Leicestershire LE11 3DW.

Tel. 01509 211664 Fax. 01509 260630

British Music Information Centre, website: *www.bmic.co.uk*

Chetham's School of Music, Long Millgate, Manchester M3 1SB.

Tel. 0161 834 9644 Fax. 0161 839 3609

Eastern Orchestral Board, 10 Stratford Place, London W1N 9AE.

Tel. 0207 629 9601 Fax. 0207 495 4710

European Guitar Teachers Association, 29 Longfield Road, Tring, Hertfordshire HP23 4DG.

European Piano Teachers Association, Jenny MacMillan, 17 Lynfield Lane, Cambridge CB4 1DR.

Tel. 01223 461916

European String Teachers Association, London Regional Centre, 17 Western Avenue, Woodley, Reading, Berkshire RG5 3BJ.

Tel. 01189 618856

Folkworks Website: *http://www.folkworks.co.uk*

Gamalan, South Bank Education Department, Royal Festival Hall, South Bank Centre, London SE1 8XX.

Tel. 0207 921 0846/0908 Website: *http://www.sbc.org.uk*

Generator North East, 69 Westgate Road, Newcastle-upon-Tyne, Tyne and Wear NE11 1SG.

Tel. 0191 245 0099

Guildhall Summer School Website: *http://www.gsmd.ac.uk*

Local HE and FE

Making Music (NFYM) 7–15 Roseberry Avenue, London EC1R 4SP

Tel. 0207 841 0110 Fax. 0207 841 0115 Email: *nfms@nfms.org.uk*

Website: *www.nfyms.org.uk*

Music Masters' and Mistresses' Association, Wayfaring, 8 Smithers Lane, East Peckham, Tonbridge, Kent TN12 5HT. Email: *mma.admin@cwcom.net*

National Association of Youth Orchestras, Central Hall, West Tollcross, Edinburgh EH3 9BP.

Tel. 0131 221 1927 Fax. 0131 229 2921 Email: *nayo.office@virgin.net*

National Children's Orchestra, Email: *mail@nco.org.uk*

National Children's Wind Orchestra, Email: *HMusicale@aol.com*

National Federation of Music Societies, 7–15 Roseberry Avenue, London EC1R 4SP.

Tel. 0870 872 3300 Fax. 0870 872 3400 Email: *info@makingmusic.org.uk*

National Foundation for Youth Music, One America Street, London SE1 0NE.

Tel. 020 7902 1060 Fax. 020 7902 1061 Email: *info@youthmusic.org.uk*

Website: *www.youthmusic.org.uk*

National Youth Orchestra of Great Britain Website: *www.nyo.org.uk*

Nottinghamshire County Council, More Able File – Music, Joan Arnold.

Opera companies

Orchestras/ensembles

Oriental Arts Tel. 01274 370190

Performing Rights Society, Copyright House, 29–33 Berners Street, London W1T 3AB.

Tel. 020 7580 5544 Fax. 020 7306 4455 Email: *info@prs.org.uk*

Pro Corda Trust (National School for Young Chamber Music Players) Leiston Abbey House, Theberton Road, Leiston, Suffolk IP16 4TB.

Tel. 01728 831354

Purcell School, Aldenham Road, Bushey, Herts. WD2 3TS.

Tel. 01923 331100 Fax. 01923 331166

Email: *purcell.school@btinternet.com* Website: *www.purcell-school.org*

Royal Academy of Music, Marylebone Road, London NW1 5HT.

Tel. 020 7873 7373 Fax. 020 7873 7374 Website: *www.ram.ac.uk*

Royal College of Music, Prince Consort Road, London SW7 2BS.

Tel. 020 7589 3643 Fax. 020 7589 7740

Email: *ssturrock@rcm.ac.uk* Website: *www.rcm.ac.uk*

Royal College of Organists, St Andrew's Church, 7 St Andrew Street, Holborn, London EC4A 3LQ.

Tel. 020 7936 3606 Fax. 020 7353 8244 Email: *rco@rco.org.uk* Website: www.rco.org.uk

Royal Northern College of Music, 124 Oxford Road, Manchester M13 9RD.

Tel. 0161 907 5273 Fax. 0161 273 8188 Email: *pat.woods@rncm.ac.uk*

Royal Scottish Academy of Music and Drama, 100 Renfrew Street, Glasgow G2 3DB.

Tel. 0141 332 4101 Fax. 0141 332 8901 Website: *www.rsamd.ac.uk*

Scottish Music Information Centre Website: *www.iamic.ie*

Society for the Promotion of New Music, 4th Floor, St Margaret's House, 18–20 Southwark Street, London SE1 1TJ.

Tel. 020 7407 1640 Fax. 020 7403 7652 Email: *education@spnm.org.uk*

Website: *www.spnm.org.uk*

Sonic Arts Tel. 0208 741 7422

Trinity College of Music, 11–13 Mandeville Place, London W1M 6AQ.
Tel. 020 7935 5773 Fax. 020 7224 6278 Email: *info@tcm.ac.uk* Website: *www.tcm.ac.uk*
Wells Cathedral School, The Music School, Cathedral Green, Wells, Somerset BA5 2UE.
Tel. 01749 679945 Fax. 01749 679939
Welsh College of Music and Drama, Castle Grounds, Cathays Park, Cardiff CF10 3ER.
Tel. 029 2034 2854 Fax. 029 2023 7639 Email: *music@wcmd.ac.uk*
Website: *www.wcmd.ac.uk*
World of Music, Arts and Dance Website: *http://www.womad.org/*
Yamaha–Kemble Music UK Ltd. Sherbourne Drive, Milton Keynes, Buckinghamshire MK7 8BL.
Tel. 01908 366700
Yehudi Menuhin School, Stoke D'Abernon, Cobham, Surrey KT11 3QQ.
Tel. 01932 864739 Fax. 01932 864633 Website: *www.brainsys.com/ymsch*

CHAPTER 11

Physical Education and Sport

Paul Beashel

Physical education and the talented performer

Throughout the world of education, intensive efforts are being made to identify and support talented students. In the area of sport these efforts are exaggerated by the political, commercial and social imperatives of individual countries. In Britain we know that the success of the Olympic teams raises morale throughout the country, and there is a consensus that our talented young sportspeople should be given every opportunity to develop their potential.

Schools have, of course, a crucial role to play in the identification and development of talent. However, there are many other parties closely involved in the development of sporting talent. These include parents, coaches, sports clubs, national governing bodies, the Youth Sports Trust, UK Sports Institute and the government. Schools can no longer work in isolation. There is a vital need for coherent planning to ensure that all the parties contribute to the ultimate success of the young sportsperson.

Physical education and sport in schools

Physical education can be considered to be the use of physical activities to achieve educational ends, while sport, on the other hand, is to do with organised, purposeful and usually competitive, physical activities. There is an obvious overlap between sport and physical education but their central focus is different. The aim of physical education is to educate the pupil, while sport may have many different purposes, for example, achieving excellence, gaining fitness, earning an income or pure enjoyment.

We teach physical education not sport in school lessons but we recognise the gifted and talented pupils we teach through their sporting prowess. Therefore, when we talk about gifted and talented pupils in PE we are talking about those who show high levels of skill in sporting activities.

Most secondary schools have developed general policies for identifying and supporting gifted and talented pupils. These policies usually include definitions of gifted and talented, mechanisms for identification and strategies for ensuring that their special needs are met. Physical educationists have not been in the forefront in developing specific programmes within their subject. However, in practice PE teachers are very adept at identifying talented and gifted pupils in order that these pupils gain sporting success for themselves and the school through competition. Recognising practical physical ability is part of PE teachers' professional training.

The essentially practical nature of PE means that pupils are required to demonstrate their ability whenever they take part in a lesson. This is not necessarily true in other subjects, where pupils can be taught but not assessed so readily. A performance is essentially a very public display of ability more likely to be seen in PE than in history, in music than in maths, in drama than in science.

In PE, pupils are routinely observed and assessed by their peers. Indeed when pupils take part in sport outside of lessons they are also assessed by their parents, their coaches and other interested spectators. Talent identification would therefore appear to be quite straightforward, however, the problem is not just one of identification of talented pupils in secondary school.

When we look at the identification of talented pupils at primary level the issue is one of opportunity. The opportunities that a primary school can offer its pupils will depend on a variety of factors, including the availability of PE and sport specialists, time given to PE within a crowded curriculum and the finances for facilities and equipment. Pupils who experience a sound physical education programme in their primary school will acquire good generic movement skills and the fundamentals of a range of sports. They will also develop confidence and a positive attitude to physical activity. This, currently, cannot be guaranteed in all primary schools.

There are relatively few physical education specialists working in our primary schools, yet it could be argued that this is where sporting talent needs to be recognised and nurtured. By the time most pupils reach the secondary school, they have probably decided whether they are good at sport or not and indeed already have preferences and dislikes for particular sports. One challenge is to identify talent early.

The girl representing her county in netball might have been even better at squash or a range of other sports had she been given an early opportunity to try them. Many other pupils may not even have had the opportunity to play netball at an early age, let alone under the guidance of a qualified specialist. How many potential rowing and netball champions have never even had the opportunity to experience these sports? Equality of opportunity in sporting terms is essential in the primary school for the full development of the nation's talent.

The government appears to have recognised this problem with the establishment of specialist sports colleges and the appointment of school sport coordinators, based in secondary schools, but working with a family of local primary schools. These coordinators are physical education specialists able to identify and develop sporting talent. This scheme is already underway in schools within the Excellence in Cities (EiC) programme and the government intends to extend it to all schools in the future.

The government's framework for talented performers

The government's Plans for Sport (March 2001) set out a strategy for PE and sport in schools. Within this strategy is the clear message that gifted and talented sports pupils in school need to be identified and supported. The report stated that youngsters with the potential to progress to higher levels of competition could only do so if they had the opportunity to discover and develop their sporting talent at school. This was why the government placed special emphasis on school sport.

In September 2001, an intensive gifted and talented programme was under way in over 1,000 secondary schools, 400 primary schools and in post-16 institutions across some 70 LEAs. This provision was made through the gifted and talented strands of Excellence in Cities, Excellence Clusters and Excellence Challenge. The government intends to spend £60m on provision for gifted and talented pupils in the financial year 2001/2002.

In participating secondary schools, this funding will enable:

- the appointment of a coordinator for the Gifted and Talented programme;
- the identification of a gifted and talented cohort comprising 5–10 per cent of pupils in each year group, at least one third of this cohort to be talented pupils with ability in art, music, PE, or any sport or creative art;
- the development and implementation of a whole school policy for gifted and talented pupils;
- the development and implementation of a distinct teaching and learning programme to meet the needs of pupils in the gifted and talented pupil cohort; and
- the provision of complementary out of school hours study support programmes.

Primary schools have a designated teacher who is supported by a lead coordinator who works with a group of schools in a cluster or partnership. In these schools, the cohort is confined to Years 5 and 6. Alongside the teaching and learning and study support programmes there is an additional scheme to improve the transition of gifted and talented pupils between primary and secondary schools.

The commitment to the early identification and support for gifted and talented pupils was reinforced in the White Paper 'Achieving Success' (September 2001). The government's policy for gifted and talented pupils in all schools seeks to:

- support the most gifted and talented in the country and in each school, particularly in disadvantaged areas;
- build on pupils' particular strengths and tackle any weaknesses, making sure they too receive a broad and balanced education;
- combine in-school learning with complementary opportunities out of school,

typically including masterclasses, summer schools and mentoring programmes;
- provide more opportunities for pupils to progress in line with their abilities, rather than their age and, where possible, achieve mastery, rather than superficial coverage of all subjects; and
- blend increased pace, depth and breadth in varying proportions according to the ability and needs of pupils. They want teachers to consider express sets, fast-tracking and more early entry to GCSE and advanced qualifications.

The government will also establish a new Academy for Gifted and Talented Youth to support and challenge gifted and talented pupils. The academy is expected to be based in a university and will develop:

- study support opportunities;
- distance learning programmes;
- mentoring programmes;
- training and consultancy services; and
- pupil assessment centres.

It will identify, develop, adopt and disseminate best practice through research and evaluation.

In addition to its specific plans for gifted and talented pupils, the government intends to implement its promise of an entitlement of two hours of high quality PE and sport each week in and out of school for all pupils. By 2004, there will be a network of 1,000 school sport coordinators based in secondary schools working in partnership with primary schools. These will provide a range of sporting opportunities to develop the talents, enrich the lives and benefit the health of pupils right across the country. Every school will be expected to arrange a full programme of high quality inter- and intra-school competitive sports and activities, when it has the services of a coordinator. The government also intends there to be 250 specialist sports colleges by 2006.

Talent identification in practice

Although the government has provided a clear framework for action, it has not determined precisely how schools, and others, should identify and nurture their gifted and talented pupils. A number of other countries have developed talent identification programmes, most notably Australia.

Talent identification in Australia

The dramatic improvement of Australian sport at Olympic and world level came as a result of a carefully constructed talent identification programme. The overall aims of their talent identification programme are to:

- raise the standard of sporting achievement by maximising the number of gifted athletes participating in certain sports;
- provide talented youngsters with the opportunity to develop their sports skills; and
- optimise potential for all individuals to achieve sporting success.

Rowing was the first Australian sport which, in 1988, adopted a systematic and scientific process of selecting talented athletes within schools and colleges. Other sports soon followed. Funding was provided for a national coordinated programme called 'Talent Search'. This was designed to help sports identify talented athletes (aged 11–20 years) and prepare them for participation in domestic, national and eventually international competition. The process aimed to assess the potential of young people across a range of sports through a single battery of tests. It also avoided the duplication of sports testing by many different sporting bodies.

Three phases for the 'Talent Search' programme were identified as school screening, sport specific testing and talent development.

School screening

PE teachers tested pupils using eight physical and physiological tests. The results went to the State Talent Search Coordinators for comparison with a national database.

Sport specific testing

The top 2 per cent were invited to take part in phase two. Phase two refined the accuracy of the tests in phase one and incorporated sport specific laboratory testing.

Talent development

Phase three was for pupils who were identified with talent for a specific sport. They were invited to join a talented athlete programme organised by the state and/or national sporting organisation.

The Australian 'Talent Search' programme is recognised as an international leader in the field of identifying potentially talented athletes and has been adopted in many different countries.

The Sport England model

Sport England has adopted the testing procedure of the Australian Talent Search programme but has decided to use it purely as a sport encouragement system. This Sport England initiative called 'Sport Search' is an interactive computer-based programme that allows secondary school pupils to find a sport that matches their own physical attributes and interests. It works as follows:

- a young person completes 11 physical and fitness related tasks during PE;
- the results are entered into a PC that is running SPORTSEARCH and is connected to the internet;

- the young person then answers a series of questions about their own sporting preferences and attitudes; and
- SPORTSEARCH provides a ranked selection of sports and information from national governing bodies of sport. These sports are selected from over 115 sports nationwide.

SPORTSEARCH advises the young person about local sporting opportunities and how to make contact with sports clubs and facilities.

In addition, the system advises young people on how to maintain and improve their fitness, access a national sports database, take part in surveys, participate in research projects and enter competitions. SPORTSEARCH was piloted during 2001 in three local education authorities that were already linked to the NGfL initiative. The pilot involved extensive consultation with schools nationwide, and the programme started in January 2002.

It is likely that, given the lack of any alternative talent identification measures, SPORTSEARCH will be used by many for this purpose.

The Youth Sport Trust model

The Youth Sport Trust established a talented and gifted programme called Junior Athlete Career Education (JACE). This programme is based on a network of specialist sports colleges and national governing bodies. The programme has two parallel strands.

The first strand in JACE supports young sports people with an educative series of workshops. Teachers are trained to deliver these workshops with supporting materials. Workshops educate young sportspeople on the merits of lifestyle management, performance profiling and performance planning. The key elements are:

- consideration of a balanced lifestyle – what it is and why it is important;
- good communication between everyone (teachers, parents, coaches) working or involved with the young sportsperson. The concept of 'Team You' is developed; i.e. the team of people important in the individual youngster's total development;
- identification of their sporting strengths and weaknesses, together with an action plan for improvement, involving parents, coaches and teachers;
- identifying and planning for 'hotspots' or clashes in their calendar year caused by competitions, training, school, exam or social commitments. These calendars are shared with all people within 'Team You'.

A workshop is also arranged for the parents of the elite young performers. This reinforces the messages delivered to the young sportspeople and enables parents to ensure that their gifted child maintains a balanced lifestyle and, at the same time, is able to achieve his or her full potential.

The second strand underpins support for these young sportspeople through a mentoring programme delivered in their own school. It aims to help them achieve a balanced lifestyle involving schoolwork, exams, training and competitions. Mentors are trained to help pupils cope with the potentially conflicting demands of home, school and sport.

The Deanes School

The Deanes is an 11–16 mixed comprehensive school in south-east Essex, with 1,020 pupils of mixed ability. In 1998 it became a DfEE designated sports college. The school was awarded the Beckwith National Innovation Award by the Youth Sports Trust in 2000, in recognition of its work with its family of schools in supporting gifted and talented sporting pupils.

Some years ago, it was realised that the school was not putting the same effort and resources into catering for the special needs of the most able compared with the least able. After a great deal of thought and effort, a policy was produced for supporting all gifted and talented pupils within the school (GATE). This has resulted in a practical system to identify the gifted and talented pupils across the curriculum, together with a programme designed to enrich their educational experiences and provide them with further challenges. The early programme looked for experiences and activities, which could be bolted on to the curriculum. Today every department has the responsibility to ensure that these pupils are challenged and motivated within their subject.

For physical education this presents a particular problem, as the needs of the gifted and talented cannot be satisfied within the normal physical education programme. An outstanding gymnast, for example, will need specialist coaching, equipment and facilities to fully develop their talent. This requires extra provision outside of the normal PE lessons.

Another potential conflict between school and sport can easily arise between examination commitments and important sporting competitions. There is always the potential for tension between the competing demands of academic and sporting success.

When the school gained sports college status, it was decided to develop a programme for supporting gifted and talented pupils, not just at the Deanes school, but also within the wider family of schools in the area. This was important because the GATE programme for sport subsequently acted as a catalyst, ensuring the full collaboration of local primary and secondary schools. The second decision, of equal significance, was to fund the appointment of a member of staff from one of the local secondary schools for one day a week to support the development of the programme. These two decisions helped to ensure the full cooperation and commitment of the physical educationists in the local schools and colleges.

The Deanes GATE programme was founded on the belief that talented young sportspeople:

- have special requirements due to their sporting success;
- need to feel valued;
- are under pressure to perform in daily school life and sport;

- want the key people around them to understand the pressures upon them;
- must keep a balance between academic work, sports training and a social life; and
- can act as positive role models to motivate other pupils.

The key aims and objectives of the programme are:

- to identify and provide a clear pathway for talented performers which allows them to fulfil their sporting potential;
- to ensure that the agreed long-term aims for talented performers influence their short-term goals in relation to training, competition and performance;
- to develop a framework to ensure that the performer and their needs are clearly placed at the centre of the programme. This will reduce the chance that the performer suffers burnout in their sport, underachievement in their academic work or disaffection with both;
- to work with a family of schools, including secondary schools, independent schools and sixth form colleges, with all relevant head teachers fully endorsing the programme and policies;
- to gain commitment and involvement from higher education, national governing bodies and the Youth Sport Trust's JACE programme;
- to extend the available resources and technical support to talented students and schools; and
- to establish registers of talented performers, both at county and national level, as well as those below this level but who show the potential to progress with further support.

The programme involves the following:

- 10 secondary schools
- 1 sixth form college
- 1 independent school
- Loughborough University
- University of Essex
- De Montfort University
- NGBs
- Youth Sports Trust
- Essex Learning Services
- Parents
- Coaches
- Teachers
- Clubs
- Active Sports
- County Development Officers
- Seconded staff

There are now over 300 young people registered on the programme. Forty-six of these pupils perform at national or international level (see Figure 11.1).

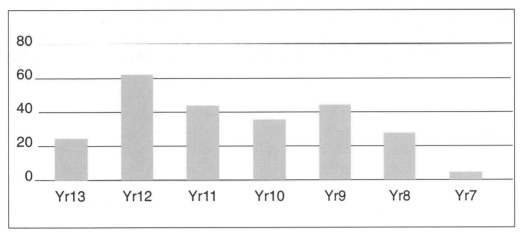

Figure 11.1 Pupils on the Deane's Gate Programme

The gifted and talented performers represent 17 different sports:

Archery   Athletics
Badminton   Basketball
Boxing   Cricket
Dance   Football
Golf   Gymnastics
Hockey   Judo
Karate   Netball
Rugby   Squash
Swimming   Tennis
Trampoline

The support programme

The programme is administered and coordinated by the Deanes Sports College. All head teachers in partner schools have endorsed the programme and its policies. A steering group has been established with a representative from each school.

Mentors in all of the partner schools have undertaken a training programme planned and delivered by the Youth Sports Trust. Staff from each of these schools have also been trained to deliver the education workshops devised by the Trust. These education workshops are available not only to students on the gifted and talented programme, but also to their parents and coaches. These workshops contribute to the individual education programmes of the talented young sportspeople.

Masterclasses are now being run in a number of different sports. Performance coaching takes place in tennis, gymnastics, badminton, trampoline, football, dance and basketball. This enables selected students to receive sports specific coaching from highly qualified coaches in the company of equally talented students from partner schools. All students on the programme are registered with the sports college physiotherapist and can receive treatment at a reduced cost.

A pilot project is under way involving six highly talented tennis players receiving regular coaching during normal lesson time. It is each student's responsibility, with help from their mentor, to ensure that any work missed is subsequently completed.

Eighty of the highest performing students receive sports science support from Essex University. This takes the form of regular fitness assessment and advice on appropriate training methods. Additionally, 34 national performers have access to lab testing at Essex University. Here comprehensive records of performance are established and digital movement analysis is undertaken.

In the near future, all students on the programme will undertake a regular programme of fitness assessment, with the younger students attending a new fitness assessment centre at Brentwood Public School. Five students are currently on the World Class Performance Programme and work closely with their sport's NGB. Students who attend competitions or training camps have the use of laptops to access school work and to keep in contact with their school through regular e-mails.

A county careers adviser, based at South East Essex College, specialising in sporting careers, is not only involved in the regular student workshops but is also available on an individual basis for career guidance.

A number of national governing bodies are working closely with the project. For example, one member of the PE staff has been joint-funded by the school and the British Amateur Gymnastics Association (BAGA) in order to run a pilot project in a number of infant/junior schools in East Basildon Education Action Zone. A gymnastics screening programme is run in each school. The children gain gymnastic experience in five different stations. One of these stations is led by a high performance coach who seeks to identify those children with gymnastic potential. Gymnastic clubs are being set up for each cluster of four primary schools within the school sport coordinator partnership, while those children who have been identified as being potentially talented are invited to attend a gymnastics club run at one of the three local secondary schools. They also have the opportunity to progress to the high performance club at South Essex Gymnastics Club. The programme is currently working with over 500 children in 12 infant/junior schools.

The programme so far

Early evaluation of the programme is very encouraging. Positive benefits have become evident through the collaborative working of schools, teachers, parents, coaches and NGBs. These benefits include:

- a greater understanding of the needs of gifted and talented performers, both in school and in the wider community;
- improved communication between all those individuals and groups involved in the programme;

- young performers feeling more valued, with higher levels of self-esteem and increased levels of motivation and aspiration;
- realisation by the NGBs of the need to be involved in the whole process of talent identification in schools and beyond.

The future

There is a danger that early specialisation in a particular sport may not ultimately be in the talented child's best interest. Spending a great deal of time and energy on one sport at the expense of a wide range of different physical activities may actually limit the opportunity to discover their potential in other sports. For example, the young swimmer training every day may not have the time to play major games or racket sports. Also early physical maturation can sometimes give a false impression of the potential ability of the young sportsperson.

Recognising these problems, it is intended to identify multitalented young sportspeople in primary school and give them the opportunity to develop a range of generic sporting skills. The programme will include, for example, the principles of games, sports psychology, nutrition, lifestyle and and future planning.

NGBs are playing an increasingly important role in the programme. It is intended that they become more involved in the construction of individual education plans and will give advice and support on fitness testing, nutrition, psychology and movement analysis for their particular sport. A vital role is to identify where different performers fit into NGBs' performance plans and to support their progress.

This is an exciting and challenging development for the school. There is a need to celebrate the success of all young sportspeople and to help to ensure the smooth passage of their sporting careers.

CHAPTER 12

Religious Education

Mark Cope

Introduction: gifted and talented?

In much of the current literature, the terms 'gifted and talented' and 'more able' are used interchangeably. In the late 1980s there were a number of interesting studies on the notion of giftedness such as R. J. Sternberg and J. E. Davidson's *Conceptions of Giftedness*, and J. Freeman's *The Psychology of Gifted Children*. There is agreement that 'gifted' students account for a very small percentage of individuals who display higher order skills in one or a number of areas.

A gifted student would also be more able, but a more able student might not be considered gifted in the sense in which this word is used in this context. A gifted student might display extraordinary abilities which, in the main, cannot be fully accounted for by the process of education. The phrase 'a God given gift' captures the feeling that the reason why someone displays a higher order skill is not fully explicable by normal rational processes. The student who can play like a concert pianist at ten or goes to university to study mathematics at twelve is truly gifted: the education system cannot really take the credit for such natural genius, apart from its willingness to encourage it.

Who qualifies as more able in the classroom?

'More able' students account for a wider group of children who can easily cope with most tasks with which they are presented and are usually the first to finish their work in class. It is difficult to give a precise percentage as to how many students should be included. In a selective school, for example, all the students might be more able: in a mixed comprehensive, with no selection policy, it would vary from year to year depending upon the nature and abilities of the students in a particular year group.

Curriculum 2000 is underpinned by a commitment to social inclusion. The government's definition of 'gifted and talented' seeks to target the much larger percentage of students who could benefit from teaching which is planned and structured for their needs rather than just the 1 or 2 per cent who are born with an exaggerated degree of talent.

Gifted and talented in RE

In this section, let us consider the notion of high ability in religion, its perceived value, and ways of enhancing it. What is unique about high ability in religion, how may it be characterised and stimulated?

In defining and identifying the gifted, talented and more able pupil in respect of the study of religion, there are a number of issues which need to be addressed. Current schemes of work, and recently revised agreed syllabi for religious education, modelled on the QCA models, identify two broad areas with which the subject needs to be concerned: learning *about* religion, and learning *from* religion. These correspond to the more familiar GCSE criteria: knowledge, understanding and evaluation. Knowledge and the understanding which you have inherited from someone else, is the bulk of the task of learning *about* religion. Your own understanding and how you judge it, or value it, sediments into what one has learned *from* religion. In planning for the gifted, talented and more able, the first is much easier to deal with than the second.

High ability is not always valued in the same way in all times and places. A key factor when judging high ability is whether or not a society deems that ability to be praiseworthy. At different times and places in history, different sorts of abilities have been held in high or low esteem, not because of their real merits, but because they are, or are not, in accord with the prevailing view at the time. During wartime, a great soldier is applauded for attitudes and decisions which in peacetime are not seen to be appropriate. In our own time, someone who is able to make vast amounts of money is prized more highly by society than a great academic or spiritual leader. In *The Republic* from the fourth century BC, Plato makes it very clear that the muses and the poets are a higher source of authority than his own logical analysis. By contrast, in the twelfth century, Thomas Aquinas, a theologian, most fully in *Summa Contra Gentiles* and *Summa Theologica*, used the newly rediscovered Aristotelian logic to become the apologist for Roman Catholic Christendom.

In addition to everything else that one might say about them, the founders of the world's religions displayed exceptional abilities in a variety of measurable ways, and also in ways not so easily measured. During the Sermon on the Mount, in Matthew chapter 5, Jesus captivated an audience with his teaching style because of its openness and accessibility to and for the masses. He seemed to be able to explain the most complex idea through a story. The prophet Muhammed encountered opposition from the rulers of his time because he suggested what appeared to them to be an over simplistic view of the relationship between mankind and God. Hear the words of Allah directly through the Quran, act upon them, and King or pauper meets God with equal status. Siddhattha Gautama bewildered his followers by doing the exact opposite of what society would have expected of the young prince. He rejected the life of luxury for a life of poverty. Again, these responses to life situations were impossible to assess using our 'normal' measures of success and failure, right and wrong, which were employed by his contemporaries.

The American comparative mythologist Joseph Campbell in *The Power of Myth*, citing the Indologist Heinrich Zimmer, said that the most important things defy expression, the second most important things are spoken about by poets and the third most important things are what may be talked about. By implication, the great religious teachers, therefore, had to use metaphor: through stories, something of the unknowable mystery becomes known.

A unique difficulty for RE

Higher ability in understanding religion has this essential difference from other school subjects. It has to take on board the fact that its greatest exponents were not, in retrospect, considered to be great because they confirmed what had gone before, but because they went beyond it. This going beyond was not easy: it involved pain and often the eventual breaking up of what had gone before. Also, many people in the world probably consider the founders of the world's religions to be slightly mad.

By implication, those who follow them might be thought to be the same: this is a prejudice with which every teacher of religious education has to contend. There is no absolute consensus as to whether spiritual intelligence or intuition actually exists. Some recent work has been done by Dinah Zohar, where she looks at the evidence for an identifiable 'spiritual quotient' in the way we have an IQ. Her research leads her to the view that there is a particular type of brain activity which accompanies spiritual thinking. In gauging higher ability in religious understanding there is a need to be aware of this propensity towards alienation. Yet, in making provision for the more able, religious education has to somehow crack open the cosy view that it is just about Jesus being nice to people. It does not square up with the actual way in which its main progenitors – all gifted and talented – proceeded. Also, this cosy view does not interest the most able minds. Yet, ironically, these difficulties may be the springboard to a positive reappraisal of how the study of religion may be facilitated.

Teaching religion presents some unique challenges in school and these are sharpened when teaching more able students. The sorts of questions which more able students raise often strike at the very foundations of the subject. High ability students want to explore such questions. It is important to be able to anticipate such questions when planning, and our continued experience should be used to inform our provision for the subject. It is from such a basis that the study of religion needs to be made meaningful to the modern mind.

The skills and abilities of more able pupils in RE

Having looked at some of the inherent difficulties and the imperatives placed upon the teacher when considering high ability in the study of religion, let us discuss the sorts of skills and abilities which are capable of being developed by the teacher.

Using professional judgement, a good teacher, without prejudice, should know which students are more able. Kelvin Peel in his research project 'An investigation into the special educational needs of more able children', emphasised how the subjective judgement of classroom teachers always seemed to be able to correct the more objective methods which were employed in the identification of more able students in a number of schools. There are observable criteria which apply to all more able students across all subjects. There is nothing unique to religious education, except in where and when the last three in the list below occur.

A more able student should show:

- an ability to concentrate upon a particular piece of work, or ponder over one fact for much longer than his/her peers;
- the ability to complete work which is set for the group as a whole quickly and accurately;
- a very high standard of presentation of work, indicating that pupils control the subject matter rather than letting it control them;
- a competence to read a source and be able to select all the key points easily;
- the capacity to see how the topic relates to other topics which have been studied, and sometimes to relate them to their wider, more general knowledge;
- a faculty to interpret the material in a way unforseen by the teacher, noticing the ambiguities and similarities in a source, which must first be resolved before choosing which line to take; and
- the capacity to approach a source with questions of his/her own, and then to generate new questions when he/she has identified the key points and the unresolved and contentious parts.

The first four may be quantified as being what a more able pupil learns about religion. The last three really propel us into the highest realms of thinking in the study of religion because they encourage an individual to take creative steps through the subject matter and beyond it to a point where they are able to frame the very parameters in which they are operating. Ordinarily, points 6 and 7 are the sort of descriptors which one may find attached to the criteria for a post-graduate thesis. But in religious education they are anticipated by the youngest child who asks: 'If there is a God, why is the world such a horrible place?' Think of this for a moment: it is the epistemological equivalent of a young child asking: 'Describe to me exactly why light cannot escape from a black hole.'

This is probably a unique characteristic of religious education as a school subject. Many of the key questions, which professional philosophers and theologians are trying to answer, are asked by more able ten-year olds. Most children ask half of them or more. As lawyers might say, they 'cut to the chase' very quickly. This has to be anticipated and planned for when making provision for the more able.

High ability in the study of religion: a university perspective

A number of lecturers in the theology department at Birmingham University were asked about how they would characterise high ability in the study of religion. Here is a summary of what they suggested.

- The ability to construct and sustain a complex argument.
- The ability to sustain and integrate a significant number of different ideas at any one time.
- The ability to be critical at the right point, fully absorbing existing knowledge and understanding before pursuing an original course.
- The ability to raise independent questions, in written and verbal forms.
- The ability to identify and use the relationships between questions within a subject area and see how they relate to other subject areas.
- The ability to present a sustainable counter-argument.
- The ability to plan and sustain a project.
- The ability to start at different points in a study and then structure this as part of the whole.
- The ability to sustain an in-depth dialogue, if the learning environment allows it.
- The ability to employ different methodologies to diverse subject matter.
- The ability to continually relate parts to the whole.
- The ability to allow reflection and practice to inform each other.
- The ability to put local knowledge into the context of a particular current or historical world view.
- The ability to be aware of the valuing process which others and you yourself are operating within.
- The ability to appreciate that conclusions might be interim and that one's evaluation of them might change with greater knowledge, understanding and experience.
- To be aware of one's moods in relation to the type of task being undertaken.
- The ability and courage to employ and integrate personal experiences and insights into the study.
- To have the courage to take adventurous steps in learning.
- The ability to be aware of the mode of perception which you yourself are using.
- The ability to use the 'destructive' elements of the pursuit of knowledge as a stage on the way to a new synthesis or reconstruction.
- Experience and 'gut' reaction would inform the teacher roughly as to whether an individual has more to develop or not.
- Ability does not always manifest itself as being able to write good essays.
- Encourage students to write as they think.
- To identify the teachable elements, and work out how to teach them.
- Mediate between the individual and the expectations of the school, university or institution.

What does this mean for the classroom teacher?

A number of key principles may be drawn together from the above which may form the basis of planning classroom work for more able pupils.

- There are elements which should foster cross-curricular skills, because they are simply good practice. (1–10)
- There are elements which are about seeing the study in a wider context. (11–15)
- There are elements which call for a high level of personal reflection and self-reflection by the person studying. (16–20)
- There are elements which inform the method of teaching and allow the teacher to respond to the individual student. (21–25)

The third and fourth groups are especially significant. They focus upon what is meant by learning *from* religion. Because religion is really about what concerns people most deeply, what Paul Tillich called 'ultimate concern', the study of religion touches students personally. It follows that if higher levels of insight, and thereby achievement, are to be reached, then self-reflection cannot be avoided in relation to the subject matter. A thorny issue presents itself here. Does this mean that one may only really understand and evaluate religion – and learn *from* it – by participating in it, i.e. by worshipping?

Where does a pupil stand in relation to the subject matter?

The founders of the world's religions were clearly 'inside' religion. Their context was one of fostering salvation and personal devotion. This is not quite what one is trying to replicate with high ability students in religious education. One is trying to develop the insight without necessarily having the personal devotion and commitment. Paul Tillich characterises this as being the difference between the *philosophy of religion* and *religious philosophy*. He explains that the philosophy of religion is about asking questions from a neutral position, showing no personal conviction either way: religious philosophy is when one asks the same questions having a personal interest in the answers.

Metaphorically, the philosophy of religion is like observing goldfish in a bowl, where one is able to see the whole bowl and all the interactions therein: religious philosophy is like doing the same, only from the position of swimming around with them. This really crystallises the central problem for the teacher of religious education who is attempting to facilitate learning for more able students. In order to do it, there has to be an opportunity, as it were, to jump in and out of the goldfish bowl.

Religion is about raising questions about life in the world with God – and offering answers. The non-confessional and inclusive imperative in state schools precludes giving answers to children which may conflict with the views of their own faith community. Also, most children now have an entirely secular world-view, so answers which are offered from any religious tradition are often interpreted to be at best challenging, and at worst irrelevant. In short, one may not raise personal questions and offer personal answers. What needs to be done, therefore, is to create opportunities to expand the range of questions and allow opportunities for individuals to frame their own answers.

The teacher of religious education has to thoroughly plan the process through which deeper levels of understanding may be reached, but not the outcome – in relation to the third and fourth groups above. Groups one and two can have definable outcomes, which are not in many ways any different from those to be found in all other subjects. It seems appropriate to concentrate upon groups three and four, as these are concerned with the more difficult problem which faces teachers of religious education. What types of questions will serve the purpose, and how may they be used?

Facilitating a deeper level of understanding through questions

If a religious education department is to try to make its subject matter appeal to more able students, then it needs to foster a climate where the freedom to ask questions is its most basic principle. This ethos should span the key stages, and should grow with the students: there is never a point at which it is more or less appropriate to generate new questions in relation to subject matter. The importance of using the right questions is older than Plato's Socratic dialogues. Robert Fisher in *Teaching Children to Think* looks at the different ways in which the right sorts of questions and manner of questioning facilitate higher levels of thinking. For the purposes of religious education, we may identify seven different types of questions which will allow one to mediate the subject matter at a higher level, and assist the teacher to deepen the pupils' understanding.

1. Closed questions
- One possible answer: 'Yes' or 'No'
- One possible answer: where a thing is located in a particular time and place.

2. Open questions
- To establish some common ground between the teacher and the students.
- To establish some general background upon which to build later, using other questions.
- To see if a student has an opinion about something and what it is. Have they thought about this before?

3. Probing questions
- Verbal and non-verbal gestures so the student feels encouraged to continue.
- Support for what the student has said already, prompting them to say more.
- Repetition of key words to focus the dialogue.

- Pausing at the right moment to encourage the student to explain something in a different way.
- Occasional 'Why?' or 'Why not?' to focus or expand a particular point.
- Questions which call for superficial and more interpretative and conceptual comparisons to be made.
- Questions which seek to extend what has already been said and lead the student to a deeper level of response.
- Hypothetical questions.
- Summary questions, which round off the dialogue and/or create a platform for a different line of questioning.

4. Existential questions

- *Personal/subjective:* How am *I* experiencing this in terms of my feelings and emotions?
- *Intersubjective:* How does *someone else* seem to be sharing this experience in terms of their feelings and emotions?
- *Universal:* What responses give a clue to something which seems to be true for everyone in all times and places, or in certain identifiable contexts?

5. Phenomenological questions

- How is this thing showing itself to me?
- What does it appear to be when I have bracketed questions of meaning and truth?
- How am I, the observer, affecting this?

6. Metaphysical questions

- Thinking through abstractly from an assumption to a conclusion.
- What seems to be the underlying trend and logic of it all?
- Things which people find it difficult to talk about.

7. Critical questions

- What conditions make this appear as it is, here and now?
- If I am being deceived, how?
- How would this appear from an opposite point of view?
- Is there anything else I need to take account of in order to consider this more fully?

Using questioning strategies in lessons: Muslim beliefs and values

Although the discussion so far gives a framework for planning, let us map out a topic in detail. It is hoped that the approach will stimulate the reader to transfer the underlying theory to different and more diverse subject matter. The topic chosen is an area which even more able students find difficult. Because the approach is generic, it can be used with any age group so long as it is scaled up or down in proportion to the specific subject matter.

It is assumed that resources are available from which the student may learn *about* the Muslim belief of *Tawhid* (the oneness of God and unity of creation), *risalah* (belief in the prophets, the Quran and Muhammed), *akhirah* (the last day and life after death), the word *Islam* (submission to God) and *al'Qad'r* (God's foreknowledge). These questions may be pursued through written work, but are primarily offered as a basis for discussion work.

Preliminary questions about beliefs and responsibilities which underpin any study of religious values

- Closed: What are the basic beliefs of the religion being studied?
- Open: What are 'basic beliefs'? What are 'duties' and 'responsibilities'?
- Existential: What are your own basic beliefs? What determines your own basic beliefs system? What do I mean by 'duty'? How do beliefs and actions influence each other?
- Phenomenological: What do I see when I watch members of a religion performing their religious duties? Why may what I observe seem strange to me?
- Metaphysical: When, for example, Muslims say 'Allah' and 'angels', what do they mean? What are the links between all the basic beliefs?
- Critical: In what sense may our basic beliefs be demonstrated to someone else? Do these beliefs undermine a person's free will? Why might someone doubt a person's beliefs? Does 'duty' conflict with free will?

Tawhid (belief in the oneness of God and the unity of creation)

These questions are generated from a basic examination of the concept of *Tawhid*. They present a canvas upon which a question set by someone else may be drawn.

- Closed: What does the word 'Tawhid' refer to?
- Open: What is 'belief'? What is 'obedience'?
- Existential: Why do human beings respond to the idea of 'Oneness'? What do I understand by 'obedience'? How have I experienced obedience and how did it make me feel? How do my beliefs affect my actions?
- Phenomenological: How do specific beliefs appear to change the way a Muslim acts? What does a Muslim do which appears to demonstrate obedience?
- Metaphysical: What does a Muslim mean by the words 'eternal' and 'absolute'? What does a Muslim mean when he/she refers to 'Allah'? What does a Muslim mean by 'sin'?
- Critical: Is a life based upon the unseen a good enough basis for choice? Does obedience undermine personal freedom? How might commitment to one particular way make me narrow minded?

Risalah (belief in the prophets, the Quran and the prophet Muhammed)

- Closed: What does 'Risalah' mean? What is meant by 'free will'? What do 'tawrat', 'zabur', 'Injil' and 'Quran' refer to? What does the word 'guidance' mean?

- Open: How do different religions treat their holy book? What is the role of a messenger? Give some examples of guidance. Give some examples of where/ when human beings exercise their free will.
- Existential: How would human beings change without freedom of choice and action? Must human beings have free will? How does guidance from someone else affect the way in which human beings behave?
- Phenomenological: What do angels, the Quran and the prophet Muhammed appear to be for Muslims?
- Metaphysical: How are angels and human beings different? How do Allah, angels and human beings relate to each other in this view?
- Critical: Can any intelligent being not have free will? Why do people find it difficult to believe in angels?

Akhirah (the last day and life after death)

- Closed: What does 'ultimate' mean? What is meant by 'justice'? What does the word 'Akhirah' refer to? What does 'Yawm-ud-din' refer to?
- Open: How do people try to maintain justice in our society? Give some examples of justice and injustice. What are some of the different ideas which you know about concerning life after death?
- Existential: Is obedience natural to us? What sorts of events stop justice taking place? How does belief in life after death change people's behaviour? Why do people seek for an ultimate meaning to life?
- Phenomenological: What does 'hell' appear to be for Muslims? How might a Muslim behave differently because of his/her belief in Akhirah? What does 'heaven' appear to be for Muslims? What do Muslims do to show that they believe in life after death?
- Metaphysical: Are heaven and hell real physical places? Do people *personally* live for ever in the Muslim view? What could reward and punishment mean in this context?
- Critical: What is difficult about believing any ideas about life after death? Are such ideas merely a way of frightening people into good behaviour? Could people be 'greedy' for heaven like for anything else?

Islam (submission to God) and al'Qad'r (God's foreknowledge)

- Closed: What is meant by 'Islam'? What is meant by 'submission'? What is meant by 'Al Q'adr'? What is meant by 'predetermined'? What is meant by 'Seal of the Prophets'? What are the 'five pillars of Islam'?
- Open: What sorts of thing do human beings willingly and unwillingly submit to? Give some examples of events, the outcome of which seems to be a foregone conclusion.
- Existential: How might a sense of your being 'chosen' affect your behaviour? Is obedience and submission natural to human beings? How might you argue that

human beings have the power to shape their own futures? How does a belief that everything is predetermined affect the way in which people might think or act?

- Phenomenological: How does a Muslim appear to show submission? How does submission appear to change the way in which a Muslim approaches life? How does being 'chosen' appear to make a Muslim act differently?
- Metaphysical: What is the relationship between Allah and mankind based upon? How does our own free will alter events? In this view, is God involved with human beings or separate from them?
- Critical: Why change your behaviour if it is all predetermined anyway? In what sense can a person have the last word about religion? In what sense is one person 'chosen' and another not? Humans must grasp the opportunity to bring about change for themselves.

Issues about teaching more able pupils in a state school

In this final section, let us consider some of the issues which are central to teaching more able students in a state school and the constraints within which the teacher of religious education works.

More able students do not, in the normal sense of the word, cause a problem. As they do not cause trouble in the classroom, and are likely to pass their GCSEs anyway, why worry? In practice, schools and classroom teachers have to prioritise: as a consequence most special needs initiatives are targeted towards those with learning difficulties. Teachers of religious education are often trying to fight for sufficient curriculum time and thinking about the needs of the more able in a subject which has only a single period a week is a luxury. Yet it is within the power of the classroom teacher to change attitudes and approaches to teaching and learning within their classroom, insofar as conditions allow.

Another important point is about the way in which the curriculum is orientated towards external examinations. The framework outlined allows a subject to develop laterally, but also embraces the important skills required by examination boards. Examination questions do not really require students to ask a full range of questions, yet it is the wider questions which most interest and stimulate the more able. The skills required for doing well in examinations need to be integrated into the teaching throughout, but made explicit to the students at the right time. If the focus of the teaching is towards an external examination, then it is sensible to draw out those questions which examiners want you to know the answers to, and show understanding of, at some stage within the course.

Examinations notwithstanding, it is important to remember that the transition or journey which a young person makes relies on their receiving a framework through which they can make sense of their own lives, indeed, gain a true experience of life. It is like climbing mountains. A novice will climb where there are plenty of natural footholds: an expert will have the independence of mind and experience to make her own. A knowledge and understanding of what has gone before are like the footholds: when a person has learned to climb, it is possible to go to new places.

One aspect which confuses the study of religion for the modern student is the relationship between collective and individual values. Modern young people have a much more heightened sense of self worth and dignity than did students only a few years ago, and this seems to be at odds with what the world's religions teach in some ways. They all teach about the personal, but very much within the context of the shared values of the faith community. It is an unresolved dichotomy at the moment which begs a question. Should a teacher challenge notions of individualism, even though they know that they seem to be swimming against the tide?

Society is essentially secular, and the students reflect these values. If more able students are to find religious education challenging and meaningful, then it is important to challenge questionable ideals and values by measuring them against those of the world religions in such a way that there can be no attempt to close off the difficult questions and issues which the students themselves bring.

Although pupils appear to be open to every influence, their minds are often remarkably closed. The narrower the mind, the wider and more sweeping the statements – and this is perhaps no more true than in religion. It is important to develop a framework through which bright and intelligent minds might be helped to navigate a very difficult subject area by shifting the emphasis in the teaching from giving answers to facilitating questions. When young people do, then, formulate answers, these will be at an altogether higher and more sophisticated level.

References

Campbell, J. (1991) *The Power of Myth*. New York: Parabola.

Cousineau, P. (ed.) (1999) *The Hero's Journey: The Life and Work of Joseph Campbell*. London: HarperCollins.

Denton, C. and Postlethwaite, K. (1985) *Able Children*. London: NFER.

Fisher, R. (1990) *Teaching Children to Think*. Oxford: Blackwell.

Freeman, J. (1985) *The Psychology of Gifted Children*. Chichester: Wiley and Sons.

MacKay, I. (1980) *A Guide to Asking Questions*. London: British Association for Commercial and Industrial Education.

Peel, K. (1993) 'An Investigation into the special educational needs of more able children', MEd thesis, University of Birmingham.

Sternberg, R. J. and Davidson, J. E. (1986) *Conceptions of Giftedness*. New York: Cambridge University Press.

Tillich, P. (1997) *Systematic Theology*, Vol. 1, pp. 8–11. London: SCM Press.

Zohar, D. and Mitchell, I. (1999) *SQ: The Ultimate Intelligence*. London: Bloomsbury.

Websites

DfEE/QCA Schemes of Work, published for each subject through 2000–2001. Online at *www.qca.org.uk*.

QCA have listed some *Methods of identifying gifted and talented children (www.standards.dfee.gov.uk/excellence/gift)*: National Curriculum tests, ability profile tests, teacher nomination, classroom observation, examination of pupils' work, subject specific checklists, generic checklists, reading tests, creativity tests, educational psychologists and the opinions of parents and peers.

Acknowledgement

Thanks to: Professor Hugh McLeod, Dr Mark Goodacre, Dr Martin Stringer, Dr John Parrat and Dr Emmanuel Larty. The dialogues I had with them are written up more fully in my unpublished *Religious Education and More Able Students* (1997), Farmington Fellowship Thesis, Farmington Library, Harris Manchester College, Oxford. I have summarised a part of this discussion in this chapter.

Index

A level   51, 79, 147, 153, 158–9
ability
   in art   76–7
   in English   27–9, 32
   in foreign languages   141–3
   general indicators of   12
   in mathematics   42–5
   musical   164–67
   specific or all-round   11, 28
   in study of religion   189–92
Academy for Gifted and Talented Youth   180
acceleration   23, 33, 53–4, 151–2, 168
Achieving Success (White Paper, 2001)   179–80
Achter, J.A.   12
Adams, Marilyn Jager   34
Adey, P.   21
aesthetic values   77
Ahmes Mathematical Papyrus   46
akhirah   196–7
Allende, Isabel   133
Aquinas, Thomas   189
architecture   94
Arnold, John H.   114
art, teaching of   76–92
Assessment of Performance Unit   94
assessment techniques and procedures   63–5, 97;
   see also formative assessment; summative
   assessment
Association of Teachers and Lecturers   30
auditing of needs and resources   160
Australia   17, 34, 180–1
autism   78
autonomous learners   149

Barak, M.   97
Baxter, M.   93
Bayliss, T.   93
Beckwith National Innovation Award   183
Bennett, N.   70–1
BICS (Basic Interpersonal Communication Skills)
   141
bilingual children   143, 157

Black, P.   138
Bloom, B.   6, 10, 95
Boston, Daniela   160
Brentwood Public School   186
Bridges, Cathy   123
British Amateur Gymnastics Association   186
British Museum   121
Buzan, Tony   65

Callow, R.   131
CALP (Cognitive/Academic Language Proficiency)
   141
Campbell, Joseph   190
Canada   19
Canale, M.   141
CASE (Cognitive Acceleration through Science
   Education)   64
Centre for Language in Primary Education   34
challenging activity, definition of   20–1, 118, 131
characteristics of gifted and talented pupils   59–60,
   97, 114–15, 130–1
checklists of pupils' abilities   15, 80, 82, 142–3, 160
chess   129
Clark, C.   76, 131
classification exercises for pupils   135–6
classroom provision   19–20, 38–40, 153
Clay, Marie   34
clockword radio   93
closed questions   194–7
comfort zone   20
community-based opportunities   6–7
concentration by pupils   15, 59, 77, 191
concept formation   135
conceptual change, model of   60–1
continuous assessment   65
coordinators (for physical education and sport)
   179–80
creativity   64–5, 69, 94–110, 129
   foundations of   109
   teaching and learning attributes for promotion of
      101–4
   with younger and with older pupils   106

critical questioning   195–8
critical thinking   76, 79
Csikszentmihalyi, M.   20, 77
Cummins, J.   141
Cunliffe, Leslie   88
curriculum   14, 18, 65, 159–60, 198; *see also*
    National Curriculum
Curriculum 2000   188

Dasgupta, S.   93
David, Jacques   88
Davidson, J.E.   188
Davidson, M.   95
Davies, Peter   130
Daw, Peter   28
Day, M.   76
de Bono, E.   64
Deanes Sports College   183–5
Dearing Review (1996)   113
debriefing   137–8
definition of gifted and talented pupils   9, 42, 64,
    165–6
Department for Education and Employment   vii
design of activities   70–1
design problems   93–4
design and technology, teaching of   93–111
diagnose and treat approach   9
diagnostic assessment   13–14
differentiation   28, 30, 79, 146–53 *passim*
distributed cognition   131
Dobson, A.   149
domains of talent   15
Doppelt, Y.   97
Dryden, Gordon   177
Dweck, Carol   137
dyslexia   77
Dyson, James   94

East Basildon education action zone   186
Eisner, E.   76
Elmer, R.   94
emotional development of pupils   8–9, 54, 107
English, teaching of   27–40
enquiry skills   129, 158
enrichment   6–7, 18, 54–7, 62, 65, 69–70, 81,
    150–3, 159, 168
Essex University   186
evaluation skills, teaching of   129, 158
examinations   33, 202; *see also* A level; GCSE
Excellence in Cities initiative   vi–vii, 7, 13, 31, 42,
    87, 179
existential questions   195–8
expectations (of students and of teachers)   106–7
extension   18, 20, 30, 62, 65, 69–70, 81, 118, 150,
    159
extra-curricular activities   65, 69, 120–1, 151

fast-tracking   53–4, 168, 180

feedback to pupils   110, 138, 149
fiction, historical   119–20
Fisher, R.   21, 194
flow, state of   20
formative assessment   110, 149
Franklin, Benjamin   70
Freeman, J.   9, 15, 62, 188
French Revolution   88

Gallagher, J.J.   18
Gardner, Howard   5, 10–11, 44–5, 164
GATE programme   183–4
Gautama, Siddhattha   189
GCSE   138, 141, 145, 147, 153, 158, 180, 189
    in history   116
    in mathematics   53
generative teaching and learning   61–2
genre theory   34
geography, teaching of   128–39
geometrical reasoning   49
giftedness   7–10, 19, 64, 96, 188
Gilhooley, K.J.   21
girls, special issues for   97, 107
Goodwyn, Andrew   27–9
Goya, Francisco   88
Greer, D.   76
group work   71–4, 131
grouping of pupils   6, 19–20; *see also* setting
    arrangements
Guernica   88
Gunstone, R.F.   60–2
gymnastics   186

Halliday, Michael   34
Henry, Lenny   27
Her Majesty's Inspectorate of Schools (HMI)   vi,
    19, 28
Hill, A.   97
historical novels   119–20
history, teaching of   113–26
House of Commons Education and Employment
    Committee   vii, 30–1, 35
Howe, M.   14, 22

identification of gifted and talented pupils   9–16,
    31–3, 78, 80, 114–15, 160, 177–81, 187, 191
    through challenge   42
    through provision   16
inclusive education   19, 116, 165
individualism   199
information and communications technology (ICT)
    116–20, 150, 154
information-processing skills   128, 158
inner speech   131
intelligence
    analytic, creative or practical   11
    entity and incremental theories of   137–8
    logical-mathematical   44

spritual 190
see also multiple intelligences, theory of
intelligence trap 64
internet, the 7, 47, 69, 79, 117, 119, 154
IQ 14, 190
Islam and Islamic art 88, 196–8

Jackson, N.E. 11
Jesus Christ 189
Joyce, James 27
Junior Athlete Career Education (JACE) programme 182, 184

Keith, George 34, 39
Kerry, T. and C. 4
key skills 128, 131, 134
keyboarding skills 40
Kimbell, R. 94–6
Krutetskii, V.A. 43–5

language learning
    English 29, 34–7
    foreign languages 140–3, 149, 157
lateral thinking 64–5
learning skills and strategies 61–2, 142, 154
learning styles 21, 61
Lewin, R. 64
lifestyle management 182–3
linguistic aptitude 142–3
listening skills 36, 149
literacy 29–30, 32, 34
    and history 115–16
Literacy Hour 30

McCormick, R. 95
McGuinness, C. 21
Maker, C.J. 19
mathematics, teaching of 42–56
mentoring 100, 106–7, 170, 186–90 *passim*
metacognition 21–2, 60–1, 73, 97, 130–2, 139–40, 157
metaphysical questions 195–8
mixed ability groups 38, 71, 80, 123
modelling of ideas 94
modern foreign languages, teaching of 140–61
Montgomery, D. 13, 17
Mozart family 166
Muhammed the prophet 189, 196–7
multiple intelligences, theory of 11, 44, 164
music, teaching of 164–72
Muslim belief 88, 196–8
Myers, R.E. 109

National Curriculum 13, 14–15, 28, 79–81, 95, 116–17, 128, 137, 141, 164, 166
    Design and Technology Working Group 94–5
    for English 14
    for mathematics 45, 49–51
    for modern foreign languages 145, 157–8
    for science 62
National Literacy Strategy 29–30, 32, 34, 160
National Numeracy Strategy 45
National Portrait Gallery 121
National Power 86
New Zealand 34
Nicholson, Ben 86
Nielson, A.B. 17–18

objectives-led approach 55
observation of emerging ability 16
Office for Standards in Education (OFSTED)
    vi–vii, 14, 28, 94–8, 116–18, 147, 149, 153, 165, 171
open questions 194–7
opinion about giftedness 12, 14

Painter, Frieda 165
parental influence 107–8
parental involvement 166, 171, 186
Pasku, Judit 166
Peel, Kelvin 191
peer pressure 108
personal style phase in development of giftedness 10
phenomenological questions 195–8
philosophy (of religion) 192–3
physical education 177–87
Picasso, Pablo 88
Plato 189
playful phase in development of giftedness 10
political pressure 34
portfolios 13
precision phase in development of giftedness 10
pressures
    on education, political 34
    on schools 95
Priory School, Orpington 123
problem-solving expertise 129
prodigies 166
progression 32–3, 62–3, 137, 145–7, 153
proof, different concepts of 51
Pullman, Philip 119
Pythagoras' Theorem 46–7

Qualifications and Curriculum Authority (QCA)
    vi, 31, 81, 88, 114, 142, 145, 149, 158
qualitatively different provision 19
questioning 81, 109, 194–7
Quran, the 189, 196

reading 38–9
    in foreign languages 153
    for pleasure 30
    problems with 77
reading qualities 35
reasoning skills 129

recognition of giftedness 9
registers of gifted and talented pupils 12, 184
religious education 188–99
Renzulli, J. 64
revelation of ability 16
Richter, Hans-Peter 119
risalah 196–7
risk-taking 109
Robinson, Tony 114
role play 124, 148

SATIS (Science and Technology in Society) 69
SATs (standard assessment tests) 13, 114
savants 77–8
scaffolding 29, 35, 148
schools
    factors in effectiveness of 3, 98–9
    management of 111, 159
science, teaching of 59–74
secular values 199
Sefton-Green, J. 109
self-monitoring by pupils 22, 130
semantic differential technique (in art) 88–90
setting arrangements 8, 53
Shayer, M. 21
Shore, B.M. 15, 21
social development of pupils 8, 54, 107, 144
social semiotics 34
SOLO (Structure of Learning Outcomes) taxonomy
    129–30
Southern Arts 86
speaking skills 36–8, 149
specialisation
    by pupils (in particular sports) 187
    by schools 180
spiritual thinking 190
sport 177–87
Sport England 181
Sport Search 181–2
sports colleges 180, 183
Stamp Advisory Committee 120–1
Sternberg, R.J. 11, 188
Stopper, M.J. 7
strands of learning 35–7
summative assessment 110, 149
Sutton, Clive 68
Swanwick, K. 172

talent-spotting 13–14
talents 96, 165–6, 178, 181
Tate Gallery, St Ives 86
Tawhid 196
Teacher Training Agency 96
teachers
    of art 79, 92
    assessments made by 13–14, 78; *see also*
    assessment techniques

of design and technology 96, 100, 105–10
effective methods used by 99
of English 29, 31, 33, 35
of geography 138
interactions with pupils 51, 56, 79, 108–9
of mathematics 45, 54, 56
of modern foreign languages 147–8
of music 166–8, 172
in physical education 178
in religious studies 190, 194
of science 70–1
student responses to expectations of 106–7
training of vii
Teare, Barry 118
tests, use of 11–12
Thales 49
thinking skills 21–3, 64, 69, 91, 97, 128–34,
    157–8
thinking styles 63
Thinking Through Geography (TTG) group 132,
    138
Tillich, Paul 193
Torrance, E.P. 109
triarchic theory 11
Tufte, Edward 132

UK Mathematics Foundation 54
UK Sports Institute 177
United States 19

values and value systems 107–10, 199
Van Tassel-Baska, J. 17
visits 81, 87, 121, 123
visual representation 76, 132
Vos, Jeannette 177
Vygotsky, L.S. 20, 29, 34–5

Wallace, Belle 164
Waring, S. 51
whole-school policies 5, 91, 179
William, D. 138
Winner, E. 78
Wittrock, M.C. 59–60
Wolverhampton Grammar School 120
Wood, D. 129
words, use of 68
World Class Performance Programme 186
writing 39–40

Youth Sports Trust 177, 182–5

Zimmer, Heinrich 190
Zohar, Dinah 190
zone of proximal development 20
Zorman, R. 10